Finding the Answers to Legal Questions:
A How-To-Do-It Manual®

Virginia Tucker
and
Marc Lampson

HOW-TO-DO-IT MANUALS®

NUMBER 174

Neal-Schuman Publishers, Inc.

New York   London

Published by Neal-Schuman Publishers, Inc.
100 William St., Suite 2004
New York, NY 10038

Library of Congress Cataloging-in-Publication Data

Tucker, Virginia, 1953-
    Finding the answers to legal questions : a how-to-do-it manual / Virginia Tucker and Marc Lampson.
        p. cm. — (How-to-do-it manuals ; no. 174)
    Includes bibliographical references and index.
    ISBN 978-1-55570-718-7 (alk. paper)
    1. Legal research—United States—Popular works. 2. Law—United States—Popular works. I. Lampson, Marc, 1949- II. Title. III. Series.

KF240.T83 2011
340.072'073—dc22
                                                                            2010036421

To my children, Kate, Jessica, and Jameson, who inspire me more than they know. And to my mother, Virginia, and my sisters, Kathy and Barbara, gone all too soon yet never far from thought or heart, inspiring me still.

—V. T.

To my mother, Helen Lampson, to my co-author, Virginia, and to my two companions for the past 18 years, Fudge and Belle, two extraordinary cats.

—M. L.

Contents

Contents

List of Figures

Foreword

It may be a cliché to say that "information is power," but this doesn't make it any less true. My own studies on information literacy, information technology, and the relevance and quality of information affirm both the importance of being able to find and use information and that people of all ages and abilities can improve their abilities to do so.

"Information is power" is particularly salient in the legal domain. Today, the most common, first-choice information-seeking strategies are to "Google" and to consult *Wikipedia*. While these tools may be sufficient for general topics such as identifying people, places, things (including products and vendors), they frequently lack the credibility and depth necessary for resolving legal or government-related problems or questions. At the same time, the explosion in information and resources resulting from online services, the World Wide Web, and extensive government and judicial digitization efforts makes it difficult for most of us to navigate through the various legal information systems and services. This is even a challenge for librarians and other information professionals.

Fortunately, we now have this highly useful and practical book, *Finding the Answers to Legal Questions*, to help information specialists and laypersons. Tucker and Lampson begin with an overview of the U.S. legal environment and of information sources on federal, state, and local levels, and they then offer practical approaches to finding and using information for common legal problems. Their advice centers on taking advantage of the most readily available information institution in society: the public library.

The heart of the practical approaches offered by Tucker and Lampson are found in Part III, "Information: Specific Legal Questions." Eight very specific chapters cover a wide range of frequently asked questions from people seeking to become better informed or trying to do their own legal work on such topics as lawsuits, family law, wills and estate planning, debt and collections, employment, and criminal law. This content is truly a must for laypersons as well as library and information professionals engaged in reference and information services.

I can also attest that this book will have lasting value across physical and virtual information settings. I am currently involved in a MacArthur Foundation–funded study of legal and health information problem solving in a virtual world (Second Life). As of this writing, we are still collecting and analyzing data, but preliminary efforts point to the importance of "first life" resources, expertise, and problem-solving abilities of information users and those attempting to help them. I can easily envision an information provider in Second Life or other virtual worlds frequently consulting Tucker and Lampson for expertise on how to better meet users' legal information needs.

Finally, writing this foreword reminds me of some of the personal legal matters and problems that I've been avoiding, such as revising my will and estate and retirement planning. The tasks seemed daunting, so I've put them off. But now I really do plan to rely on this book for the necessary context, resources, direction, and confidence to tackle these important matters.

Mike Eisenberg
Dean Emeritus and Professor
Information School, University of Washington

Preface

Where do people go to get answers to their legal information questions? If they don't have an attorney, how do they learn to navigate the court system or prepare pleadings to file with a court? Where do they turn when they need to translate legalese into language they can understand?

People find sample forms in stationery stores, do-it-yourself booklets, software packages, and innumerable websites of varying value and relevance, but how does a person know where to start? How does the average person become familiar with the workings of the local court and its rules and processes? Some communities offer free legal clinics staffed by lawyers volunteering their time, others provide legal services based on income level, and still others have court-provided facilitators (paralegals) to assist with paperwork. And, all across the country, people call on their public libraries with questions involving legal information. Small to medium-sized public libraries are unlikely to have staff with legal experience or much in the way of reference materials to assist these patrons.

Audience and Purpose

Finding the Answers to Legal Questions: A How-To-Do-It Manual is intended for librarians, paralegals, laypersons, and students without a background in law who need to find answers to legal questions. It is particularly recommended for public library staff faced with reference questions involving legal information and dealing with challenges of providing a basic legal reference collection. The focus here is on public libraries that are of small to medium size; large public libraries may have legal reference staff or even their own law libraries within an extended library system. The book is not aimed at law library staff who are familiar with legal research and the legal system and who often have legal experience or education.

The book is also for students preparing for careers in public libraries who need to be conversant with the U.S. legal system, the workings of the courts, and common questions that are likely to arise. It is also appropriate for paralegal students needing an introduction to the justice system and many of the most frequently encountered demands for basic legal information.

In short, the audience for this book includes:

- librarians and library staff at public libraries providing reference services and encountering questions about legal information;
- students preparing for a career in public libraries;
- students learning the basics of finding answers to legal questions; and
- members of the general public looking for legal information.

The four major aims of this book are:

- to provide a general introduction to the structure of the legal systems in the United States;
- to provide an overview of the most used legal information sources on the federal, state, and local levels, in all formats;
- to provide a guide to finding legal information about the most frequently encountered legal problems faced by laypersons; and
- to provide a guide for "collecting" and managing basic legal resources in the context of a public library.

How to Use This Book

The book is organized into four parts, with three appendixes:

- Part I, "Foundation: Legal Information Overview"

Part I explains the structure of U.S. legal systems as reflected in the structure of legal information resources. It begins with background information to establish a basic understanding of what is meant by codes, statutes, laws, and regulations. The chapters provide an overview of primary law—statutes, regulations, and case law—and explain how secondary sources can help the novice legal researcher. Recommendations and how-to instructions are included for finding primary law in print sources, free websites, and pay-for-view databases.

- Part II, "Preparation: Understanding Legal Information Needs"

This part begins with a discussion of the complexities of the reference interview when legal information is involved. Librarians can provide legal information but cannot provide legal advice, and library patrons trying to do their own legal work will frequently ask for "advice." The librarian's role is that of navigator, not advisor or advocate. Part II introduces the reader to basic legal research, including citation and keyword searching as well as issues such as jurisdiction and checking for the most current information. Part II continues with coverage of resources beyond the public library, such as legal aid organizations, and considerations when choosing a lawyer.

- Part III, "Information: Specific Legal Questions"

Part III describes common questions or information scenarios typically encountered by laypersons seeking legal information. Throughout this section it is essential to keep in mind that state and local statutes and court rules will vary, and this book cannot address each jurisdiction.

The eight chapters in Part III each cover an area of law that generates the questions most frequently asked by people trying to do their own legal work. Each chapter typically includes the framework for the area of law (whether it is governed by state or federal law, for example, or a combination), a "getting started" section (what a person needs to know to begin finding answers in that area of law), frequently asked questions and helpful ideas for finding answers, and "resources recaps," summarizing important print and online sources covered in individual sections or the chapter overall.

The questions in Part III were determined through a combination of the authors' experiences and an informal survey of reference librarians at public libraries. There seems to be general agreement on the most commonly asked legal questions: "When American families are asked to describe their legal needs, the topics that come up repeatedly are housing, personal finance, family and domestic concerns (usually in conjunction with divorce and child support), wills and estates, and employment-related issues" (American Bar Association, 2009).

- Part IV, "Collection: Building a Basic Collection or Website"

Part IV is intended for public library staff wanting to create a basic website, or perhaps just a single webpage, with links to relevant legal information for their local community. It also provides advice on how to build a small hardcopy collection at minimal cost. The first two chapters cover print sources that are not available online or in pay-for-view databases and discuss the general nature of free legal information on the Internet—megaportals, law school library sites, public library sites—and how it differs from what is included in pay-for-view databases like Lexis and Westlaw. These chapters provide tips on how to sift through and evaluate self-help law books and websites, often an intimidating array and host to unique concerns such as jurisdiction, relevancy, bias, and authenticity. The final chapter provides how-to information for creating a basic website of legal links and building a small, low-cost collection of print resources.

- Appendixes

Three appendixes supplement the legal sources described in the book. Appendix 1 is a glossary of legal terms highlighted throughout in the book and also includes a list of recommended online legal dictionaries. Appendix 2 summarizes the most essential, go-to-every-time legal resources available online and for free discussed throughout the book. These resources include case law, federal statutes and regulations, court rules, tribal law, legal forms, and more. Appendix 3 is a directory of online resources for legal information from all 50 states. It collects in one place the URLs for free online sources for state statutes, regulations, courts, and case law. Updates for the appendixes can be found at the authors' website (www.GetLaw.net).

Finding the Answers to Legal Questions offers a unique, how-to-do-it approach to legal information and legal research. With a wealth of recommended legal resources, organized for efficient lookups, and its focus on the needs of the generalist reference librarian, paralegal, and layperson, this book is packed with practical suggestions to help you understand the legal system, locate appropriate resources, and quickly find answers to legal questions.

Don't Forget

Many library users do their own research. Some do it to learn how to represent themselves, and some do it to be more knowledgeable in working with an attorney they may retain to help them with their legal matters. This latter course of action is highly recommended; in addition to doing one's own legal research, one should consult with an attorney if at all possible either for a one-time consultation or for representation. Just as a person might look on the Internet for information about a prescription drug or a surgical procedure, this would be no substitute for the advice of a physician.

Especially when it comes to criminal matters, anytime one's liberty is at stake, that person is strongly advised to seek legal counsel and to seriously question whether self-representation is wise.

Reference

American Bar Association (ABA). 2009. *Guide to Wills and Estates.* "Preface." Chicago: American Bar Association.

Acknowledgments

No book—particularly a book about finding information—is ever the result of one person's thoughts and ideas. This one is no exception. My co-author, Marc Lampson, is the first person I want to thank most deeply; he is both a gifted explainer of the legal system and its layers, twists, and turns, and he is a calm and patient encourager.

Next, there are the questioners themselves—the patrons at my public law library and the laypersons, attorneys, and courthouse staff—without whom there would be no quest for answers at all. I am particularly grateful to the many lawyers I have come to know in Bellingham, Washington, who have been so supportive of the law library and its law librarian. They are champions of the law library's mission and always there to cheer me on in helping members of our community navigate the court system and find the legal information they need. The Whatcom Dispute Resolution Center and LAW Advocates in Bellingham are shining examples of mediation and legal aid services, and I am pleased to have been able to serve in a small way within those organizations. Their volunteers and staff are making this world a better place.

My students in the MLIS program at San José State University's School of Library and Information Science have also been a part of this book. They never cease to astound me with their curiosity and commitment to the profession of librarianship; they are its future, and it is a bright one, full of surprises. If finding answers to questions is my craft, then teaching about "finding" is my passion.

I have included my sisters and my mother in this book's dedication and also acknowledge them here, for they had everything to do with my learning to put words together and to paper. My sister, Kathy, was my first editor when I sent her my earliest poetry; she had to learn while still in college how to deal with an author's tender ego and ultimately made editing her profession. My sister, Barbara, could put words together on her feet in front of an audience and each person felt she was speaking directly to him or her. My mother, Virginia Sr., school principal and sculptor, knew better than anyone how learning and information can transform lives.

Marc wishes to acknowledge all the hard work of his co-author, Virginia Tucker. The book was largely born of her inspiration and has come to completion largely due to her dedication, persistence, and discipline.

She also designed the template for what I think are some of the book's most original chapters, those on the specific topical areas of legal practice. My students in LIS programs, paralegal programs, and law schools over the years have also contributed to the book by teaching me better how to convey the complexity of finding legal information. Specifically, students in my spring 2010 legal resources course at San José State University's School of Library and Information Science contributed the links for the state law appendix.

Both authors wish to express our sincere appreciation to the Neal-Schuman editorial and production staff, most notably Sandy Wood and Charles Harmon. Thank you for your endless supply of encouragement.

Foundation: Legal Information Overview

Part I is an introduction to the legal system in the United States, explaining the connections between the structure of this system and the structure and organization of legal information. The chapters provide an overview of primary law—statutes, regulations, and case law—and explain how secondary sources can help the novice legal researcher. Recommendations and how-to instructions are included for finding primary law in print sources, free websites, and pay-for-view databases.

The Structure of the Legal System in the United States

Getting Started Finding Legal Information

"Only one-third of Americans can even name the three branches of government, much less say what they do," former Supreme Court Justice Sandra Day O'Connor told Jon Stewart in her appearance on the *The Daily Show*. She said a nationwide survey in 2009 reported this statistic, and she has launched a website, OurCourts.Org, to try in some small way to educate Americans about how our government is organized. She thought part of the problem was that schools had stopped teaching "civics," and the tagline for her website is "21st Century Civics." If you are looking for legal information, it will help you a great deal to learn or be reminded about the three branches of government, what they do, what kind of law they make, and how our legal system is organized generally. Legal information is organized in a way that reflects the structure of the legal system, and it is this organizational structure that is the subject of this chapter.

Fifty-One Legal Systems

We say "the" legal system, but really there are *at least* 51 different legal systems in the United States; the federal legal system is one, and the legal systems in each state are the other 50. These systems exist entirely separate from one another. Of course, there are times when you need information from both the federal and state systems, but usually your first step is to decide which legal system governs the legal problem you are researching. Deciding this question concerns the problem of "**jurisdiction**," and Chapters 3 and 4 will help you decide whether the federal system or a state system is the proper "jurisdiction" for your legal question. Once this is decided, you will want to know what type of law you need and which governmental unit makes that type of law, leading you deeper into understanding how legal systems are organized. The good news is that the organization of the 51 legal systems is often very similar.

The Rule of Threes

We often learn about subjects by dividing them into their component parts. To learn about our legal systems, dividing into three parts works in several ways: there are three types of primary law made by three different branches or separate units of government, and these days this law is found in three distinct realms: in print, online, and in pay-for-view databases. This is a bit of a simplification, but it works well as a learning device.

Three Types of Primary Law

The three types of primary law on both the federal and state levels are **enacted law**, **case law**, and **regulatory law** (see Figure 1.1). The goal of most legal research is to find the primary law that applies to a given legal problem. The legal field distinguishes between primary law and secondary sources. Secondary sources are defined as "commentary about the law" and are thoroughly discussed in Chapter 2. In this chapter the focus is on the three different types of primary law created by three different branches or units of government.

Figure 1.1. Types of Primary Law	
Type of Primary Law	**Subtypes**
Enacted Law	Constitutions, statutes, ordinances, court rules
Regulatory Law	Administrative rules, regulations, and sometimes administrative decisions in individual cases
Case Law	Cases interpreting statutes and regulations and cases making law in the absence of statutes and regulations (often referred to as "common law")

Three Branches of Government

The three branches of government, federal or state, are the legislative, the executive, and the judicial branches. Each branch makes a particular type of primary law (Figure 1.2).

Legislatures Enact Statutes

The type of law that is most often needed to resolve legal questions is that type of primary law made by the legislative branch: enacted law, often called "statutory law." Thus, the United States Congress enacts federal statutes; state legislatures enact state statutes. On the local level, elected bodies of people, analogous to legislatures, enact local ordinances. The best broad term then for this type of law enacted by elected bodies of

Figure 1.2. Three Entities and Three Types of Primary Law		
Branch or Unit	**Type of Primary Law**	**Published in Hard Copy As...**
Legislature	Statutes	Session laws Statutory codes
Courts	Case law, opinions, decisions	Case reporters Case digests
Administrative Agencies (may be part of the Executive Branch or may be an "independent" governmental agency established by legislature)	Regulations (and sometimes administrative decisions in specific cases)	Administrative registers Administrative codes

people is enacted law. **Constitutions** are best considered enacted law, too, because, while not enacted by legislatures, constitutions and information about them can be found in the same places as statutory law. The same is true of court rules.

The legislative branch of government in the federal system is known as a "bicameral" institution, or "two houses," collectively known as the United States Congress and is comprised of the United States House of Representatives and the United States Senate. Those two "houses" of Congress must, usually by a majority vote, agree to enact the same piece of legislation. Once that is done, the president must agree to sign that legislation and when that is done, the legislation becomes "the law," known as a federal statute.

All states, save one, also have a bicameral legislative branch with two houses similar to the U.S. Senate and the U.S. House of Representatives, though on the state level these two houses may have different names depending on the state. The California Legislature, for instance, is comprised of the California Assembly and the California Senate. Whereas in Georgia the two houses are known collectively as the Georgia General Assembly, consisting of the Georgia State Senate and the Georgia House of Representatives. Nebraska, by contrast, is the only state to have a unicameral legislature. It consists of only one "house," called the Nebraska Unicameral Legislature. Regardless of the exact name of the legislative branch, state legislatures act very similarly to the United States Congress in that once the legislature enacts a piece of legislation it must be signed by the governor of the state and then it becomes "the law," usually referred to as a "state statute."

Statutes are published in hard copy first as "session laws" right after they are enacted, and then once they have been categorized by subject— a process called "codification"—they are published in statutory codes. But today, finding state and federal statutes has become increasingly easy as the legislatures have assured that robust websites publish not only existing statutes but sometimes proposed legislation and historical statutes as well. Usually finding these sites is a matter of typing the name of the legislative branch into a search engine. Be sure, however, that the site you find is the "official" site, usually with a URL that ends in ".gov" or sometimes the state abbreviation followed by ".us," such as "ne.us."

Administrative Agencies Promulgate Regulations

The administrative agencies of government, which are sometimes part of the executive branch and sometimes independent agencies set up by legislatures, create or "promulgate" regulatory law. These are the rules and regulations that govern how the administrative functions of the government are to be carried out. Rules and regulations are also created on the local level.

Hundreds of administrative agencies exist in the federal system and hundreds exist in nearly every state. These agencies are charged with "administering," or carrying out the functions of government, from making sure the roads and bridges get built to making sure that children are not living in dangerous, hurtful homes. The agencies issue many regulations about how the agency itself is to function and regulations that govern the area of the agency's expertise, such as occupational safety and health, or transportation, or labor relations, and so on.

Agency regulations pertain to all of the sectors of society or industry that are administered by the agency. These regulations are therefore said to carry out a "quasi-legislative" function in that the regulations resemble the statutes issued by legislatures. But often administrative agencies carry out a "quasi-judicial" function as well, deciding on individual cases governed by its regulations rather than merely issuing broad-reaching regulations.

The individual decisions about individual cases resemble judicial opinions, which is the reason they are viewed as "quasi-judicial." These decisions are sometimes published in a publicly accessible way and sometimes not. Sometimes the decisions are sent out only to the individuals involved, and sometimes the decisions are published in hard copy "reporters" or loose-leaf services. These services are discussed in the second chapter and, where applicable, in individual chapters on specific legal topics.

The legal researcher will often be looking for administrative regulations and sometimes administrative decisions. Generally, regulations are published in hard copy first as proposed and then as final regulations in administrative registers and then subsequently in administrative codes arranged by agency or topic. While administrative regulations can be found online, this is not as certain as the online publication of statutes.

Finding administrative decisions in individual cases, however, can be more difficult. But the determined researcher may find them in loose-leaf reporters, or at the agency itself, or if necessary through public record requests. Again, increasingly these decisions can be found online, but it may take some persistence and assistance.

Courts Make Case Law

The judicial branch of government, whether state or federal, issues legal opinions, decisions, or cases. You may also hear it called "judge-made law." All of these terms are used interchangeably, but in legal research terms it is most often referred to as "case law." You will also hear the phrase "common law" in reference to case law. Most case law involves the interpretation of enacted law or regulatory law, but when a case decides a legal question where there is no statute or regulation, that is what is more precisely meant by "common law." The broader term for all judicial decisions is case law.

Case law is published first as "slip opinions" and then in case reporters. Private publishers of case law also summarize the cases and arrange those summaries by subject matter in sets of books called case digests. Chapters 3 and 4 discuss reporters and digests more fully.

You will learn in the following section that not all case law has equal weight and not all of it is published, but it is usually very important because it most often interprets the law that is enacted by legislatures or promulgated by the administrative agencies because the meaning of enacted or regulatory law is often ambiguous. The weight or importance of the opinions or decisions issued by the courts varies according to the level of court that writes the opinion.

Three Levels of Courts

The rule of threes works well for learning the structure of the court systems in the United States too. Generally, a court system has three different levels: trial courts, intermediate appellate courts, and final appellate courts (see Figure 1.3). The final appellate courts have the highest authority in any court system, and so it is best to think of courts in a hierarchy.

Figure 1.3. Three Levels of Courts			
Levels of Courts	**Names of Federal Courts**	**Names of Sample State Courts**	**Function**
Final Appellate Courts	United States Supreme Court	California Supreme Court	Court of Last Resort—In most cases parties must petition this court for review, there is no "right" to appeal to this court except in limited situations.
Intermediate Appellate Courts	Court of Appeals	California Court of Appeals	First Level of Appeal—In most cases parties have a "right" to appeal to this court.
Trial Courts	United States District Courts	County Superior Courts	Fact Finders

Trial Courts

At the lowest level, and the level with which many patrons are likely to be concerned, is the trial court level. Trial courts are the type of courts with which most people are familiar because they make for good drama on television and in movies. Trial courts are where witnesses testify, where jurors sit to decide cases, where evidence is presented, and where the trial judge presides. Before television, many people found entertainment by attending trials in the courts of many cities; then came *Perry Mason*, and hundreds of similar programs, and more recently we had *Boston Legal.*

Most people who begin a lawsuit, or who are being sued, or who are in trouble with the criminal justice system, will begin in trial court. Thus, a library patron will often be most concerned with trial courts, and legal information will be important for the patron to find. This information includes court rules, especially. Court rules are often considered to be part of "enacted law," not because an elected body enacts it but because rules are often made a part of enacted law collections.

"Case law," however, is a little more problematic when discussing trial courts. As far as finding legal information, though trial courts may be very important to the individuals involved in a lawsuit or trial, the decisions or other documents issued by a trial court are not the type of legal information that is typically of concern to legal researchers.

First, a decision of a trial court is not "**precedent.**" Though a trial court decision binds the parties involved, it does not bind anyone aside from those parties. Such a decision in fact does not even bind the judge who might have issued the decision. That judge may be faced with the same legal issue the next day and decide it differently, probably based on the differing facts, but perhaps because of an advocate who changes the judge's mind.

Second, as a consequence of trial court decisions not being precedent, they are not "published" in the usual sense of the word, at least in most state legal systems. This will often lead to confusion for a patron seeking such decisions or documents. Public library patrons may not understand that trial court decisions or other documents related to a case in a trial court are not precedent and are not readily available.

Until recently, you could get a copy of a decision or other document from a trial court only by going to the clerk's office for the court involved. Usually the clerk's office will help someone access and, perhaps, copy decisions and court documents from the case file that the clerk's office maintains on specific cases. To get the case file, you will usually need the case name and the docket number, though most clerks' offices will have a way of looking up the docket number if you have the names of the parties.

Third, however, is that the future is uncertain. In the past few years, decisions and documents filed in a trial court have become available online in some court systems. This is a fast-changing and controversial area of information access because it raises fundamental questions of how "public" public information should be. While most trial court documents and decisions have always been considered, in theory at least, as "public," they were not readily and easily available. As they now become easily available online, concerns over the privacy and possible misinterpretation or misuse of those documents become significant social concerns.

Access to trial court decisions, and even documents, in the federal system has always been a little different than access to state trial court decisions. A small percentage of federal trial court decisions have for a long time been published in a set of books called the *Federal Supplement*. See Chapter 3 on federal law for a discussion of this set.

Intermediate Appellate Courts

Appellate courts are very different from trial courts. Appellate courts do not decide "facts" as trial courts do but rather decide whether the law was properly applied by the trial court to the facts as determined in the trial court. Appellate courts do not hear testimony, admit exhibits, or empanel juries. This is something that people unfamiliar with the legal system often fail to understand. People often think if they "appeal" their case to the appellate court that they will get another chance to testify and present evidence to yet another court. This will not happen because of the different roles different courts play: the facts in a case are determined by the trial court and are set forth in the "record" that the trial court sends to the appellate court when a case is appealed.

Appellate courts look at this "record" as it was made at the trial court—usually transcripts of what went on at the trial court and documents and exhibits that were submitted to the trial court—then read and listen to arguments, usually from attorneys, about whether there was some legal error that occurred at the trial court level. Eventually, the appellate court will issue a decision, also called an opinion and sometimes referred to as a "case," that will state whether there was error at the trial court and why or why not. These opinions, if "published," become precedent that all trial courts governed by the appellate court issuing the opinion must follow in the future.

Finding these opinions is therefore often an important task for someone looking for legal information about a particular topic. How to do this will be discussed further in the chapters on federal and state primary sources. For now, we want to keep the focus on the structure of the legal system and of the courts.

Structurally, appellate courts are usually of two levels: the intermediate appellate courts and final appellate courts. "Intermediate" appellate courts are called this because they are between the trial courts and the final appellate courts. Most states have intermediate appellate courts. Often they are called courts of appeal, but not always. In California they are, but in New York the Court of Appeals is the state's final, highest appellate court. New York has two levels of intermediate appellate courts, the appellate divisions, divided into four judicial departments, which hear appeals from the county courts, and the lower appellate courts, which hear appeals from district, city, town, and village courts.

The practical lesson for people looking for legal information is to be guided not so much by the name of the court but by its role and its place in the structure. The published opinions of intermediate appellate courts, given those courts' role between trial courts and final appellate courts, will generally be precedent, or mandatory authority, only for those trial courts under its jurisdiction. This is most easily demonstrated by the intermediate appellate courts in the federal system.

The intermediate appellate courts in the federal system are often called circuit courts of appeal, or just federal courts of appeal. They are divided into 13 different "circuits," given this name historically because judges of those courts would literally ride the circuit—the towns and cities within the geographic territory governed by the court—on horseback or other means of transportation. A map of those circuits, demonstrating that it is a geographic designation, can be found at www.uscourts.gov/images/CircuitMap.pdf.

Thus, the federal trial courts within the jurisdiction of the different circuit courts of appeal must follow the opinions from the circuit court of appeal that governs its geographic territory. More specifically, this means that the federal trial courts, called United States District Courts, in the geographic area governed by, say the 11th Circuit Court of Appeals (the federal district courts in Georgia, Florida, and Alabama), are under an obligation to construe the law on any particular legal issue in the way that the 11th Circuit Court of Appeals has done. In other words, the published opinions of the 11th Circuit Court of Appeals are "mandatory authority" for those courts and litigants in those courts within the 11th Circuit: Georgia, Florida, and Alabama.

Consequently, someone looking for what the federal courts have said is "the law" on a particular issue governed by federal law must first determine what federal circuit court governs the geographic area in which the legal issue arises. Sometimes this can be quite complicated, but in most instances it entails simply looking at a map, such as the one cited previously, and determining which circuit court governs the federal district courts in the state where the question arises. So, if the query arises in California, the opinions of the Ninth Circuit Court of Appeals in the federal system would be "mandatory authority" unless of course the United States Supreme Court had decided the issue differently. If the query arises in Texas, then the opinions of the Fifth Circuit Court of Appeals would be mandatory authority in the absence of contrary decisions from the United States Supreme Court.

This same geographically based jurisdiction will be true in most states concerning those states' intermediate appellate courts. Those intermediate appellate courts will usually be divided into "divisions" or "departments" or some other designation, and the trial courts within the geographic jurisdiction of those divisions or departments will be under an obligation to follow the opinions of the intermediate appellate court for the trial courts' geographic area. Again, rely on the court's role and position in the structure rather than the names of courts to understand what legal information is needed, in this instance which court opinions are mandatory and which are not.

The best thing to do is to find a hard copy or online resource that will quickly and easily tell you the structure of the courts for the state in which you are interested. For instance, a handy structural rendering of the court structure in New York can be found at www.courts.state .ny.us/courts/structure.shtml. As you might expect, the more populous the state, the more complicated the legal system will be. North Dakota, a state less populated than New York, has a relatively uncomplicated court system: www.ndcourts.com/court/Brochure.htm.

Finding opinions of the intermediate appellate courts will be discussed further in Chapters 3 and 4. For now it is best to note that not all opinions of the intermediate appellate courts are published. The ones that are published are considered "precedent." The ones that are not officially "published," while you can find them on the court's websites and even in pay-for-view databases such as Westlaw and Lexis, will usually have a note at the beginning stating that the opinion is not to be cited because it is not a published, precedential opinion.

Final Appellate Courts

The final appellate court in the federal system is the United States Supreme Court. What it says is "the law" regarding any legal issue arising under federal law is "the law" for all federal courts, everywhere, and for that matter, for all state courts when those state courts are applying or interpreting federal law. Finding legal information from and about the United States Supreme Court is therefore extremely important and is often the sort of legal information people seek. The decisions of the United States Supreme Court are often the leading news of the day and therefore people frequently want more information about these decisions. As a consequence, there are many places one can find information about the decisions of this court. We will review many of these in the chapters that follow, particularly the chapter on federal primary sources, but for immediate information about very recent cases one can always begin with the website of the United States Supreme Court (www.supremecourtus.gov/).

All states will also all have final appellate courts, or "courts of last resort" as they are often called. Again, the names of those courts will often differ from state to state. In Montana and Virginia, for instance, as in many states, the final appellate court is called the "Supreme Court." But in Massachusetts, the final appellate court was originally the Superior Court of Judicature, but today is called the Supreme Judicial Court.

Usually the final appellate courts in both the federal and state systems publish all of the opinions those courts write (see Figure 1.4). In other

Figure 1.4. Hierarchy of Mandatory Authority	
Federal System	**State System**
U.S. Constitution	
	State Constitution
Federal Statutes	State Statutes
Federal Administrative Regulations	State Administrative Regulations
U.S. Supreme Court Decisions	State Supreme Court Decisions
Intermediate Appellate Court Decisions	Intermediate Appellate Court Decisions

words, in contrast with the intermediate appellate courts, which publish only a small percentage of opinions those courts write, final appellate courts publish all of the opinions written by that court. Finding those opinions then, in the sources discussed in Chapters 3 and 4, is often less of a problem than finding opinions of the intermediate appellate courts. One can usually be assured that if one finds an opinion from the final appellate court it is precedent unless of course it has been subsequently overruled by later court opinions or sometimes by the legislature.

Conclusion

Understanding the overall structure of the legal system will help people seeking legal information find that information. If the researcher knows that there are three types of primary law and that those three types are created by three different governmental entities and that in most cases those entities will publish, often chronologically and also topically, the primary law it creates, then the researcher will be able to track it down more easily. Tracking down this law, however, often starts with consulting sources that provide the researcher with an overview or summary of the law on a particular topic. This overview can be found in what the law calls secondary sources, which are discussed in the next chapter. Chapters 3 and 4 return to the primary sources of primary law in the federal and state systems.

Secondary Sources and Practice Materials

Finding "**primary law**," as discussed in the prior chapter, is usually the goal of legal research. But you can be helped to that goal with the **secondary sources** discussed in this chapter. These sources are not primary law and therefore are not likely to be cited to or used by a court as "authority," but these sources will help the researcher understand and find the primary law that can then be used as authority in a legal dispute.

Secondary Sources Generally

Secondary sources are often the best place for the novice researcher to start in finding legal information. Primary law consists of enacted law (constitutions, statutes, ordinances), case law, and regulations, but often it is difficult to get an overall sense of what "the law" is about a specific topic, especially if you merely compile several pieces of primary law. A secondary source will summarize, synthesize, and explain seemingly disparate pieces of primary law for you; it can also be a valuable starting place to learn about the terminology of an area of law.

A secondary source is to the law what a movie review is to the movie. A movie reviewer will summarize a movie and explain whether he or she liked it or not, but it is often best to go see the movie yourself. Similarly, a secondary source will tell you about the law, what the law says, and sometimes why the law is "good" or "bad," but a secondary source is not the law itself. Secondary sources therefore are often not the final step in legal research because usually secondary sources will lead the researcher to the next step, finding statutes, cases, and regulations that constitute the law itself.

But the researcher should exercise caution in using secondary sources. First, the secondary source may be wrong about its summary or its analysis of "the law." Some secondary sources have gained significant reputations for accuracy and reliability; many secondary sources, however, have no reputations at all. This is especially true of legal commentary you might find on the web. Second, secondary sources often attempt to make a general summary of the law on a specific point and in so doing may gloss over significant differences and variations that may exist. Third, secondary sources can become out of date quite quickly. The law changes all of the time. A specific court case on one day can significantly alter the legal landscape on a particular issue. It is hard for secondary sources, especially in print, to keep up with the ever changing law. With these precautions in mind, however, the novice researcher should always consider using secondary sources first.

Practice materials are related to but are not exactly the same as secondary sources. These materials advise legal professionals how to do very specific actions within the legal system and may also include model forms or templates that a person may modify and file in court or elsewhere. Consequently, practice materials can be very helpful to nonlawyers trying to navigate the legal system on their own. But extreme caution and good judgment should also be exercised in using these materials because they are only guides, not absolute blueprints.

What follows is a general discussion of the types of secondary sources and practice materials you can find. All of the secondary sources described can be found in print. Many of them can also be found in the pay-for-view databases, such as Westlaw and Lexis, though what is available will depend on the level of subscription for which you or your library has paid. To date, a very limited number of the secondary sources discussed can be found on the "free" web.

While some examples are provided, discovering all of the secondary sources that may exist in a specific library or online will depend on using the library's catalog, seeking the help of a knowledgeable librarian, and searching online with some knowledge provided by this book and other sources. Very useful and well-known secondary sources pertaining to specific legal areas will be discussed in later chapters on general research strategies (Part II) and on specific legal topics (Part III). The secondary sources are discussed beginning with the most useful for nonlawyers.

Secondary Sources: In Print

Legal Encyclopedias

Legal encyclopedias can help you get started, but they can also mislead. They do exactly what other encyclopedias do: summarize what is known about a particular topic and point the reader to other secondary sources and, most importantly, to the primary sources relied on in the summary. Each volume of an encyclopedia is usually organized in a similar fashion, with the summary being the most prominent part of each page, but with footnotes supporting that summary often constituting a major portion of the page. Both the summary and the footnotes can be useful. Although a number of access points exist for encyclopedias, usually the best starting point is to use the separate index volumes that are usually called a "Descriptive Word Index." These sets are designed for lawyers and nonlawyers, so you do not need to know specialized legal vocabulary to use the index. Use words related to the problem you are researching, focusing on such things as the people, the place, the legal dispute, or the property involved. The index will often direct you to other subject terms for your topic, too. If this approach does not work, try using the same concepts but using words that are more specific or more general.

The precautions mentioned previously, however, are particularly true in consulting the main topic volumes: encyclopedias are often very general and dated. Two major legal encyclopedias, described next, have been published in the United States for decades and are often the resources you can find in a library. A few states, California and New York for example, have legal encyclopedias about the laws in those states; some states have sets of books that resemble encyclopedias, though the sets are not necessarily called encyclopedias. Here is a quick review of some of these resources.

National Legal Encyclopedias

Corpus Juris Secundum (*CJS*) and *American Jurisprudence 2d* (*AmJur2d*) are the two major legal encyclopedias that have been published for decades. While there are subtle differences between the two, both are generally reliable and often consulted and even occasionally cited in legal pleadings. *CJS* claims to summarize all of the federal or state statutes and cases pertaining to the specific topics covered in the set. It also gives the researcher "topic and key numbers" that relate to other sets of books from the same publisher. *AmJur2d*, on the other hand, claims only to selectively summarize some of the thousands of cases and statutes that may pertain to any particular legal topic. Both sets, however, can provide a valuable overview of the law on a specific topic, and both sets have ample footnotes to lead you back to the primary sources you will ultimately need.

Localized Legal Encyclopedias

Twenty-two states have legal encyclopedias that summarize their laws and legal system. If you are looking for legal information about California law, for example, two legal encyclopedias will be useful: *California Jurisprudence, 3rd* (*CalJur3d*) and *Witkin's Summary of California Law*. Some will dispute whether the latter title is an "encyclopedia," but it serves the same function. Other states have sets of books that are either called encyclopedias or that fulfill the same function, such as *Colorado Law Annotated, 2d*; *Louisiana Civil Law Treatise*; and *Michigan Law and Practice Encyclopedia*. The Harvard Law School's Law Library website provides a list of the national and state legal encyclopedias by title, so check that list to see if the state you are interested in has a legal encyclopedia. See www.law.harvard.edu/library/research/guides/united_states/alr_legal_encyclopedias.html.

Note that most national and state legal encyclopedias are updated by pocket parts, which are little pamphlets inserted in the back of the book containing information that is more recent than the main volume. But even these pocket parts are not always dependably published or up to date, so be sure to check the publication date on the first page or two to see how recently it was published.

Treatises

Treatises are most often multivolume sets of books that provide encyclopedic coverage of a very specific topic in the law. Thus, rather than a geographic orientation as with the national and state encyclopedias, treatises have a topical orientation and often bear the name of their original writers or compilers, though those writers may be long gone. *Corbin on Contracts*, *McCormick on Evidence*, and *Prosser and Keaton on the Law of Torts* are a few examples of the better known and well-respected treatises.

Sometimes these multivolume sets are reduced to single-volume "hornbooks" or "student editions" designed to be accessible to law school students as they are studying specific topics. These shorter, more compact versions can often be quite helpful to new legal researchers. A large variety of other single-volume books, also designed with the law student in mind, can also be useful for legal researchers. The Thomson West publishing company publishes a "nutshell" series of books that are very short summaries about specific topics in the law, and these are usually written by very well respected and authoritative authors. A variety of study guide summaries of the law, particularly case law, are published primarily for the law student market and are not usually helpful to the legal researcher.

Treatises, hornbooks, student editions, and nutshells have structures that are similar to encyclopedias in that the law is summarized in the narrative portion of the work but the narrative is amply supported by numerous footnotes to the primary sources on which the summary relies. In sum, these types of secondary sources can be very useful to the researcher, and in the case of single-volume editions, can often be quite affordable as well for a library or individual collection.

The library catalog is often the best lead to finding these types of secondary sources. Additionally, *Legal Books in Print* and a publication titled *Specialized Legal Research* can also be helpful in identifying treatises and other secondary sources that fall into this category. In Part III of this book, we discuss how to research specific legal topics and any treatises on those topics are listed there.

Practice Materials and Forms

Practice materials and forms are a huge category of legal information materials. While some of these materials fit the general description of secondary sources as "commentary on the law," often practice materials are not commentary but instruction. These materials are intended to instruct legal professionals how to do very specific tasks in the legal system. As such, these materials can be very useful for the self-help litigant. But the sheer number and variety of these materials can be daunting. Furthermore, the materials are sometimes difficult to navigate and to understand and can easily mislead those unfamiliar with the legal system and those in too big of a hurry.

Those cautions in mind, the effort to find and to collect such materials pertaining to your jurisdiction and your specific legal needs can be worth the time it takes. Examples include *AmJur Trials*, *AmJur Proof of Facts*, *Causes of Action*, and a large number of sets using a variation on the title of "pleading and practice materials." These materials may be found for working within the federal system and for working within the legal systems of each state. A library card catalog or patient shelf browsing are often the best ways to identify what materials a particular library has available.

Most of these sets include legal forms. Legal forms and sample documents present problems in themselves. While it is true that many legal documents appear to consist of arcane language and obscure formulations, these problems with legal documents are perpetuated by legal form books. The forms are best used as starting points, but not as something that has to be copied and used word for word. More often than not, if the basic format of a form is followed, then the language can be plain and simple.

In addition to form "books," many legal forms now appear on the web. Some of the sites containing these forms are merely a way of getting the user to buy a product either in hard copy or as an electronic copy. These forms have all the same problems that hard copy forms do: they are full of arcane and obscure language that need not be used, are of questionable reliability, and are of questionable usefulness across different jurisdictions. You should therefore exercise extreme caution in using form books or forms from the web.

Increasingly, however, court systems themselves are developing online form banks. Some of these sites are merely the forms, but some sites provide interactive guides about how to fill out the forms properly. If someone searching for legal information is in need of a form, the best initial search is to find out if the court where the form will be filed has a website, which it should, and then to see if the court's website provides forms.

Loose-Leaf Services

"Loose-leaf services" or "loose-leaf reporters" got their name because typically they are published in three-ring binders, though the format may vary widely. They are published this way so they can be easily and frequently updated. This updating is necessary because the subject matter of many loose-leaf services concern areas of the law in which statutes, cases, and especially administrative rules and regulations play a significant role. Administrative rules and regulations change frequently, and cases interpreting those regulations are often issued by the courts. A loose-leaf service both collects together into one set all of the law and related material pertinent to a specific legal topic *and* permits easy updating by removing one page and inserting another.

What loose-leaf services may exist for a researcher's specific legal information need will generally be determined by the same methods mentioned previously regarding treatises: a library catalog, *Legal Books in Print*, *Specialized Legal Research*, and consulting information and legal professionals. But locating a pertinent loose-leaf service is only part of the battle. These services tend to be large sets of interrelated subsets, and it often takes time to learn how to use them. Because the publishers want them to be marketable and therefore useful, most loose-leaf reporters or services will contain prefatory material in one or all of the volumes telling the researcher how to use the set. The effort made to locate and use loose-leaf services is often worth it for even the novice researcher because they are very efficient tools, gathering all pertinent material into one set and giving some assurance that the material is up-to-date.

American Law Reports

A very useful secondary source, though perhaps beyond the needs of most nonlawyers looking for legal information, is the series titled American Law Reports (ALR) that exists in many different sets such as *American Law Reports*, Fifth Edition, and *American Law Reports— Federal.* These sets of books publish articles, which the set calls "annotations," that focus on very, very specific legal topics. Each annotation gathers together the cites to the statutes and cases that concern that very specific topic, often summarizing those statutes and cases and providing an analysis of what appears to be the "majority" and "minority" points of view on those legal issues.

The various sets in the ALR series are unlikely to be found in many public libraries. The researcher going to the depth covered in ALRs is well advised to seek out these sets at local county law libraries or law school libraries. A reference librarian at those libraries will no doubt be helpful in showing you how to find the information in the set that you need.

Legal Periodicals

Legal periodicals, or "serials," come in a wide variety of formats. The first category, law reviews or journals, will often be beyond the needs of most nonlawyers, and certainly most nonacademics, and will be collected in hard copy only by large county law libraries and academic law libraries. However, the diligent researcher may be rewarded by pursuing articles in these journals. The second category, legal newspapers and magazines, are even more varied. Sometimes they are of little use to the researcher looking for legal information in the sense of legal analysis or primary law. But this will vary by jurisdiction. Some local legal newspapers may be the first to publish recent, important cases or may have very good analyses of recent legislation. It is therefore hard to generalize.

A variety of access points exist for legal periodicals. One would be reading in a court opinion or elsewhere a reference to an article in a periodical. Then it is a matter of known item searching and the article can usually be tracked down fairly easily. Another access point is a reference in annotated statutory codes. These codes are discussed in Chapters 3 and 4, but briefly, annotated statutory codes publish not only statutes themselves but references to other research material, including articles in legal periodicals. A third access point, and one familiar to most library researchers, are indexes. The two major indexes for major legal periodicals are the *Current Law Index* and the *Legal Resource Index.* CD versions of these indexes appear in some libraries. Finally, versions of these indexes are available in Westlaw and Lexis.

Law Reviews/Journals

In general, "law reviews" and "law journals" are phrases that are used interchangeably and refer to scholarly serials that are published most typically by law schools often on a quarterly basis. Journals publish very in-depth articles on specific legal topics and issues. Some journals are dedicated to a specific topic area such as animal law or telecommunications law; other journals, particularly those bearing the name of the law school, are more general and are likely to publish articles on a wide variety of legal issues and topics.

The chief value of these articles is that ordinarily the writer has collected into one place references to all of "the law"—statutes, cases, and regulations—that pertain to the article's topic and has critically analyzed that law. So the articles are valuable often solely for the references collected in the footnotes, even aside from the scholarly analysis provided in the article. But the intellectual content—the analysis and critical stance of the articles—may sometimes have a significant impact in the field generally and sometimes in court decisions. Thus, for the researcher, finding an article on a topic of interest in a law journal can be a significant find: the article will often provide an overview of the area of law with which it is concerned, will discuss significant cases or legislation, will sometimes provide a legally and intellectually sound critique, and will collect in the footnotes references to primary law that it might take a researcher months to compile.

For the person looking for a specific case or a specific statute, recourse to legal periodicals would be a waste of time. Even someone wanting more depth might find the effort in tracking down articles in law reviews beyond their needs, but since users come with a dizzying array of needs and talents, law reviews may sometimes be exactly what is needed.

Legal Newspapers, Magazines

Legal newspapers and magazines may be published privately as a commercial enterprise; by national, state, or local bar associations; by lawyer organizations of various kinds; or by trade or industry associations. Some of these publications may be collected by county law libraries or academic libraries. Some of the publications are indexed by the national indexes mentioned previously, but many are not.

Except for those few publications that exist in some localities that publish recent full-text court opinions from usually local courts, the effort to find articles in legal newspapers and magazines may not be worth the effort. While it is true that many interesting articles may be published in these publications, it is unlikely that such articles will ever be critical pieces of information in most legal information finding.

Of course there will always be the seeker intent on finding every article ever written by a particular judicial nominee, for instance, or finding a particular bar association's view of a specific legal issue. In those cases, the seeker is best directed to a local governmental or academic law library.

Restatements

A final category of secondary sources must be mentioned for the sake of completeness, but it is a source that even lawyers rarely use: the *Restatements of the Law*. There are many sets of *Restatements*, each concerning, generally, areas of the "common law" (judge-made law) or decisional law. Those areas tend to be the "oldest" in the legal arena: property, contracts, torts, among others. These areas of the law developed largely through judicial decisions, the more careful sense of the phrase "common law." The trouble with this sort of development is that thousands and thousands of cases purport to state "the law" on any particular common law topic.

Thus, in the 1930s a group of legal professionals and academics decided to "restate"—collect together and summarize and then state in condensed principles—what "the law" appeared to be about the various subtopics in property, contracts, and torts. This effort continues today, and the volumes that contribute to that effort, the *Restatements*, are understandably voluminous and complex. Except for the most gifted, ambitious, determined legal information seeker, the *Restatements* are usually best left to the scholars.

Secondary Sources: Pay-for-View Databases

The two major pay-for-view databases for legal materials are Westlaw and Lexis. Both of these databases can provide access to many of the secondary sources listed previously, particularly legal encyclopedias, ALRs, some treatises, some practice materials, and many legal journals and law reviews. However, several cautions should be observed.

First, exactly how many of these sources you can access depends entirely on the level of your subscription to these services. These services provide a befuddling array of levels of access. A public library subscription, if available at all, is likely to be more limited than a university library subscription, which is likely to be far more limited than a university law library's subscription, and access to those libraries with fuller subscriptions will depend largely on your status as student, faculty, or neither. Second, though both of these services provide "credit card" access, it can be very costly. This is especially true for secondary sources, for which you are less likely to have a specific citation to a specific section. Browsing and noodling around can be quite expensive on these databases. Third, because browsing is expensive in these databases, serendipity is less likely to occur in these databases than in print.

With these precautions in mind, and if inexpensive, broad-based access to one of these two databases is available to you, it will be worthwhile for two main reasons: powerful search engines and hyperlinked references. For instance, finding an ALR annotation on one's topic of interest can be easy with the sophisticated search engines provided in these databases, and because annotations collect citations to many primary sources, accessing those primary sources is just a click away within Westlaw and Lexis. Many public law libraries, usually housed in the county courthouse, provide free or cheap access to one or both of these databases.

Secondary Sources: Free Online Access

The web has made great strides in access to free legal information over the past decade, but access to the secondary sources discussed is still nonexistent. You will not find legal encyclopedias, ALRs, *Restatements*, or authoritative practice and form books on the web. You will find many sites selling "legal forms." You will find lots of law firm websites offering various levels of advice.

You may also find all sorts of "commentary" on "the law" looking like secondary sources. Extreme caution should be exercised in relying on such commentary. As the famous *New Yorker* cartoon advises, "No one on the Internet knows that you're a dog." Or an idiot with an ax to grind.

However, at least two exceptions to this exist. The first one is the Cornell Legal Information Institute (www.law.cornell.edu/). In this book we will mention this resource many times. It provides both primary law and, to a much more limited extent, commentary on that law. In particular, it has a "Law About" function that can get you to explanations "about the law" of specific topics. You can access it at topics.law.cornell .edu/wex.

The other exception to the rule that no *reliable* secondary legal sources exist on the web is the University Law Review Project (www.lawreview.org/). Its name is self-explanatory. It provides the researcher with free access to one of the chief types of secondary sources, law reviews.

Conclusion

It takes time to learn how to use most secondary sources, but the effort is well worth it, especially for someone new to legal research. Public libraries are likely to have only a few, if any of these sources. Big public libraries may have legal encyclopedias and maybe a few treatises. To access most of the secondary sources discussed previously, you will need to go to a public law library. This too is worth the effort, and the help you can receive there from law librarians will make you glad you made the trip.

Finding Federal Law:

Legal Information in the Federal System

Introduction

Federal law includes the U.S. Constitution, federal statutes, federal regulations, federal case law, and federal court rules. These sources are considered "primary law" in the federal system. This primary law is usually the ultimate goal of any legal researcher because only it will be mandatory authority. However, the researcher might not *start* with primary sources, but may instead need a guide to find them.

Secondary sources provide an overview of and citations to federal primary law. Most secondary sources about federal law are not about federal law in general, but about *specific areas of the law* that are governed by federal law. Secondary sources regarding specific areas of the law are discussed in Part III of this book in the chapters on specific legal topics. The next section introduces a few general or comprehensive secondary sources about federal law.

General Secondary Sources for Federal Law

American Law Reports—Federal

Specific legal issues within federal law are often researched in the set called *American Law Reports—Federal*, or ALR Fed for short. As explained more fully in Chapter 2 on secondary sources, the ALRs are volumes of articles on very specific legal topics. These articles, which ALR calls "annotations," pull together citations to the primary law sources (statutes, cases, regulations) and some secondary sources concerning the topic and discuss briefly what those sources say. The annotations give the reader an overview of where the law stands on the particular topic being researched. These annotations are very valuable because they save the researcher hours of tracking down the sources cited in the annotation; moreover, the annotations summarize those sources. The careful researcher will not rely entirely on those summaries, but will track down the original sources. But the annotation helps the researcher decide whether it is worth the effort to track down the original sources. *ALR Fed* has a separate index and the index is the best entry into the hard copy volumes of the set. *ALR Fed* is also available on Westlaw and Lexis, depending on one's subscription. For the serious researcher, *ALR Fed* is a valuable resource, and it is worth the trip to a law library or might be worth paying for a session of Westlaw or Lexis.

Practice and Procedure and Form Books

Federal court litigation is complex. It is governed primarily by the federal rules of civil procedure. You can, and should, consult separate compilations of these rules, and these are discussed in this chapter. But if you are planning to be or are already involved in federal litigation and want thorough information about the literal "rules of the game" for that litigation and how courts have interpreted those rules, two federal practice sets stand out:

▶ Moore, James William, Daniel R. Coquillette, et al. 2009. *Moore's Federal Practice*. New York: Mathew Bender. Also on Lexis.

▶ Wright, Charles Alan, Arthur R. Miller, and Mary Kay Kane. 2010. *Federal Practice and Procedure*. St. Paul, MN: West Group. Also on Westlaw.

These two sets are organized by rule number for each federal rule of civil procedure. So, for instance, if you want to know how to begin a lawsuit in federal court, you would look at federal rule of procedure (FRCP) 3. The rule says, "A civil action is commenced by filing a complaint with the court." You might need a little help with just exactly what this means, and so by going to the volumes in the two sets listed previously you would find ample information.

But this rule also mentions filing a "complaint." You might not know what a complaint looks like. Form books provide samples so you can see different types of complaints. Three sets of form books may be useful to you for federal litigation. As with all form books, the forms reprinted in these sets should be adapted to one's particular needs and used only as beginning points. Federal pleading documents—the documents used in litigation in federal court—are often a bit more technical than documents used in state courts, so using the forms in these sets of books will often help people avoid common mistakes:

▶ *American Jurisprudence Pleading and Practice Forms Annotated*. 2010. Rochester, NY: Lawyers Co-operative.

▶ Moore, James William, et al. 2002. *Moore's Manual: Federal Practice Forms*. Albany, NY: Mathew Bender.

▶ *West's Federal Forms*. 2009. St. Paul, MN: West Group.

Treatises

Treatises on federal law are likely to be specific to specialized areas, such as federal rules of evidence, federal law of employment discrimination, federal law of eminent domain, and so forth. Some of these are discussed in the special topic chapters of this book. But if you are looking for a treatise on a specific topic that is an aspect of federal law not discussed in those chapters, you will find treatises most easily by consulting a law library's online catalog or talking to a law librarian or possibly a practitioner in that area of the law.

For resource updates, visit this book's companion website at

▶ *www.GetLaw.net*

RESOURCES RECAP		
General Secondary Sources for Federal Law		
	Resource	**Notes**
American Law Reports— Federal	▶ *American Law Reports—Federal, ALR Fed.*	In print and in Westlaw or Lexis
Practice and Procedure Treatises and Form Books	▶ *American Jurisprudence Pleading and Practice Forms Annotated.* 2010. Rochester, NY: Lawyers Co-operative.	
	▶ Moore, James William, et al. 2002. *Moore's Manual: Federal Practice Forms.* Albany, NY: Mathew Bender.	
	▶ Moore, James William, Coquillette, Daniel R., et al. 2009. *Moore's Federal Practice.* New York: Mathew Bender.	Also on Lexis
	▶ *West's Federal Forms.* 2009. St. Paul, MN: West Group.	
	▶ Wright, Charles Alan, Arthur R. Miller, and Mary Kay Kane. 2010. *Federal Practice and Procedure.* St. Paul, MN: West Group.	Also on Westlaw

Free Web Sources for Federal Law

The sources discussed in this section are a bridge between the secondary sources discussed previously and the primary law sources discussed after this section. These sources have some secondary material, "commentary on the law" broadly speaking, but these sources also serve as "portals" to primary law.

The federal government and others improve access to federal law sources on a daily basis. The sites listed in the following section are often listed in this book because they provide wide-ranging access to all types of law, but our focus here is federal law.

Government Sites

GPO Access (www.gpoaccess.gov), the Government Printing Office's website, is a great place to begin. It provides access to the Constitution, federal statutes, federal regulations, and federal case law and provides a wealth of other information. Thomas (thomas.loc.gov), a website from the Library of Congress, is most noted for information about *pending* legislation, but it too has a wealth of other information, including the *Congressional Record*, treaties, committee reports, and more. USA.gov (www.usa.gov), another federal government site, is much broader than the other two, but one may need this breadth at times. One of its values is that it goes beyond federal law and provides links to state and local sources.

Educational Institutions' Sites

The single best site for free, online legal information on both federal and state law is from the Cornell Law School's Legal Information Institute. It has a specific section devoted to federal law, www.law.cornell.edu/federal. There you will find much of what GPO Access provides but often in an easier to use format. For instance, you will get easier access to the federal rules of civil procedure at this site than anywhere else.

The University of Michigan provides another fairly comprehensive site for links to federal materials at www.lib.umich.edu/government-documents-center/explore/browse/federal-government/251/search/?. It suffers from being almost too comprehensive and is organized alphabetically, which is not terribly helpful. But in the right-hand column, one can filter all of the entries by subtopic, such as executive branch, legislative branch, judicial branch, and this filtering makes the site a little more usable.

Private Company Sites

Although not providing broad access to all federal law, lexisOne (law.lexisnexis.com/webcenters/lexisone/ and www.lexisone.com) provides limited free case law. It is limited by how many years of case opinions are available and by which courts are available. Its coverage of case law changes and is described at www.lexisone.com/freecaselaw/coverage.html.

For resource updates, visit this book's companion website at

▶ **www.GetLaw.net**

RESOURCES RECAP		
Free Web Sources for Federal Law		
	Resource	**Notes**
Government Sites	▶ GPO Access: www.gpoaccess.gov ▶ Thomas: thomas.loc.gov ▶ USA.gov: www.usa.gov	Government Printing Office's website Website from the Library of Congress
Educational Institutions' Sites	▶ Cornell's Legal Information Institute, "Law by Source: Federal": www.law.cornell.edu/federal ▶ University of Michigan Library, "Explore Government Documents: Federal Government": www.lib.umich.edu/government-documents-center/explore/browse/federal-government/251/search/?	Specific section devoted to federal law Comprehensive site of links to federal materials

Primary Law: U.S. Constitution

If you do a Google search on the "United States Constitution" you will come up with nearly 15 million results. Similarly, if you walk into a law library you will find thousands of books, and a good portion of those, whether obvious or not, will be somehow related to the U.S. Constitution. So, where to begin?

Answering this question depends on what you want. If all you want to know is what exactly the First Amendment says, then all you have to do is find an authoritative text of the U.S. Constitution. Most often people will be interested in how has the language of the Constitution been interpreted by the courts. For this information, you will need to go to some of the following resources.

Secondary Sources on Constitutional Law

Two constitutional law treatises come highly recommended:

▶ Nowak, John E., and Ronald D. Rotunda. 2007. *Treatise on Constitutional Law: Substance and Procedure.* St. Paul, MN: Thomson West.

Nowak and Rotunda's *Treatise* is a well-respected, up-to-date, multivolume set providing the reader with an excellent overview of most of the important areas of federal constitutional law. This work is a thorough and very practical set that has as its task simply describing what the U.S. Constitution says and how it has been interpreted by the courts.

▶ Tribe, Laurence H. 2000. *American Constitutional Law.* New York: Foundation Press.

While equally well respected and comprehensive, Laurence H. Tribe's *American Constitutional Law* takes a much more theoretical approach to the topic. For those interested in a unique, very scholarly, interesting approach to the topic, Tribe is your man. If one wants a straightforward explanation, however, use Nowak and Rotunda.

General Sources

Print

Print copies of the U.S. Constitution can be found in thousands of places. If you are in a library with a fairly large legal collection, the easiest way to find the U.S. Constitution in hard copy is in the volumes dedicated to the Constitution in one of these three sets:

▶ U.S. Code (**USC**)

▶ U.S. Code Annotated (USCA)

▶ U.S. Code Service (USCS)

The virtues and shortcomings of these sets are discussed fully in the section on U.S. statutes, also known as "federal statutes," and they are discussed in the next major section of this chapter. Because researchers will most often want something more than the simple wording of the

Constitution, particularly citations to cases that have interpreted the language, the researcher will more likely want to go to USCA or USCS. These two sets provide a section called "Notes of Decisions," which give a short summary and a citation to specific cases that have interpreted the language in any particular section of the U.S. Constitution. This is particularly helpful because these cases can be hard to find on the free web, which offers relatively primitive subject searching capabilities, and can be expensive to find in the pay-for-view databases.

Websites

One of the areas the free web excels in is providing information about the U.S. Constitution. As you can imagine, some of it is wonderful, and some of it is not to be trusted. First, the federal government's site for the text of the U.S. Constitution is part of the GPO Access site mentioned previously: www.gpoaccess.gov/constitution/index.html. Second, a wide-ranging, entertaining, interesting, and authoritative site for the Constitution is the National Archives' website (www.archives.gov/exhibits/charters/charters.html). You will see that it has not only the Constitution but also the Bill of Rights (the first ten amendments to the Constitution), the Declaration of Independence, and other important documents. The site provides scanned copies of the original documents as well as text-only versions. Third, we have mentioned the Cornell site

For resource updates, visit this book's companion website at

▶ **www.GetLaw.net**

RESOURCES RECAP		
Primary Law: U.S. Constitution		
	Resource	**Notes**
Secondary Sources on Constitutional Law	▶ Nowak, John E., and Ronald D. Rotunda. 2007. *Treatise on Constitutional Law: Substance and Procedure*. St. Paul, MN: Thomson West. ▶ Tribe, Laurence H. 2000. *American Constitutional Law*. New York: Foundation Press.	
General Sources—Print	▶ U.S. Code (USC) ▶ U.S. Code Annotated (USCA) ▶ U.S. Code Service (USCS)	
General Sources—Websites	▶ Cornell's Legal Information Institute, "United States Constitution": www.law.cornell.edu/constitution/constitution.overview.html ▶ GPO Access, "Constitution of the United States: Main Page": www.gpoaccess.gov/constitution/index.html ▶ House of Representatives, "Educational Resources": www.house.gov/house/Educate.shtml ▶ National Archives, "The Charters of Freedom": www.archives.gov/exhibits/charters/charters.html ▶ University of Chicago, "The Founders' Constitution": press-pubs.uchicago.edu/founders/	Specific section devoted to the U.S. Constitution

(www.law.cornell.edu/constitution/constitution.overview.html). It has a specific section devoted to the U.S. Constitution. Fourth, part of the House of Representatives' website (www.house.gov/house/Educate .shtml) provides information not found elsewhere. Its links specific to the Constitution, however, will take you to the National Archives site, second on our list. Finally, many sites exist that provide historical perspectives on the Constitution. For example, try "The Founders' Constitution" from the University of Chicago (press-pubs.uchicago.edu/ founders/).

Primary Law: Federal Statutes

Pending Legislation

People will often be interested in legislation that they have heard about in the news. Often this legislation is only proposed or pending. Tracking it down can sometimes be tricky, but try the following sources.

Websites

Print sources do exist for pending legislation, but it takes a long time for printed sources to arrive in a library. For pending legislation, therefore, there is no substitute for free web sources. We have mentioned both of these sites before but in a different order because Thomas is tops for pending legislation, otherwise known as legislative "bills":

- GPO Access, the Government Printing Office's website: www.gpoaccess .gov
- Thomas, a website from the Library of Congress: thomas.loc.gov

People will most often want to find pending legislation when they have heard about or read about a "bill" or "law" that Congress is considering. If you know the bill number, your search may be easier, but you can still find the bill using some key words or phrases.

Current Statutes

Many people are unfamiliar with the term "statutes," yet it is the type of "law" that most of us think of as "the law." Statutes are those pieces of law that are enacted, that are voted on by legislative bodies. When we are talking about federal statutes, that legislative body is the U.S. Congress, which is made up of two houses, the U.S. Senate and the U.S. House of Representatives.

You can find federal statutes in hard copy or online at many free websites. If you have a specific citation to a statute, either print or free online sources will be relatively easy to use. If you do not have a specific citation and you want a statute about a topic but are not exactly sure how that topic is categorized, you will have to do a subject search in either the index volumes for the print sources listed below or in Westlaw or Lexis. If you do not have a citation but are pretty sure of the topic you are

---

CLOSER LOOK

How a Bill Becomes a Law
Briefly, you will recall that in the legislative process, somebody, usually a senator or a representative, introduces a "bill," a proposed piece of legislation, into the house of Congress to which he or she was elected. The bill then goes to an appropriate committee of that house. The committee holds hearings on the bill and either passes it out of committee or fails to do so. If it is passed out of committee it goes to the full body. If it is passed it then goes to the other house of Congress. At that house it goes through the same committee process, and if the full body passes the bill and the president signs it, the bill then becomes a public law (P.L.) and is published. At this stage it is most often referred to as a "slip law" because it is published in hard copy on pieces of paper, "slips."

The next stage is known as "**codification**," a term given to the following process: The slip law is sent to the code reviser's office and that office assigns it a title number and a section number. These numbers are assigned according to the subject matter to which the statute belongs. It is then published in the federal statutory code. It is at this stage that the bill has become a law and then is referred to as a "statute."

QUICK TIP

Interpreting Citations to Federal Statutes

A federal statutory citation will most often look something like this: 42 U.S.C. § 1983. The first number is the title number, the number that pertains most closely to the subject of the statute. Title 42, for instance, holds statutes pertaining to the "public health and welfare." A pretty broad topic. The abbreviation means "United States Code" and tells you the citation must be to a statute because the USC publishes statutes. The funny double s symbol that comes next merely means "section." So, if you wanted to find the statute referred to by this citation, you would go to one of the sets discussed in this chapter or one of the websites that publishes the U.S. Code and find title 42 on the spines of some of the hardcopy books or a link to Title 42 on one of the websites, and then you would find the particular volume of title 42 that holds section 1983.

interested in, you may be able to find statutes on that topic at the Cornell site discussed in the following Websites subsection.

Print

Three hardcopy sets hold federal statutes:

- ▶ U.S. Code (USC)
- ▶ U.S. Code Annotated (USCA)
- ▶ U.S. Code Service (USCS)

The first one, the U.S. Code, is the official code published by the U.S. government. Most researchers will rarely use this set. First, it tends to be slow in publishing updated material. Second, it publishes only the statutes and nothing else. Often, researchers want the "something else." That is, they want to know most often how the courts have interpreted these statutes, or they may want to know what law review articles have said about issues pertaining to these statutes, or they may want a lead in learning about the history of these statutes. For this material, the researcher will go to the other two sets, called annotated codes, because these sets annotate or provide notes about the statutes.

Most important, annotated codes provide a section called "Notes of Decisions." These notes are paragraph summaries about the facts and rules decided in specific cases and citations to those cases. Therefore, the researcher looking for case law that has interpreted a statute, or a specific portion of a statute, will find annotated codes irreplaceable. Consequently, a good rule of thumb when looking for statutes in print is to always go to one of the annotated codes—USCA, published by West, or USCS, published by Lexis.

Websites

On the web, just as with print editions, there are also the "official" sources and the unofficial sources. But the "annotated" and "nonannotated" distinction used in the print sources is less clear on the web. For one, on the free web it is difficult to find notes of decisions that summarize and cite to cases that have interpreted the statute in which one might be interested. In other words, most of the federal statutory law that you will find on the free web will be simply the statutes themselves, without any helpful "annotations."

The official site for current federal statutes, arranged by subject matter in the typical title and section citation order so you can browse for what you are looking for, is www.gpoaccess.gov/uscode/browse .html. If you do not know the title and section number, you can find an online searchable version at the GPO Access site at www.gpoaccess .gov/uscode/.

If you do not have a statutory cite but a public law number, which will look something like P.L. 108-1, meaning the first bill passed by the 108th Congress, you have two familiar but more specific choices: In Thomas, start at thomas.loc.gov/bss/d111/d111laws.html and then find the right session of Congress. For GPO Access, start at www.gpoaccess.gov/ plaws/index.html.

If you are looking for federal statutes online and you do not have a specific citation but are pretty clear about the topic, try browsing the list of topics associated with the statutory title numbers at Cornell Law School's Legal Information Institute site (www.law.cornell.edu/uscode/).

For resource updates, visit this book's companion website at

▶ *www.GetLaw.net*

RESOURCES RECAP		
Primary Law: Federal Statutes		
	Resource	**Notes**
Pending Legislation	▶ GPO Access: www.gpoaccess.gov ▶ Thomas: thomas.loc.gov	
Current Statutes and Court Rules—Print	▶ U.S. Code (USC) ▶ U.S. Code Annotated (USCA) ▶ U.S. Code Service (USCS)	
Current Statutes and Court Rules—Websites	▶ GPO Access, "United States Code: Main Page": www.gpoaccess.gov/uscode/	If you have a statutory cite
	▶ GPO Access, "Public and Private Laws: Main Page": www.gpoaccess.gov/plaws/index.html	If you have a public law number
	▶ Thomas, "Browse Public Laws": thomas.loc.gov/home/LegislativeData.php?&n=PublicLaws&c=111	If you have a public law number
	▶ Cornell's Legal Information Institute, "U.S. Code": www.law.cornell.edu/uscode/	For federal statues by topic, using statutory title numbers to search

Primary Law: Federal Cases

Case law and "case reporting" are central to our entire legal system. Ours is a legal system built on "precedent," on preceding decisions that are to be followed in future cases on the same issue. The idea is that current legal disputes should be decided in the same way as those disputes were decided in the past unless there is a very good reason for not doing so. This is a principle called "stare decisis." As a consequence of this principle, it is very important that people be able to find out how courts have decided similar legal disputes in the past, which is the whole reason why court opinions (the terms "opinions," "decisions" and "cases" are often used as synonyms) get published.

Case opinions are published in two different ways: in **reporters** and in **digests**. Reporters publish the full text of court opinions, including "value-added" material such as synopses of the opinions, and "**headnotes**," little paragraph summaries of the holdings in the cases.

In contrast to case reporters, case digests do not publish the full text of opinions but publish paragraph summaries of the issues or holdings that have been decided in those cases, accompanied by a citation to the

---

CLOSER LOOK

Lifecycle of a Court Opinion

The process of publishing full text court opinions is important too. Different courts have different practices, but the way that the U.S. Supreme Court does it is explained here because it is the most important court in the land and because many courts will follow its example. All opinions include the majority opinion, any concurring or dissenting opinions, and a syllabus or synopsis of the case prepared by the reporter's office.

Bench opinions are the first versions to appear. On the day an opinion is announced by the court, these bench opinions are available immediately to the press and public in a printed form through the Court's Public Information Office. These same opinions are immediately distributed electronically by way of the Court's Project Hermes and are available by subscription for a fee. However, many of the free web sources subscribe to this service and make these opinions available on those sources' websites.

The next generation of an opinion is a "**slip opinion**," published several days after the bench opinion. These slip opinions may contain corrections not appearing in the bench opinion. They are available for free from the Court's Public Information Office and for a fee from the Government Printing Office. They are also available on the U.S. Supreme Court's website and remain there until the hardbound volume containing the opinion is published, about a year after the opinion was originally announced. These slip opinions are often collected by **depository libraries** throughout the United States. In general, most governmental law libraries and academic law libraries are depository libraries, but few public libraries are depository libraries, at least for these opinions.

The third generation of opinions are called "preliminary prints" but are more often known as "advance sheets" or "advance pamphlets." These are paperbound pamphlets containing several opinions that were announced within a similar time frame. These pamphlets also contain lots of other information aside from the opinions themselves, including tables and indexes. These pamphlets are available for a fee from the GPO.

Finally, the fourth and final generation of opinions appear in the bound volumes of the *United States Reports*. This is the final and "official" version of the case. Any discrepancies between any of the generations of a specific opinion are resolved by resorting to this final, official printed version. Electronic copies of these bound volumes are available at the court's website going back only to 1991.

---

full text of the opinion. Thus, if you want to find cases on a particular topic you will start in digests, not in reporters.

United States Supreme Court

Print

REPORTERS: Because of their importance, you may find opinions of the U.S. Supreme Court in a wide variety of sources, from newspapers to magazines. But consistently, and historically, these opinions have been published in three hardbound sets:

▶ *Supreme Court Reporter*

Abbreviated S. Ct. in case citations, this set is published by Thomson West Publishing Group and includes synopses of opinions, headnotes, and the key topic and number system that integrates the content of the opinions into the entire West digest system.

▶ *Supreme Court Reports, Lawyers Edition*

Abbreviated L.Ed.2d in case citations, this set is now published by LexisNexis. It includes "value-added" material similar to the *Supreme Court Reporter*, including synopses and headnotes but not topic and key numbers.

▶ *United States Reports*

  Abbreviated U.S. in case citations, this is the official version of the opinions and is published by the federal government. In disputes over the exact wording of an opinion these reports are the final word.

Another print source is *United States Law Week*, a "loose-leaf reporter" (a set of three-ring binder publications) designed specifically to have up-to-date opinions, hence its three-ring binder format that is easily updated by insertion of new opinions.

DIGESTS: Case digests are sets of books that publish short paragraph summaries of cases, organized by topic. If you want to find an opinion on a particular topic and you do not know of any actual cases about that topic, the best place to begin is in a case digest for the court and jurisdiction that is pertinent to your legal problem.

  Several digests publish summaries of opinions from the U.S. Supreme Court. In general, use the "smallest" or most focused set you can find. These digests will likely be found, if anywhere, at large governmental law libraries, such as county law libraries, or academic law libraries, such as those associated with a law school.

  It takes some time to learn how to use digests. Look at the beginning of the set or of each volume in the set and you are likely to find an overview of all the topics covered in the set. The topics are also most often printed on the spine of each volume. But sometimes you are not sure what topic would cover the area you are researching. If this is true, look for the volumes that say "Index" or "General Index" or "Descriptive Word Index." In these index volumes, look up words related to the topic you want to research and you are likely to find entries next to those words that tell you what topic volume to look in for your interests. Go to that topic volume and notice that it will be divided into many subtopics, sometimes called "key numbers" if you are using a West digest, as most of them are. Once you have identified a subtopic pertaining to your area of interest, turn to that subtopic and you will find short paragraph descriptions of holdings in case opinions that pertain to that topic. Usually following that description will be a citation to the full text of that opinion, which you will then want to track down in the appropriate set of case reporters.

  Listed here are the digests containing summaries of U.S. Supreme Court opinions. The digests are listed from the most specific, smallest ones, to the largest ones:

▶ *United States Supreme Court Digest*

  This is the one to use if you are interested *only* in opinions from that court.

▶ *Federal Practice Digest*

  This digest has several series. If you are looking for recent cases, look in the most recent series, or the highest numbered series, which presently is *Federal Practice Digest*, 4th Series, which digests opinions from 1975 to the present. Furthermore, this digest is bulkier and therefore a little more burdensome to use because it digests opinions not only from the U.S. Supreme Court but also from the federal courts of appeal and the federal district courts as well as opinions from the bankruptcy courts, the courts of claims, and military courts, all courts that are beyond the scope of this book and are of rare use to average public library patrons. (Note that the opinions of bankruptcy courts are digested in a separate, more focused digest, West's Bankruptcy Digest.)

▶ *Decennial Digest*

This is the "granddaddy" of all digests. The *Decennial Digest* is the massive sets of digests that digest every case from every court, state and federal, in the United States since 1897. Though the overall set is a digest, it is really a series of digests published every ten years, hence the name "decennial." This digest is so huge and so expensive that it is unlikely you will find it in most libraries; some academic or public law libraries may have it, but often many of its volumes are in storage off site somewhere. Due to its size, it is also very difficult to use and difficult to use wisely. We would recommend that if you find you must use the digest you either take a day off from work or you ask an experienced, expert law librarian familiar with this digest to help you.

Websites

Case law, particularly opinions from the U.S. Supreme Court, are increasingly moving to the web. Budget-minded public libraries, therefore, are increasingly less likely to collect the expensive and space-consuming hardbound volumes of these opinions and are more likely to suggest to patrons that they find these opinions online.

Because of the importance of U.S. Supreme Court decisions, and because many people are interested in those decisions, the web offers many, many places to find these decisions. It is important in accessing cases on the Internet to keep in mind the process or the "generations" of opinions and to keep in mind that the final, official version of a case is always the bound, printed volume. Listed here are the most useful and reliable websites that provide free access to opinions. Other sources exist, such as Westlaw, but sources that require some form of payment are not listed. Each site listed, however, will be different in coverage— that is, in how many years of opinions are online, in searchability, and in comprehensiveness (some sites publish all opinions, some publish only "selected" opinions). So at each site carefully investigate coverage, searchability, and comprehensiveness before you decide that what you are looking for is not at the site.

The official website for opinions from the U.S. Supreme Court is www.supremecourtus.gov/opinions/opinions.html. Note that this site is most useful for recent opinions and that it publishes opinions only from 1991 forward. You will find here bench opinions that are then replaced by slip opinions, which will then be replaced by the final official version once a hardbound volume is printed.

Cornell's Legal Information Institute website, mentioned many times in these pages, has a special section devoted entirely to U.S. Supreme Court decisions (and more) in its "Supreme Court Collection" (www.law.cornell.edu/supct/). This is a "one-stop shopping" site and is highly recommended. It has very recent decisions, a complete collection of decisions since 1990, and selected "historic" decisions prior to 1990.

The archived, older decisions can be accessed by topic, author, and party name. Among other useful resources, the site contains links back to the official site of the U.S. Supreme Court and the site we discuss next, the "Oyez" site.

The "Oyez" site (www.oyez.org/) is a wonderful site, especially if you are interested in the U.S. Supreme Court beyond the mere publication of its decisions. For instance, at this site you can hear oral arguments before the court, read biographies of the justices, read news from and about the court, view the court's argument calendar, find cases organized by year and topic, and more. The "Oyez" site is also highly recommended.

If you are looking only for comprehensive coverage of decisions from the U.S. Supreme Court, for free, from 1781, a very handy site is LexisOne (www.lexisone.com/). In addition to the favored sites discussed previously, the list of free sources for U.S. Supreme Court opinions also includes the following: Findlaw, Loislaw, FedWorld, GPO Access, QuickLaw, and VersusLaw. These are easily accessed by name online.

United States Courts of Appeal (aka "Circuit Courts")

Print

REPORTERS: The chronological publication of the decisions of all of the circuit courts of appeal in the federal system is in a set of books called the *Federal Reporter*. These have been published over the years in several sets; for instance, the *Federal Reporter*, Second Series, and since 1988, the *Federal Reporter*, Third Series. These are abbreviated in case citations, respectively, as F.2d and F.3d. Thus, when you see a case citation to one of these sets you will know that the opinion cited comes from the one of the federal circuit courts of appeal.

DIGESTS: To find case opinions by subject matter, or topic, from the federal circuit courts of appeal the best and longest standing print source is a set called the *Federal Practice Digest*. Like the reporters, these sets have been published in different series, based on chronology. For decisions since 1975, look in the *Federal Practice Digest*, Fourth Series. For earlier cases, look in the earlier series.

Websites

As with opinions from the U.S. Supreme Court, opinions from the U.S. circuit courts of appeal are available from a dizzying number of sites, made even more dizzying by the varying levels of coverage available at each—from comprehensive to selective cases, and dating sometimes from the 1880s and sometimes only back to the 1990s or 2000s. Therefore, when you are using one of these sites be sure you check to see the coverage of the site before you decide you cannot find something you know exists.

First, keep in mind that precedent, those opinions that *must be* followed and are therefore considered mandatory authority, is a jurisdictional question determined by geography; federal circuit courts of appeal are divided up by geographic areas. Determine what circuit court is mandatory authority for the area in which you live or in which the legal issue you are interested in arises. Then focus your research for opinions on that jurisdiction. Each circuit has its own official website that publishes some of its opinions. Look there first.

For instance, in the ninth circuit, which covers all of the western states, the website is www.ca9.uscourts.gov/opinions/. It is not immediately apparent at this site, however, that there are opinions from this court at this site going back only to 1995. But this site has other useful and interesting material, including court rules and audio recordings of arguments before the court. These general precautions should guide you in any other jurisdiction as well because website coverage will vary by jurisdiction. If you are not sure which federal circuit court is mandatory authority for your location, a few places to begin are the U.S. courts' website (www.uscourts.gov/courtlinks/) and Villanova School of Law's Federal Court Locator (www.law.villanova.edu/Library/Research%20 Guides/Federal%20Court%20Locator.aspx). These sites should lead you to the websites for the right court for your area and to the decisions from those courts.

In addition to the official sites you find through the process in the preceding paragraph, federal circuit court opinions may also be found at many other sites. The site claiming the "oldest" opinions is Open Jurist (www.openjurist.org/), an admirable attempt to provide free access to all case opinions, including those from the circuit courts. It is most helpful at this site if you already have the *Federal Reporter* cite for the case for which you are looking. This site also has a Google search function within the opinions collected there. In addition to sites we have mentioned many times such as Cornell and Findlaw, whose coverage varies, many other sites collect cases back to only 1950. These include the following: Justia (cases.justia.com/us-court-of-appeals/) and the Public Library of Law (www.plol.org/Pages/Search.aspx).

United States District Courts

Print

The publication of opinions from the federal trial courts follows the general pattern of case publication. The opinions are published chronologically in reporters and topically in digests, as follows:

REPORTERS: For the chronological publication of the decisions of all of the federal district courts, the trial courts in the federal system, known officially as the U.S. district courts, you will look in a set of books called the *Federal Supplement.* These have been published in two sets, the *Federal Supplement* and the *Federal Supplement,* 2nd Series. These are abbreviated in case citations, respectively, as F. Supp. and F. Supp. 2d. Thus, when you see a case citation to one of these sets you will know that the opinion cited comes from the one of the U.S. district courts.

DIGESTS: To find case opinions by subject matter, or topic, from the federal district courts, the best and longest standing print source, as discussed in the previous section, is the *Federal Practice Digest*. Like the reporters, these sets have been published in different series, based on chronology. For decisions since 1975, look in the *Federal Practice Digest*, Fourth Series. For earlier cases, look in the earlier series.

Websites

While the U.S. district courts, the trial courts in the federal system, have to follow as mandatory precedent the opinions of the federal circuit courts for their area and the opinions of the U.S. Supreme Court, the U.S. district courts themselves do not have to follow what other district courts have held in prior decisions, nor do they need to follow prior decisions of the same district court. Partly for this reason, far fewer opinions from the district courts are published in any accessible form, but you can find them on the web.

First, follow the sites listed previously regarding finding the right federal circuit court for your area to find the right district court for your area. Once you have found the right court, access its website and you are likely to find at least recent opinions from that court. Beyond these official sites, some of the "unofficial" sites we have mentioned in many places may also publish a limited number of opinions from the U.S. district courts. Start with Cornell: www.law.cornell.edu/federal/districts .html#circuit.

Because of the spottiness and unpredictability of finding district court opinions on the web, this category may be one example of when it is best to travel to a law library to find these cases in print.

Other Federal Courts

The federal court system, though we simplify to say there are three levels, in truth has a number of specialized trial courts, including bankruptcy courts, courts of claims, tax court, courts of international trade, and courts related to the military and veterans. With the exception of the bankruptcy courts, these courts are the province of very specialized areas of the law and will not be discussed further in this book.

Bankruptcy

Print

Decisions from the federal bankruptcy courts are published in print in *West's Bankruptcy Reporter*, most likely available only in large county or state law libraries and perhaps in the largest academic libraries. For finding decisions from the federal bankruptcy courts by topic, there is *West's Bankruptcy Digest*, again, most likely available only in large county or state law libraries and perhaps in the largest academic libraries.

Websites

Start with Cornell (www.law.cornell.edu/federal/districts.html#circuit). The bankruptcy courts will vary in how opinions are published on the web. Locate the bankruptcy court that concerns the issue you are researching, and with good luck it may be a court that publishes its

For resource updates, visit this book's companion website at

▶ **www.GetLaw.net**

opinions. But again, because of the spottiness and unpredictability of finding federal trial court opinions (which is what bankruptcy decisions would be considered) on the web, this category is another example of when it is best to travel to a law library to find these cases in print.

RESOURCES RECAP		
Primary Law: Federal Cases		
	Resource	**Notes**
U.S. Supreme Court—Print	**Reporters** ▶ *Supreme Court Reporter* ▶ *Supreme Court Reports, Lawyers Edition* ▶ *United States Law Week* ▶ *United States Reports* **Digests** ▶ Federal Practice Digest ▶ United States Supreme Court Digest	Abbreviated S. Ct. in case citations Usually abbreviated L.Ed.2d in case citations A loose-leaf reporter Abbreviated U.S. in case citations
U.S. Supreme Court—Websites	▶ Cornell's Legal Information Institute, "Supreme Court Collection": www.law.cornell.edu/supct/ ▶ LexisNexis, "lexisONE: LexisNexis Research": law.lexisnexis.com/webcenters/lexisone/ ▶ Oyez, "The Oyez Project: U.S. Supreme Court Oral Arguments, Case Abstracts, and More": www.oyez.org/ ▶ Supreme Court of the United States, "Opinions": www.supremecourtus.gov/opinions/opinions.html	 Official website for Supreme Court opinions
U.S. Courts of Appeal—Print	**Reporters** ▶ *Federal Reporter*, first through third series **Digests** ▶ *Federal Practice Digest,* Fourth Series	aka "Circuit Courts" For earlier cases, look in the earlier series.
U.S. Courts of Appeal—Websites	 ▶ United States Courts, "Court Locator": www.uscourts.gov/courtlinks/ ▶ Villanova University School of Law, "Federal Court Locator": www.law.villanova.edu/Library/Research%20Guides/Federal%20Court%20Locator.aspx ▶ Justia, "U.S. Court of Appeals Cases and Opinions": cases.justia.com/us-court-of-appeals/ ▶ Open Jurist: openjurist.org/ ▶ Public Library of Law: www.plol.org/Pages/Search.aspx	Each circuit has its own official website that publishes some of its opinions. Look there first. To find the mandatory authority for your location To find the mandatory authority for your location U.S. District Courts-Print Reporters Federal Supplement
		(Cont'd.)

RESOURCES RECAP *(Continued)*		
Primary Law: Federal Cases		
	Resource	**Notes**
U.S. District Courts—Print	**Reporters** ▶ *Federal Supplement* ▶ *Federal Supplement*, Second Series **Digests** ▶ *Federal Practice Digest*	
U.S. District Courts— Websites	▶ Cornell's Legal Information Institute, "Federal Law Collection": www.law.cornell.edu/federal/districts.html#circuit	First, follow the sites listed previously for finding the right federal circuit court for your area to find the right district court for your area.
Other Federal Courts: Bankruptcy— Print	▶ *West's Bankruptcy Digest* ▶ *West's Bankruptcy Reporter*	
Other Federal Courts: Bankruptcy— Websites	▶ Cornell's Legal Information Institute, "Federal Law Collection": www.law.cornell.edu/federal/districts.html#circuit	First, try locating the bankruptcy court's website.

Primary Law: Regulations (Administrative Law)

Federal administrative agencies impact many aspects of our everyday lives, whether we are aware of it or not. People will often be interested in worksite safety, airline safety, the weather, space travel, and on and on. Very often these areas of interest will be significantly shaped by federal administrative agencies, designated by the "alphabet soup" we often find in our daily news: the Occupational Safety and Health Administration (OSHA), the Environmental Protection Agency (EPA), Federal Aviation Administration (FAA), National Oceanic and Atmospheric Administration (NOAA), the National Aeronautics and Space Administration (NASA), to name just a few of the hundreds of these agencies.

These administrative agencies will publish rules and decisions that govern the area of the agency's expertise, how the agency itself functions, and sometimes individual cases brought before the agency. This varied material is often referred to collectively as "**administrative law**."

More specifically, the rules that govern the area of the agency's expertise and its own processes are called "administrative rules and regulations" and are published in a "code," much like statutory codes. Finding these rules and regulations is the subject of this section and most closely resembles statutory research. To find administrative decisions that govern individual cases, look for a loose-leaf service—discussed in Chapter 2—or find the website for the agency that issued the decision. This will not be a sure bet, but it is a start.

First, the researcher will want to determine the agency that is of interest. A good place to start is Louisiana State University Library's listing at www.lib.lsu.edu/gov/. From this site you should easily find the website for the agency in question. Given the hundreds of websites, the coverage of each will vary, but more and more of these agencies are posting the regulations that the agency promulgates or follows.

Print

Finding federal agency rules and regulations has traditionally begun with the *Code of Federal Regulations*, the **CFR**. Some public libraries will have this paperbound set, and many county and academic libraries will have it too. The *CFR* is organized by agency and publishes the permanent regulations for each agency. If the researcher does not have a specific citation to a regulation, start with the general index. Proposed rules and regulations pertaining to federal administrative agencies must be published in the *Federal Register*. Most libraries that have the *CFR* will also have the *Federal Register*.

Websites

Rather than jumping right in to websites for separate agencies, a researcher may benefit from a general overview of the federal administrative agencies and their processes. For this you can begin at the U.S. Government Manual (www.gpoaccess.gov/gmanual/). You can find this source in print as well. As the official manual of the U.S. government, it will provide the reader with a comprehensive overview of the administrative agencies of the federal government.

A very good research guide to federal administrative materials is published on the web by the Law Librarians' Society of the District of Columbia (www.llsdc.org/fed-reg-cfr/). The Law Library of Congress has a similar guide (www.loc.gov/law/help/administrative.php). The Georgetown Law Library publishes a tutorial about the administrative process and how to research this material, which can be found at www.ll.georgetown.edu/tutorials/admin/index.cfm.

Several good portal sites exist too. For instance, a good portal, linking one to the online *CFR* and *Federal Register* and other pertinent information is "RegInfo.gov" (www.reginfo.gov/public/).

You may begin also by jumping right in to the two primary sources: the *CFR* and the *Federal Register*. For the *CFR* online you have at least two choices: the government's GPO Access site (www.gpoaccess.gov/cfr/index.html) or Cornell's site (cfr.law.cornell.edu/cfr/). A governmental, but experimental and unofficial electronic site, is the e-CFR, which attempts to integrate very new regulations into the existing *CFR*: ecfr.gpoaccess.gov/cgi/t/text/text-idx?c=ecfr&tpl=/index.tpl. The electronic version of the *Federal Register*, from the government, is available at www.gpoaccess.gov/fr/index.html. Finally, a very interesting governmental site that seeks citizen input into the administrative regulatory process is regulations.gov (www.regulations.gov/search/Regs/home.html#home).

For resource updates, visit this book's companion website at

▶ *www.GetLaw.net*

RESOURCES RECAP		
Primary Law: Regulations (Administrative Law)		
	Resource	**Notes**
General	▶ Louisiana State University Libraries, "Federal Agency Directory": www.lib.lsu.edu/gov/index.html	To find the federal agency that might concern your topic
Print	▶ *Code of Federal Regulations* ▶ *Federal Register*	
Websites	▶ Georgetown Law Library, "Administrative Law Research Tutorial": www.ll.georgetown.edu/tutorials/admin/index.cfm	Tutorial about administrative process and how to research this material
	▶ GPO Access, "Code of Federal Regulations: Main Page": www.gpoaccess.gov/cfr/index.html	Online access to the *CFR*
	▶ Cornell's Legal Information Institute, "Code of Federal Regulations": cfr.law.cornell.edu/cfr/	Online access to the *CFR*
	▶ GPO Access, "Electronic Code of Federal Regulations, e-CFR": ecfr.gpoaccess.gov/cgi/t/text/text-idx?c=ecfr&tpl=/index.tpl	Governmental, but experimental and unofficial electronic site, integrating new regulations into the existing *CFR*
	▶ GPO Access, "The Federal Register: Main Page": www.gpoaccess.gov/fr/index.html	Online access to the *Federal Register*
	▶ GPO Access, "U.S. Government Manual: Main Page": www.gpoaccess.gov/gmanual/index.html	Overview of federal administrative agencies and their processes
	▶ Law Librarians' Society of the District of Columbia, "Research Guide to the Federal Register and the Code of Federal Regulations": www.llsdc.org/fed-reg-cfr/	Guide to federal administrative materials
	▶ Law Library of Congress, "Administrative Law Guide": www.loc.gov/law/help/administrative.php	Guide to federal administrative materials
	▶ RegInfo.gov, "Dashboard": www.reginfo.gov/public/	Portal linking to the online *CFR* and *Federal Register* and other pertinent information

Primary Law: Federal Court Rules

All federal courts at all levels have rules about how litigants are to get things done in those courts. If you are suing someone or being sued and working on your own in federal court, you will have to find the rules for the court where the litigation occurs. You will find the Federal Rules of Civil Procedure, the Federal Rules of Criminal Procedure, the Federal Rules of Evidence, and the Federal Rules of Appellate Procedure. These rules apply nationwide—the first three in all U.S. district courts, the latter set in the U.S. courts of appeals. The U.S. Supreme Court has its own set of rules as well.

Remember, for the district courts and the circuit courts of appeal there will be local rules that apply to a specific district court or circuit court that supplement the nationwide rules. For example, say you are working in the U.S. district court for the Western District of Texas. The Federal Rules of Civil Procedure (FRCP) will govern civil actions in that court, as they govern all district courts, but there will also be a specific set of local rules for the Western District of Texas that you will need to follow as well as the FRCP. These local rules may give further requirements such as page limits or time frames within which certain actions must be taken. As an example, you can go to that court's website to find all of these rules (www.txwd .uscourts.gov/rules/default.asp). It is likely your local U.S. district court will have a similar page of links to these rules as well as its own local rules.

Print

In print, you will find many sources for federal court rules. First, you are likely to find a single volume set that contains most of the rules of nationwide application. This is often a handy and portable format. These single volumes are usually published annually and sometimes may be included in a volume that also contains state court rules. Some may also contain the local federal court rules. The local rules for the all of the federal courts in the United States is available in print in a seven-volume loose-leaf, *Federal Local Court Rules*, Third Edition (1997–2010). Second, look in the annotated statutory code, the USCA or the USCS. These sets publish not only the rules but also notes of decisions that summarize and cite to cases that have interpreted the rules. Third, if you are very serious about litigation in federal court, you can go to the two sets of books mentioned in the first section of this chapter, Wright and Miller's *Federal Practice and Procedure* and *Moore's Federal Practice*. These sets provide practitioners with very detailed and scholarly treatments of the federal court rules. Both sets cover the civil, criminal, and appellate rules. The Wright and Miller set also covers the federal rules of evidence.

Websites

Online, you can find just the text of the Federal Rules of Civil, Criminal, and Appellate Procedure as well as the Federal Rules of Evidence in PDF format at a website provided by the House Committee on the Judiciary (judiciary.house.gov/about/procedural.html). As noted, you are also likely to find the court rules on a specific federal court's website. The advantage of finding them there is that you are likely to find the local rules as well. To find your local federal court's website, start with the U.S. courts' website (www.uscourts.gov/).

For the rules plus summaries and citations to cases that have interpreted the rules, access the USCA on Westlaw or the USCS on Lexis. Finally, for in-depth, scholarly treatment of the rules, remember that the Wright and Miller set is available through Westlaw and Moore is available through Lexis.

For resource updates, visit this book's companion website at

▶ *www.GetLaw.net*

RESOURCES RECAP		
Primary Law: Federal Court Rules		
	Resource	**Notes**
Print	▶ *Federal Local Court Rules*, 3d. 1997–2010. St. Paul, MN: Thomson West.	Provides the local rules for all of the federal courts in the United States
	▶ Moore, James William, Daniel R. Coquillette, et al. 2009. *Moore's Federal Practice*. New York: Mathew Bender.	Also on Lexis
	▶ U.S. Code Annotated (USCA)	
	▶ U.S. Code Service (USCS)	
	▶ Wright, Charles Alan, Arthur R. Miller, and Mary Kay Kane. 2010. *Federal Practice and Procedure*. St. Paul, MN: West Group.	Also on Westlaw
Websites	**Example** ▶ Western District of Texas, "Appellate, Federal, and Local Court Rules": www.txwd.uscourts.gov/rules/default.asp	Find a U.S. district court website with the rules. It is likely your local U.S. district court will have a similar page of links to these rules as well as its own local rules.
	▶ House Committee on the Judiciary, "Procedural Documents": judiciary.house.gov/about/procedural.html	For rules in PDF format

Conclusion

Federal law is vast. Cut it down to manageable size by keeping in mind its parts: the Constitution, statutes, case law, administrative rules and regulations, and federal court rules. If you are looking for a "known" piece of law, usually because you have a citation to a section of the Constitution, or to a statute, or a case or regulation, then finding that known piece of law and being able to correctly interpret the citation and find the resource holding the full text referred to in the citation is relatively simple.

When you do not have a specific citation, research will be a harder. Searching by subject matter is always challenging, but that search will often begin with statutes or regulations and sometimes with the Constitution, depending on the legal issue. Learning that the statutory code and the regulatory code are divided into "titles," according to subject matter, will make the topical search of these sources a little easier. Finding case law by subject matter may pose the greatest challenge. If this is the problem posed, finding one case that is "on point" should be the goal. With one relevant case in hand, finding additional cases on point is easier because you can use the topic and key number system in the West digests and one can use a case citator to find later cases that cite the case in hand and that will more likely be "on point." The chapter in this book specifically about the process of legal research should help you with making research decisions.

Finding State and Local Law

Introduction

Primary sources in the states generally resemble primary sources on the federal level. You will find constitutions, statutes, case opinions, regulations, and court rules. These are published in a similar way to the federal counterparts. You will also find some secondary sources specific to some states, but those were discussed generally in Chapter 2.

This chapter first lists some "all in one" websites as good beginning points for research on the laws in the individual states. Second, the chapter discusses each type of primary law in the states generally and how to find this law. Third, the chapter covers local primary sources, such as county, city, or village laws. Finally, the chapter sets out some resources for tribal law and federal Indian law research.

All-in-One Websites

In traditional legal research in print sources, the typical approach was centered on the type of law for which one was looking. Each type of primary law had its own set of books. The web has altered this approach because often at one single website the researcher may find several different types of law: statutes and regulations and maybe even opinions. Or, alternatively, you may find a single portal site that has collected together hyperlinks to other websites that give you access to one or all three types of primary law. In short, you are more likely to find an "all-in-one" source on the web than in the print world. The researcher will still likely be seeking a particular type of law, such as statutory law, but instead of going to separate sets of books you go to one website. This "all-in-one" approach seems to be particularly true in finding state primary sources. Following is a list of such sites for state primary law research.

Arguably the best access on the web to a comprehensive list of state statutes, regulations, and agencies is the Washburn University School of Law's site (www.washlaw.edu/). This site is the best place to begin a

Finding the Answers to Legal Questions

QUICK TIP

Quick List of Top Websites for State Law

1. Washburn University School of Law's site: www.washlaw.edu/
2. Cornell Legal Information Institute: www.law.cornell.edu/ statutes.html
3. American Association of Law Libraries' "State Law Toolkit": www.aallnet.org/sis/lisp/toolkit.htm
4. State and Local Government on the Net: www.statelocalgov.net/index.cfm
5. Public Library of Law: www.plol.org/Pages/Search.aspx
6. Justia: www.justia.com/index.html
7. Gavel2Gavel (statutes and regulations, mostly for the states): www.re-quest.net/g2g/codes/state/index.htm#OK
8. Links to the main website for each state government: www.gksoft.com/govt/en/us.html
9. Also see Appendix 3 for more links.

For resource updates, visit this book's companion website at

▶ **www.GetLaw.net**

state law search if you are not already familiar with a specific state's websites for statutes and regulations. Once you are at the Washburn homepage, look on the right-hand navigation column and you will see "States." Look for your state under that heading.

A second site is also arguably the best. As is often mentioned in this book, the Cornell Legal Information Institute website is superb. For hyperlinks to a specific state's constitution, statutes, regulations, and court opinions, go to www.law.cornell.edu/statutes.html.

A third all-in-one site and a relative newcomer is a site prepared and hosted by the American Association of Law Libraries at www.aallnet.org/sis/lisp/toolkit.htm. This site provides a list of states. Clicking on the link for the state you are interested in will yield a listing of many state-specific websites for that state. These lists appear to often have been prepared by librarians at law libraries in the specific states involved, so it should be very authoritative.

Fourth, another impressive site is provided by "State and Local Government on the Net" (www.statelocalgov.net/index.cfm). This page will give you a list of the names of the states. Click on one of the names and you will be taken to another page that lists a wide variety of government sites for the state you clicked on. These links frequently include the state legislature, the state courts, and the administrative agencies in that state.

Fifth, the Public Library of Law claims to provide access to all types of state (and federal) primary law (www.plol.org/Pages/Search.aspx). Sixth, another resource for linking to state law is Justia (www.justia.com/index.html). Again, scroll down the page a little and you will find "US States." A seventh site that lists links to all the statutory and administrative codes for all the states is a site from Gavel2Gavel (www.re-quest.net/g2g/codes/state/index.htm). Like many sites, some of the links are outdated, but with some persistence these links may get you to the

RESOURCES RECAP

All-in-One Websites

	Resource	Notes
State and Local Law	▶ American Association of Law Libraries, "Public Libraries Toolkit": www.aallnet.org/sis/lisp/toolkit.htm	For state law research
	▶ Cornell's Legal Information Institute, "Constitutions, Statutes, and Codes": www.law.cornell.edu/statutes.html	
	▶ Gavel2Gavel, "State Laws, Codes, and Statutes": www.re-quest.net/g2g/codes/state/index.htm	Provides statutes and regulations, mostly for the states
	▶ Governments on the WWW: United States of America: www.gksoft.com/govt/en/us.htm	For links to the main website for each state government
	▶ Justia: www.justia.com/index.html	
	▶ Public Library of Law: www.plol.org/Pages/Search.aspx	
	▶ State and Local Government on the Net: www.statelocalgov.net/index.cfm	
	▶ Washburn University School of Law: www.washlaw.edu/	

codes you need for your state. Then it will be a matter of subject searching within those codes.

Finally, if these seven sites do not help, a comprehensive list of links to the main website for each state government can be found at www.gksoft.com/govt/en/us.html. Although this site says it was last updated in 2002, the links for the state governmental websites all seem up to date as of late 2009. You have to scroll down on the page quite a distance to see the links to the states.

All of these sites are "free." If you can afford it, there is always Westlaw and Lexis. Or if you are lucky enough to live close to a public library or law library that provides free access to such sites to patrons, this is a solution too. Many county law libraries now provide free access to these databases for a limited amount of time to patrons. Those libraries will likely charge for printing out the results of searches, but often the search itself is free. If you do not want to pay for printing, writing down the citations to the cases you find will work, then track down the cases in print. Some libraries may let the researcher copy results to a disc or a portable memory device.

State Constitutions

Yes, every state has its own constitution distinct from the federal constitution. While the federal constitution is the "Supreme Law of the Land" for the entire nation, state constitutions are the highest law of the state they concern. State constitutions cannot conflict with the federal constitution and cannot take away any rights granted by the federal constitution, but state constitutions may actually give additional rights or protections to the state's citizens over and above those granted in the federal constitution. Article 1, § 25 of the California constitution, for instance, provides that the people "shall have the right to fish upon and from the public lands." No such right exists in the federal constitution.

To find a specific state's constitution in print, it is usually easiest and cheapest to find the state's annotated code. Usually the constitution is in the first few volumes of the set. If one has access to a large law library and wants perhaps to compare different states' constitutions, the multi-volume set from Oceana *Constitutions of the United States, National and State* is the best place to start.

You can find state constitutions online too. Aside from the "all-in-one" sites listed, another place to start online to find a specific state's constitution is the FindLaw index of hyperlinks to those constitutions (www.findlaw.com/11stategov/indexconst.html).

Be careful when looking at state constitutions. Some states have had a few constitutions over the years, so be sure you are looking at the current one. Alabama, for instance, posts both its current constitution, from 1901, and its pre–Civil War constitution of 1819, which has provisions regarding slavery.

As with the federal constitution and statutes generally, the words of any state's constitution will be the subject of litigation and court interpretation. Therefore, the researcher will usually want to find case law interpreting any constitutional provision. To do this most easily and cheaply, find the constitution in the state's annotated statutory code usually available at large public libraries and law libraries. If a print copy of the code is not available, Westlaw or Lexis will likely have an annotated code for the specific state you need. As noted, many county law libraries now provide "free" access to these databases for a limited amount of time to patrons.

For resource updates, visit this book's companion website at

▶ *www.GetLaw.net*

RESOURCES RECAP		
State Constitutions		
	Resource	**Notes**
Hard Copy or Pay-for-View		Use the annotated code for your state as your first resource.
Hard Copy	▶ Columbia University, Legislative Drafting Research Fund. 1974/2009. *Constitutions of the United States, National and State.* 2nd ed. Dobbs Ferry, NY: Oceana Publications.	
Online	▶ FindLaw, "State Resources: State Constitutions": www.findlaw.com/11stategov/indexconst.html	See also the all-in-one sites (pp. 45–46).

State Statutes

When a state's legislature enacts and the state's executive signs new legislation, it is first published as a **"session law."** Most legislatures meet for specific periods of time called legislative "sessions." Most often this new law will be given a number, usually beginning with the session number and then a simple number pertaining to the chronology of its passage. So a newly enacted law might be labeled 83-101, meaning the 101st bill enacted by the 83rd session of a particular state's legislature. However, such a designation provides no clue to what topic the legislation pertains. Consequently, the new legislation gets "codified."

Statutory Codes

Codification is simply the process of assigning to new legislation a numerical designation that indicates the subject matter to which it pertains. This is done so that people can track down legislation based on subject matter rather than by the date the legislature enacted it. So in most states a volume number or "title" number of that state's code will hold all of that state's currently-in-force statutes on a particular subject matter such as the penal code, or labor, or real estate. Once this numerical designation is assigned, it becomes known as a "statute" and is published in the statutory code.

A specific state government will usually publish that state's statutory code, and it will usually be just the statutes themselves. But researchers usually want to find cases that have interpreted those statutes, and the best way to find citations to those cases is in an annotated code. Many private publishers, but usually Thomson West or Lexis, will publish print versions of these annotated codes. If you are using print sources, the best practice is to use the annotated codes, which provide the researcher with citations to cases and other supporting material in addition to the statutes themselves.

You will also likely find the statutory code for your state on the web. The places to start are the list of "all-in-one" sites listed previously, the state law appendix in this book, the Cornell Legal Information Institute's listing of state statutes by topic at topics.law.cornell.edu/wex/state_statutes, or a simple Google search "X statutory code," where X is the name of the state in which you are interested. Keep in mind, however, that statutory codes are updated very often because legislatures will amend or repeal current statutes and create entirely new ones. Some states' statutory code websites may alert you to these changes and some may not. Therefore, you should always look for the most current legislative developments in your state. Usually the place to start will be the websites for your state's legislative bodies, usually a senate (or an assembly) and a house of representatives, though the names may differ between the states.

State Session Laws

Some state governments will publish the newly enacted legislation for that state. These are usually called "session laws" and will first be published in some sort of paperbound format and then later in hardbound format. In some states, however, a private publisher such as Thomson West will publish these session laws, first as pamphlets, often called "advance sheets" or "legislative advance sheets." Eventually these session laws are published in hardbound volumes organized by the legislative session that enacted the laws. In some states, both the government and the private companies will publish this material in two or more different sets. On the web, look for these session laws in the same way you look for state statutory codes discussed in the prior subsection.

Court Decisions Interpreting Statutes

To find citations to court opinions that interpret statutes, two of the best methods are these. One, consult the annotated statutory code for the specific statute in which you are interested. Two, use the state

> For resource updates, visit this book's companion website at
>
> ▶ *www.GetLaw.net*

RESOURCES RECAP		
State Statutes, Session Laws, and Citations to Court Decisions Interpreting Statutes		
	Resource	Notes
Hard Copy or Pay-for-View		Use the annotated code for your state and any advance sheets or legislative service pamphlets for that code as your first resources.
		(Cont'd.)

RESOURCES RECAP *(Continued)*		
State Statutes, Session Laws, and Citations to Court Decisions Interpreting Statutes		
	Resource	**Notes**
Hard Copy or Pay-for-View *(Cont'd.)*		For citations to court decisions interpreting statutes, aside from the annotated codes, use state statutory code citators.
Online	▶ Cornell's Legal Information Institute, "Topical Index: State Statutes": topics.law.cornell.edu/wex/state_statutes	See also the all-in-one sites (pp. 45–46).

statutory citator, using the statutory cite for the specific statute you are researching. Citators are explained in Chapter 5.

State Administrative Law

Just as on the federal level, much of the work of state government is carried out by administrative agencies. These agencies run under rules the agencies create ("promulgate" is the official word). The agencies also create rules, also more specifically known as "regulations," for the arena of life or industry that each agency administers. For instance, a state's department of transportation will run by certain rules. Those rules might govern the contract bidding process, such as for companies that will actually bid to build the highways. But the department of transportation will also "promulgate" regulations for exactly how those highways are to be built: the composition of the asphalt, the width of specific roadways, maybe even how those highways are to be striped. All of these rules and regulations will be published somewhere and usually under the umbrella of the agency involved.

A good place to begin is this book:

▶ Nyberg, Cheryl Rae. 2000. *State Administrative Law Bibliography: Print and Electronic Sources.* Twin Falls, ID: Carol Boast and Cheryl Rae Nyberg.

State Regulatory Codes

Not too many years ago, these administrative rules and regulations could be very hard to find. Often states lacked a comprehensive administrative code and one would have to depend on each individual agency to publish its regulations. This has changed to some degree in some states, but finding state regulations can still be a challenge.

State administrative codes are analogous to statutory codes in that they publish material by subject matter and that subject matter is often assigned a specific "title" or volume number. In the case of administrative codes, however, often the specific subject matter and the specific title or volume number will pertain also to a specific administrative agency. For instance, the regulations of the state department of corrections will all

---

QUICK TIP

The Internet—and the National Association of Secretaries of State—have made finding state administrative codes much easier. The researcher can find links to the administrative codes at www.administrativerules.org. Once at that site, look at the left navigation panel and click on "Codes and Registers." Then you will see in the middle of the page another link for "Administrative Rules Online by State." Click on that link and voila—you will see a list for every state and separate links for each state's codes and registers.

be published under the same section of the code and under the same title or volume number.

If the researcher already knows that the regulations being sought are from a specific department or administrative agency, then usually scanning the spines of the administrative code or scanning its table of contents will specify where to look for that specific agency's regulations. If the researcher knows only the subject matter and not the agency, then the administrative code will likely have an index organized by subject entries that will then provide cites to appropriate sections of the code concerning specific subjects.

State Regulatory Registers

The relationship between administrative codes and registers is similar to the relationship between statutory codes and session laws. Registers publish brand new administrative rules and regulations, usually before those regulations have been "codified" and placed in the code. And administrative rules and regulations tend to change even more frequently than statutes.

But registers are also unique. Administrative agencies are required to publish not only "new" rules and regulations but also *proposed* rules and regulations, before those rules and regulations go into effect. This is very important because these proposed rules are published so that the public has an opportunity to comment on those rules. Comments can usually be made in writing or through testimony. One can also sometimes challenge rules and regulations if they were not published prior to going into effect or were published with insufficient time for public comment.

Administrative registers may have different names in different states, but the type of material contained in them will be published somewhere, usually in a paperbound version.

Court Decisions Interpreting Administrative Law

Usually there is no annotated administrative code, so the best way to find citations to court opinions interpreting state administrative regulations

QUICK TIP

As noted regarding administrative codes, these state administrative registers are now easily accessible online through the website provided by the National Association of Secretaries of State (www.administrativerules.org). Once at the site, look at the left navigation panel and click on "Codes and Registers." Then you will see in the middle of the page another link for "Administrative Rules Online by State."

For resource updates, visit this book's companion website at

▶ *www.GetLaw.net*

RESOURCES RECAP		
State Administrative Law, Administrative Codes, and Registers		
	Resource	**Notes**
General		For court decisions interpreting administrative rules and regulations, use the citator for the state administrative code.
Print	▶ Nyberg, Cheryl Rae. 2000. *State Administrative Law Bibliography: Print and Electronic Sources.* Twin Falls, ID: Carol Boast and Cheryl Rae Nyberg.	See also the all-in-one sites (pp. 45–46).
Online	▶ National Association of Secretaries of State, Administrative Codes and Registers Section: www.administrativerules.org	For access to administrative codes and registers

is to use the citator for the state administrative code, if possible. Citators are explained in Chapter 5. Alternatively, you can use case digests, explained in the next section.

State Court Decisions

In general, state court systems will be organized in a similar way to federal courts: there will be a trial court level, an intermediate appellate court level, and a final appellate court level. It is likely too there will be specialized courts, municipal courts, district courts, or other courts often referred to as "courts of limited jurisdiction." These courts might be traffic courts or small claims courts or other sorts of courts.

Opinions from Trial Courts or Courts of Limited Jurisdiction

Usually the researcher will not be looking for decisions or opinions from courts of limited jurisdiction or from the state trial courts. This is because these decisions have no "precedential" impact; that is, the decisions impact only the parties involved in the litigation that is the subject of the decision or opinion, but it will not govern how the same question or issue will be decided in other cases involving other parties.

Two exceptions to this lack of publication may occur. First, the researcher may be one of the parties involved in the litigation or may be researching on behalf of one of those parties, but often the parties will have received the decision, usually by mail, and there is no need to look further. Sometimes, however, the researcher may not be a party but may know by one way or the other of a trial court decision that may be of interest, despite the decision's lack of precedential value. In this situation, the researcher will usually have to have the parties' names and the docket number for a specific case. With this information, the researcher would have to go to the office of the clerk of the court involved to retrieve a hard copy of the file. But this leads to the second exception: more and more trial courts are beginning to post to the web information—and sometimes entire documents, including decisions—from cases that are before the trial courts. This is one of the most widely divergent areas of practice in legal information gathering today, and no generalizations can be made. Therefore, there is no single way to determine whether this material is available. Start by either trying to find the website for the trial court involved or by calling the clerk's office for that trial court to determine what is and is not available.

Finding State Appellate Court Decisions in Hard Copy

The person looking for court opinions or decisions will most of the time be looking for published appellate court decisions, opinions from the intermediate or final appellate courts in a particular state. These opinions will be published in hard copy in separate sets, most likely, one for the intermediate court and one for the final appellate court. Sometimes these sets will be published by the state government, sometimes by a private company, sometimes by both.

The researcher should also know about "West's National Reporter System," also sometimes referred to as the "regional reporter system." Thomson West, formerly West Publishing, publishes the opinions of the intermediate and final appellate courts of all of the states in sets divided into seven geographic regions. For instance, the decisions from the intermediate and final appellate courts of 15 western states are all published in one set of books, the *Pacific Reporter*. If you want to know which regional reporter publishes your state's opinions, the easiest way to find out is to go to lawschool.westlaw.com/federalcourt/NationalReporter Page.asp. Once you have identified the regional reporter that publishes court opinions for the state in which you are interested, the best way to find cases is to go to that regional reporter's digest. How to use these digests is explained in Chapter 5.

Finding State Appellate Court Decisions for Free Online

What is available for free on the web will vary widely. If the researcher does not already know of a website that publishes a specific state court's opinions, the place to begin on the web is the comprehensive directory for state court websites available from the National Center for State Courts (www.ncsc.org/WebDocumentLibrary/IR_CourtSites.aspx). If this does not get you to the opinions, start by going to the state government's website. Also, see the state law appendix in this book. Finally, a comprehensive list of links to the main website for each state government is available at www.gksoft.com/govt/en/us.html. Although this site currently states that it was last updated in 2002, the links for the state governmental websites all seemed up to date when this book was written. Once you find a specific state government's main site you are likely to find on that site a link to a site or two or three for opinions from that state's appellate courts.

After you have found a specific appellate court's website, the challenges continue. First, the best way to find opinions on these sites is usually if you already know the case name or the names of parties involved in a specific case. If you do not have this information, then some sites will provide you a brief synopsis of a case without having to click on the link for the full opinion, and this may help you find cases of interest. A second challenge is that these state appellate court sites, often maintained by the courts' administrators, will post only very recent opinions, though the sites may provide a link to older, "archived" repositories. So if you are looking for a specific opinion that is older than three or four months, you are likely to have to look to a site other than the issuing court's site.

If you do not have the name of a specific case you are looking for and you are looking for cases by subject matter or topic, you will have a harder time. Consider accessing Westlaw or Lexis. Remember that many county law libraries provide some "free" access to these databases. This access is often limited to federal materials and materials for the state in which the county library resides. So it will be harder for you to find cases from a "foreign" jurisdiction—a state outside of the one in which you are doing research—through this free county law library access, if it exists at all.

Sometimes you will be faced with having to pay Westlaw or Lexis for per search access. If you have a case name or citation, this search will be relatively quick and inexpensive. If you are searching for cases by topic, however, it is likely to get expensive. Consider instead looking for cases by topic in the hard copy materials such as annotated codes and case digests for your state's cases. Once you identify case names and citations for cases that seem to pertain to your topic, then you can either access those cases in hard copy, or, if not available, by a quick per search access by case name in Westlaw or Lexis.

> For resource updates, visit this book's companion website at
> ▶ *www.GetLaw.net*

RESOURCES RECAP		
State Court Decisions*		
	Resource	**Notes**
Online	▶ Westlaw, "West's National Reporter System": lawschool.westlaw.com/federalcourt/NationalReporterPage.asp	To determine which regional reporter prints your state's court opinions
	▶ National Center for State Courts, "State Court Web Sites": www.ncsconline.org/D_KIS/info_court_web_sites.html	To find citations online See also the all-in-one sites (pp. 45–46).

* Court decisions from the appellate courts of a particular state may be published in hard copy by the state government in an "official state reporter," or they may be published only by a private company, or your state may have both.
Court decisions from your appellate courts will also be published in hard copy in the regional reporter from West.
To find citations to court decisions by topic, consult your state's digest of case law or the digest for the regional reporter system.

State Court Rules

All courts at all levels will have rules about how litigants are to get things done in those courts. If you are suing someone or being sued and working on your own, you will have to find the rules for the court where the litigation occurs. Remember that there will be rules that may apply statewide to all state trial courts, for instance, or to all state appellate courts. There is also likely to be a set of "local court rules." For example, you may be in a trial court for a specific county, so you will need to know both the statewide rules that apply to those county courts as well as the local court rules for that specific county.

In print, you will find several sources for court rules. Look first for a single volume of your state's court rules. These are usually published annually and will likely have all the court rules of statewide application. Whether those single volumes also publish the local court rules will vary by state.

Second, look in the annotated statutory code for your state. Very often the court rules are published as a part of the statutory code, and the bonus in finding the rules there is that you will also be able to find, as in any annotated code, citations to cases that have interpreted those rules.

Third, look for a set of books that are published for legal practitioners in your state. Many states have such sets, and usually in those sets you will find the statewide court rules often along with scholarly commentary about how the rules work and how they have been interpreted.

Online, you are likely to find court rules in several places as well. Most courts now have websites, and very often that is the best place to find both the statewide rules that apply in that court and the local, specific court rules for that court. If you have trouble locating a specific court's website, try the National Center for State Courts' "Court Web Sites" page (www.ncsc.org/WebDocumentLibrary/IR_CourtSites.aspx). You may also find court rules at the same site you find your state's statutory code. As noted, statutes and rules are often published in the same place. Finally, if you have access to Westlaw or Lexis, your state's court rules are likely accessible through those databases and often with annotations similar to those in annotated codes.

For resource updates, visit this book's companion website at

▶ *www.GetLaw.net*

RESOURCES RECAP		
State Court Rules		
	Resource	**Notes**
Online Directory	▶ National Center for State Courts, "State Court Web Sites": www.ncsc.org/WebDocumentLibrary/IR_CourtSites.aspx	To find a particular court's website

State Executive Materials

Although in most instances the average library patron will not often need legal information from a state's executive, its governor, at times there may be a call for such material. In those instances, the place to start is the comprehensive list of links (www.gksoft.com/govt/en/us.html) to the principal website for each state government.

For resource updates, visit this book's companion website at

▶ *www.GetLaw.net*

RESOURCES RECAP		
State Executive Materials		
	Resource	**Notes**
Online Directory	▶ Governments on the WWW: United States of America, "State Institutions": www.gksoft.com/govt/en/us.html	To find the main website for each state government

Other State-Specific Resources

Because it is hard to generalize about state primary sources, persistence and creativity may be needed to find useful materials. Often organizations or associations may be very helpful in learning about or finding state legal resources. For instance, many state or county or city bar associations publish "self-help" materials for citizens of their localities. These might include "how to do your own will in this state," or "how to contest a traffic ticket," or any number of other scenarios. Moreover, many of these bar associations may also have free or low-cost lawyer referral services. If you find that you need to retain an attorney but do not know where to begin, consider looking for bar associations that may provide you a way to locate an attorney.

You can start to locate these bar associations in the phone book or on the web just by searching for "X bar association," which could be a state bar association, a county bar association, or a city bar association in many of the largest cities. Additionally, here are three FindLaw websites that will help you.

▶ FindLaw, "Legal Associations and Organizations," for legal and law-related associations: www.findlaw.com/06associations/index.html

▶ FindLaw, "National and Specialty Legal Associations": www.findlaw.com/06associations/national.html

▶ FindLaw, "State and Local Legal Associations": www.findlaw.com/06associations/state.html

For resource updates, visit this book's companion website at

▶ *www.GetLaw.net*

RESOURCES RECAP		
Other State-Specific Resources		
	Resource	**Notes**
Online Directories	▶ FindLaw, "Legal Associations and Organizations": www.findlaw.com/06associations/index.html	For legal and law-related associations
	▶ FindLaw, "National and Specialty Legal Associations": www.findlaw.com/06associations/national.html	For national and specialized legal associations
	▶ FindLaw, "State and Local Legal Associations": www.findlaw.com/06associations/state.html	For state and local bar associations

Local Law: Primary Sources

A surprising number of legal issues and problems will involve local law—that is, county, city, or village charters and ordinances. "Charters" are analogous to constitutions on the state and federal levels. They are the foundational documents for local governmental entities. The term **"ordinance"** is the name usually given to enacted law on the local level, those rules and regulations made by city or county councils or similar elected bodies of people. Some traffic and many parking rules or laws will often be controlled by city or county ordinances. Fire, building, zoning, land use, housing, and environmental rules and regulations are frequently found at the local level, either exclusively or having concurrent application with state rules and regulations in these areas.

If generalizations are hard to make about state primary sources, it is even more difficult to make generalizations about city or county primary sources. Finding these resources can often be very frustrating. Because of the very localized nature of the materials, your local county law library or public library or city or county building may be the best place to start. Also, the clerk's office of the city or county in question is a place to begin your query, either in person, on the phone, or increasingly, on the web. Some of this material—charters, ordinances, regulations—may be published in print and be available at local libraries or governmental agencies.

Finally, however, one of the best all around, single sites for this material is posted and kept up-to-date by the Seattle Public Library Municipal Codes site (www.spl.org/default.asp?pageID=collection_municodes). Though the authors of this book are from the Seattle area, this website is recommended not out of provincialism but because it is repeatedly and highly recommended by legal information experts everywhere.

> For resource updates, visit this book's companion website at
> ▶ *www.GetLaw.net*

RESOURCES RECAP		
Local Law		
	Resource	**Notes**
Primary Sources*	▶ Seattle Public Library Municipal Codes: www.spl.org/default.asp?pageID=collection_municodes	Highly recommended by legal information experts everywhere
* Because of the very localized nature of the materials, your local county law library or public library or city or county building may be the best place to start. Also, the clerk's office of the city or county in question is a place to begin your query, either in person, on the phone, or on the web. Some of this material—charters, ordinances, regulations—may be published in print and be available at local libraries or governmental agencies.		

Tribal Law and Federal Indian Law: Primary Sources

A final set of primary sources important in the United States are those sources related to tribal law. Under federal law (Constitution Article 1, Section 8), Native American tribes have semiautonomous status, and tribes may create laws to govern their enrolled members and lands. Thus, tribal primary sources may include sources similar to the ones discussed throughout this book: constitutions, enacted law (such as statutory law or ordinances), regulatory or administrative law, and opinions or other documents from tribal courts. Legal research concerning tribal law may also often involve treaties.

On the web, the place to begin for tribal law research is the National Indian Law Library (NILL), maintained by the Native American Rights Fund. The site, specifically the "Tribal Law Gateway" (www.narf.org/nill/triballaw/), provides access to tribal codes and other materials for many tribes. This website has recently announced that Westlaw and NILL will be working together to provide greater access to tribal law materials on the NILL site and elsewhere, so look for this site to be increasingly useful. Many individual tribes also have their own websites, which often will provide access to tribal law materials. A simple Google search with the tribe's name is the place to start. Additionally, the NILL site also provides a short guide on how to do tribal law research at www.narf.org/nill/resources/guide2.pdf.

What often makes these tribal primary law sources even more challenging is whether or to what extent the laws relate to the laws of other "sovereigns." The interrelationships between tribal sovereignties and local, state, and federal jurisdictions or "sovereignties" are highly complex. If you spend much time exploring these complex interrelationships, you will be moving from tribal law research to federal Indian law research. But such research might involve both tribal law research and research in the state and federal materials discussed in the early chapters of this book.

If you plan to do much work in this arena, you will want to begin with an overview of federal Indian Law. A reliable, relatively inexpensive and up to date source is William C. Canby's *American Indian Law in a Nutshell* (5th ed., 2009), which is available for sale or at many law libraries. You may also want to get a copy, through a law library or interlibrary loan, of the following article: David Selden and Monica Martens, "Basic Indian Law Research Tips—Part I: Federal Indian Law," *The Colorado Lawyer* 34 (May 2005): 43. Part II of this article is the "short guide" mentioned previously, which has been recently updated for the web: www.narf.org/nill/resources/guide2.pdf.

For resource updates, visit this book's companion website at

▶ *www.GetLaw.net*

RESOURCES RECAP		
Tribal Law and Federal Indian Law		
	Resource	Notes
Primary Sources	▶ Canby, William C. 2009. *American Indian Law in a Nutshell.* 5th ed. St. Paul, MN: West Group. ▶ National Indian Law Library (NILL). n.d. "Tribal Law Gateway." Available: www.narf.org/nill/triballaw/. ▶ Selden, David, and Monica Martens. 2005. "Basic Indian Law Research Tips—Part I: Federal Indian Law." *The Colorado Lawyer* 34. Available: www.narf.org/nill/bulletins/lawreviews/articles/coloradoLawyerArticle-fed.pdf. ▶ Selden, David, and Monica Martens. 2005/2007. "Basic Indian Law Research Tips—Part II: Tribal Law." *The Colorado Lawyer* 43. Available: www.narf.org/nill/resources/guide2.pdf.	

Preparation: Understanding Legal Information Needs

Part II introduces how to conduct basic legal research, including citation and keyword searching as well as determining jurisdiction and checking for the most current information. It begins with discussion of the reference interview and the complexities involved in assessing legal information needs and the particular sensitivities related to legal information versus legal advice. Resources beyond the public library are described, including public law libraries, law school libraries, and community organizations that provide free legal assistance. Part II also covers considerations when choosing a lawyer.

Legal Research Basics

This chapter gives an overview of the process of legal research. Most of this book is about the legal system and about what sources of legal information are available generally and on specific topics. This chapter gives you a strategy for finding that legal information in the context of a legal research question and assumes you will consult the rest of this book as needed during that process. The first section of this chapter addresses the complexities involved in assessing the legal information needs of others as well as the particular sensitivities related to "legal information" versus "legal advice." Though the material in the first section should be helpful in framing one's research tasks, if you are reading this chapter because you are doing legal research for yourself, you may wish to jump directly to the section in this chapter titled Techniques for Finding What Is Needed; it introduces the processes and methods for doing basic legal research, preparing the reader for the specific, common questions addressed within the chapters in Part III. The final section of this chapter helps the researcher learn more sophisticated research techniques to build on what is found using the more basic research techniques.

Deciding What Legal Information Is Needed

The Reference Interview for Legal Information Needs

The reference interview for a legal information need involves several special considerations. If you are a librarian embarking on a reference query that reveals the information need to involve legal questions, these are choppy waters indeed. Always in the forefront of the reference interaction is that library staff may assist patrons in locating sources to help with their legal research, but in most states it is illegal for anyone other than a lawyer to provide legal advice, and even recommending appropriate legal reference sources can be interpreted as a form of advice.

Put succinctly, librarians may assist people in finding answers but may not provide legal answers. This distinction is vital, and it is reflected in the title of this book. Of course, ultimately, the "answer" will depend on the facts of the person's case and the interpretation of those facts and the law that is rendered by a judge or fact finder. These issues and related concerns are discussed in more depth in the section of this chapter titled Legal Information versus Legal Advice. In this section, concerns about and recommendations for handling the reference interview itself are covered.

Almost every person initiating a reference question who has a legal information need also has some level of anxiety surrounding that need. It may be related to the need itself—urgency for dealing with a collection agency's notices, for example—or the inability to hire an attorney or often simply the usual lack of knowledge about legal information generally. It may also be that it is next to impossible to articulate the need itself because the situation is so fraught with emotion and intensely personal. In this way, the need for legal information is similar to the need for medical information in that it is usually urgent, personal, and involves multiple "fear factors" about the unknown. With legal questions, these factors include the peculiarities of legal terminology, different types of legal sources and publications, strict court rules, the hierarchy of court systems, and the roles of the different players in those systems, such as judges, lawyers, court clerks, and, of course, self-represented litigants. As a result, the initial phase of the interview may well be spent defusing emotions, fears, and embarrassment before it is possible even to begin eliciting background and assessing the information need. The very situations that bring people into a library most frequently with legal questions are those most loaded with anxiety and distress:

- Probate: a person is typically handling grief and possibly family bickering while at the same time trying to cope with creditor claims on the estate of the loved one.

- Divorce: even a "good" or "positive" divorce is painful during the process.

- Parenting plans: making decisions for children of any age is one of the hardest things many people will ever do, whether married or unmarried.

- Lawsuits of any kind: pursuing or defending against a lawsuit always rates high on the stress scales. Justice Learned Hand perhaps put it best, "Dread a lawsuit beyond anything short of sickness and death" (Learned Hand, Justice of the U.S. Court of Appeals, 2d Circuit, 1924–1961).

As experienced reference librarians know so well, the library user's initial question is, more often than not, not the real question (Ross et al., 2009). This is certainly true for legal information questions, and the reference interview must be conducted with particular skill and tact. Much has been written about conducting reference interviews in a variety of settings; some of the key types of problems that arise with legal information needs are:

1. **The user begins with a very broad and general question.**
   In this situation the initial question may not even be recognizable as a legal information question. Example: Initial question is "Do you have anything on housing?" The real question turns out to be "What are my rights as a tenant during an eviction?"

2. **The user asks for something specific but it does not match the real question.**
   This occurs frequently when a user is faced with legal documents the user does not understand or perhaps the user has already concluded what legal actions are appropriate. Example: Initial question is "Do you have a summons form?" The real question turns out to be that the user needs to know a person's rights in corresponding with a debt collector.

3. **The user does not understand how the legal system is structured.**
   This problem often arises when it is not clear which court or public agency is responsible for handling the person's complaint or concern. Example: The initial question is "How do I file a case with the U.S. Supreme Court?" The real question is "What are the state laws about what a landlord is responsible for?"

4. **The user does not understand how legal resources are organized.**
   It is challenging to gain an understanding of how statutes, annotated statutes, regulations, case reporters, self-help books, and the variety of secondary sources combine to provide the foundation of legal information. In this area, law librarians can be of great help to library users and nonlaw librarians alike (see Nyberg, 2004). Example: The initial question is "Do you have a book on radar?" The real questions are "What are the laws related to using radar to detect speeding?" "What recent cases have interpreted these laws?"

5. **The user does not know the legal terminology to use.**
   Just as in most specialized fields with their own vocabularies, like medicine or library science itself, the legal field has authoritative terminology that will appear in court pleadings, statutes, and case law. To make it even trickier, legal information has more than its share of Latin terms. A concise legal dictionary like *Black's* (Garner, 2009) is necessary to and affordable by even a small public library. Example: The initial question is "My neighbor is trying to take over part of my backyard by building a fence and shed over the property line. How do I find what the laws say about this?" The real question may be addressed by looking up terms like "adverse possession" and "civil trespass."

6. **The user does not have enough information to get started.**
   Example: The initial question is "I got a call from someone saying he is going to start garnishing my wages. Can he do that?" The real question cannot be answered without more information about who is calling and what debt and/or creditor

might be involved. For the present moment, it can help to address some preliminary or groundwork questions such as "What are my rights as a debtor?" "What is a debt collector prohibited from doing?" "How do I find out more about this debt?"

Handling a reference interview by telephone presents additional challenges. This includes the need to communicate during the conversation the boundaries on what can be provided—legal information not advice—which is typically easier to establish during an in-person interview in the library setting. Virtual reference via other forms of remote communication like e-mail, live chat, and instant messaging is likewise demanding of extra considerations. Many people may in fact prefer to use the telephone, e-mail, or chat precisely because it affords a greater level of privacy for asking legal questions. Telephone calls in particular can provide a sense of anonymity, much desired when a person is embarrassed about the information need.

Frequently a combination of communication modes may be used, as when an initial inquiry arrives in an e-mail and the follow-up is by telephone or in-person. The same reference interview skills are needed: open questioning, listening, confirming, and summarizing. For further information about conducting a reference interview, see:

▶ Ross, C. S., K. Nilsen, and M. L. Radford. 2009. *Conducting the Reference Interview*, 2nd ed. New York: Neal-Schuman.
▶ Whisner, Mary. 2002. "Teaching the Art of the Reference Interview." *Law Library Journal* 94, no. 1: 161–166.

With all of this in mind, it is clear that fielding legal information queries and conducting successful reference interviews take practice and patience—and plenty of both. The other two fundamental prerequisites are close attention to the differences between legal information and legal advice and to whether the question involves state or federal law (i.e., the question of jurisdiction). These two prerequisites are covered in the next two sections.

Legal Information versus Legal Advice

Librarians helping people find legal information are often asked for legal advice, directly or indirectly. Librarians should not give legal advice. Giving legal advice when one is not an attorney is considered practicing law without a license (unauthorized practice of law) under statutes throughout the United States; only licensed attorneys are allowed to give legal advice.

Giving legal advice should be avoided not only because it is against the law but because it is a bad idea for several reasons. First, giving bad, or even sometimes good, legal advice to a library patron may jeopardize that patron's liberty, children, shelter, or property. Second, the patron who is later unhappy about losing something dear, based on bad advice received, may seek some sort of recompense from the person who provided that advice. Third, patrons asking for advice do not always provide all of the information necessary to understand the context in which the advice is sought. The facts of a legal scenario are as important as the law involved and the facts may be hard to elicit. The patron may be embarrassed, secretive, deceitful, uninformed, or just forgetful about facts. Giving advice based on partial information is not a good idea. Professional and ethical librarians want to give the best help and information possible, but in the legal context this is not always possible given frequent vagaries of both the facts and the law. Indeed, it is precisely those vagaries that lead patrons to need legal advice when they are seeking legal information.

Unfortunately, there is often a fine line between advising someone about *how to find* the law and advising someone about *what to do with the law one finds.* It is almost painful sometimes to not give answers the patron needs. Reference librarians tend to like helping people, especially people in difficult situations. So when the librarian has helped a patron find a legal form in a form book, it is tempting and seemingly "natural" to answer the patron's follow-up questions: Is this the right form? Is this the only form I need? How do I fill out this form? Can you fill out this for me? Where do I file this? When should I file it? It is very hard to resist answering these questions, especially when the answers are sometimes easy to find, but the person providing such advice is likely giving legal advice. It is safest, though sometimes difficult, to keep directing the patron back to the sources to find the answers.

The difference between advice about how to find the law and what to do with the law once it is found sometimes depends on the research task. If a patron has a citation to a case or a statute and simply needs help in tracking down the document represented by the citation, then no legal advice is likely to be exchanged. However, if the patron finds the document and then asks the meaning of it, or how it can be interpreted, or what should be done in light of it, or how to act in accord with it or in opposition to it, that patron is likely asking for legal advice.

Many libraries have a publicly posted and plainly written policy about the issue of legal advice. Such a policy eliminates some of the dangers discussed here by reminding library staff of the issue and possibly soothing the hurt feelings of patrons asking for more help than the librarian can provide. The written policy might include a list of local legal service providers that may be able to provide the legal advice the patron is seeking. For a sample policy and for further resources on and discussion of the distinction between advising how to find legal information and advising what to do with it, see the following:

▶ Healey, Paul D. 2002. "Pro Se Users, Reference Liability, and the Unauthorized Practice of Law: Twenty-five Selected Readings." *Law Library Journal* 94, no. 1: 133–139.

▶ Southern California Association of Law Libraries, Public Access to Legal Information Committee. "Chapter 4. Legal Reference vs. Legal Advice." In *Locating the Law: A Handbook for Non-Law Librarians.* Available: www.aallnet.org/chapter/scall/locating/ch4.pdf (accessed May 15, 2010).

For resource updates, visit this book's companion website at

▶ **www.GetLaw.net**

▶ State, Court, and County Law Libraries, a Special Interest Section of the American Association of Law Libraries. 2009. *Unauthorized Practice of Law Toolkit.* Available: www.aallnet.org/sis/sccll/toolkit/unauthorized _practice.htm (accessed May 15, 2010).

RESOURCES RECAP

Legal Information versus Legal Advice

	Resource	Notes
Print and Online	▶ Healey, Paul D. 2002. "Pro Se Users, Reference Liability, and the Unauthorized Practice of Law: Twenty-Five Selected Readings." *Law Library Journal* 94, no. 1: 133–139.	
	▶ Southern California Association of Law Libraries, Public Access to Legal Information Committee. "Chapter 4: Legal Reference vs. Legal Advice." In *Locating the Law: A Handbook for Non-Law Librarians.* Available: www.aallnet.org/chapter/scall/locating/ch4.pdf.	
	▶ State, Court, and County Law Libraries, a Special Interest Section of the American Association of Law Libraries. 2009. *Unauthorized Practice of Law Toolkit.* Available: www.aallnet.org/sis/sccll/toolkit/unauthorized_practice.htm.	

Techniques for Finding What Is Needed

Jurisdiction

The first question to answer in almost every legal research task is what jurisdiction's law is needed? The term *jurisdiction* has various meanings in the law, but for the purposes of most legal research it is a question of which sovereigns' laws govern a particular legal issue. The answer is almost always either federal or state.

Sometimes a court case or legal issue will be governed by both federal and a particular state's law, but in setting about your research task you must decide which jurisdiction's law to pursue first. Other times you will not know whether you need federal or state law, and this becomes your first research question; again, to answer it you will need to decide which jurisdiction to investigate first.

For some situations there are easy answers to the jurisdiction question. If a person is a defendant in a civil or criminal case, then there will be a document that started the case—a ticket, a complaint, an item of information, an indictment—that will specify whether the basis of the suit is federal or state, most likely by citing to statutory law, or sometimes other types of law. By examining this initial document and deciphering its citations to the law, the jurisdiction question can be resolved. The next section in this chapter discusses how to decipher citations.

If a person is a plaintiff in a civil suit that has already been filed, then once again the document that began the case will specify the jurisdiction's law relied on in the suit. Examine that document closely. If a person is a *potential* plaintiff in a civil suit, one that has not yet been filed, then the answer to the jurisdictional question may be more difficult.

If the basis for the potential suit is solely a federal statute, then the answer to the jurisdictional question is "federal," even though the plaintiff *may* often file the suit in state or federal court. If the basis for the potential lawsuit is solely a state statute or is based on mandatory state common law, then the answer to the jurisdictional question will be the state that enacted the statute or the state whose courts wrote the common law opinion. Sometimes a lawsuit may be based on *both* federal and state law, in which case you must research both jurisdictions' laws, but this can be done only one jurisdiction at a time.

Now, here are the harder situations. Sometimes the researcher will not know whether a potential lawsuit or an emerging research task involves state or federal law, in which case this becomes the first research task: to determine which one applies. A good starting strategy is to read the first two chapters of this book about the legal system and secondary sources and then to find secondary sources that concern the research question. If none can be identified, start with federal statutory law, then go to state statutory law. If this is not helpful, do some subject searching in federal cases, then in state cases. The issue might not be solely governed by case law, but if you find cases concerning the issue of interest, then those cases are likely to cite to mandatory authority—statutes, most likely—or administrative law that may pertain to the issue. From those you can glean the correct jurisdiction.

Through this process the researcher is likely to have answered the question of which jurisdiction's law governs the legal issue of interest. In this process, a search will likely result in citations to primary law—statutes, case opinions, administrative regulations—that may govern the issue. The researcher is then ready to tackle the easiest research task, using a citation to find a "known item" in the law. But if the search has yet to locate a "good" citation to a known item, then a first step might be to look at some secondary sources, discussed briefly in the next section.

Secondary Sources

Secondary sources are often a good place for a researcher to begin, especially in researching an unfamiliar area of the law. Secondary sources can provide you with an overview of a specific area of the law, can provide you with a working vocabulary for further searching, and may provide you some leads to primary sources. If you have little idea of where to begin in researching a particular issue, secondary sources are highly recommended and Chapter 2 gives a thorough discussion of what secondary sources are, how to find them, and how to use them.

Citations: Known Item Searching

The easiest legal research task is when starting out with an accurate and complete citation to a known item: a statute, a case, a regulation, an ordinance, a law review article, etc. A person may have come upon this citation through a wide variety of means, so, assuming the citation is accurate, then the only difficulty will be in interpreting the citation.

Case citations generally follow the same pattern, regardless of the jurisdiction. Here is an example: *Lemon v. Kurtzman*, 403 U.S. 602, 91 S. Ct. 2105, 29 L.Ed.2d 745 (1971), shown in Figure 5.1. The italicized portion is the name of the case, based on the **litigants**. The first number here, 403, will be the volume number. The letters in the middle, U.S., will be an abbreviation for the reporter, here the *United States Reports*, that holds the full opinion. The second number, 602, is the page number where the opinion starts. But notice there are three similar sets of numbers and abbreviations here. This is because there are three different "reporters" or sets of books that publish opinions. So the second set of numbers and abbreviations in this citation means that this case will be found in volume 91 of the set of books titled the *Supreme Court Reporter* and the case will begin on page 2105; the opinion will also be found in volume 29 of the *Supreme Court Reports, Lawyers Edition, 2nd Series* beginning on page 745. The case was published in 1971, as shown in the parentheses. These three sets of numbers and abbreviations are known as **parallel citations**. Most state court opinions will follow a similar pattern, although often state court opinions are published in only one or at most two sets of books, so there will be fewer parallel citations.

Decisions from the U.S. District Courts are published in the *Federal Supplement* and those from the U.S. Courts of Appeals are published in the *Federal Reporter*. See Figure 5.2 for examples of citations from both of these case reporters. (There is also the *Federal Appendix* containing courts of appeals decisions from most of the U.S. circuit courts that were not selected for inclusion in the *Federal Reporter*; these opinions are generally considered to hold less precedential value.)

Statutory citations may vary widely state to state. Usually, however, there will be a title or volume number, an abbreviation for the name of the code in which the statute is printed, and there will be a section or chapter number. Here is the federal prototype: 42 U.S.C. § 1983 (see Figure 5.3). This means title 42 (look for the volumes with "42" on the

---

Figure 5.1. U.S. Supreme Court Case Citation

Lemon v. Kurtzman, 403 U.S. 602, 91 S.Ct. 2105, 29 L.Ed.2d 745 (1971)				
Litigants	Official Citation	Parallel Citation from Supreme Court Reporter (S.Ct.)	Parallel Citation from Lawyer's Edition, Second Series (L.Ed.2d)	Year
Lemon v. Kurtzman Plaintiff v. Defendant	403 U.S. 602 volume page	91 S.Ct. 2105 volume page	29 L.Ed.2d 745 volume page	(1971)

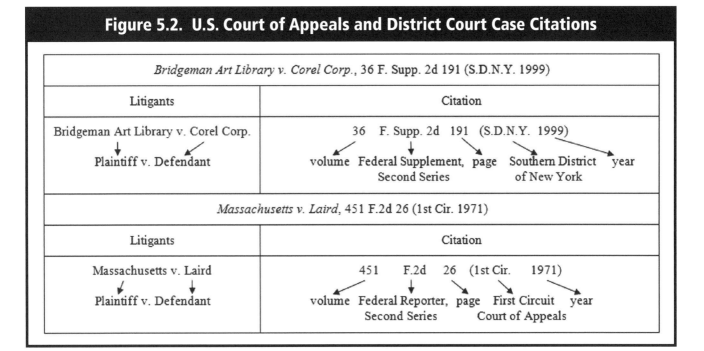

Figure 5.2. U.S. Court of Appeals and District Court Case Citations

spines) and section 1983 (look for the volumes with both Title 42 and section numbers that would include 1983). States will vary: Wash. Rev. Code 50.04.294 means title 50, chapter 4, section 294 of the Washington Revised Code. But Calif. Code of Civ. Proc. § 116.540 means that the California statutory collection does not have numbers for volumes or titles but is divided up into separate "codes" that are given descriptive names, here the California Code of Civil Procedure.

Administrative codes will vary as well. On the federal level, 23 CFR § 1.2 means title 23 of the *Code of Federal Regulations*, section 1.2. Citations to the regulations in the administrative codes of the states are likely to vary widely but will probably be similar to one of the versions of the statutory cites illustrated in the prior paragraph or the federal regulatory cite in this paragraph.

Figure 5.3. U.S. Code Citations

Title	Section	Publisher
42 U.S.C. "U.S. Code"	§ 1983	U.S. Government Printing Office (GPO)
42 U.S.C.S. "U.S. Code Service"	§ 1983	Lexis [Annotated Version of Code]
42 U.S.C.A. "U.S. Code Annotated"	§ 1983	West [Annotated Version of Code]

The good news is that usually, after you have worked with legal materials for awhile, interpreting these citations becomes second nature because you start to see very similar citations over and over. Fortunately, too, there is ample online help. Here are a few helpful websites:

▶ Sonoma State University Library: "How to Read a Legal Citation": libweb.sonoma.edu/research/subject/legalcitation.html

▶ University of Wisconsin Law Library: "Interpreting Legal Citations": library.law.wisc.edu/services/find/guides/subject/legalcitations.html

▶ West Texas A&M: "Interpreting Legal Citations": www.wtamu.edu/library/govt/casecite.shtml

Occasionally, however, a citation may be a complete puzzle. One possibility is that it is a typo or another simple mistake. But sometimes what causes trouble are unfamiliar abbreviations for the sets of books that once housed these materials. If all these methods do not help resolve a citation puzzle, one can call a law library for help in deciphering it or consult a copy of *Bieber's Dictionary of Legal Abbreviations* (Prince, 2001).

Finally, two things should be noted. One, legal citation, though it grew up in the print universe, remains the primary way to find specific legal material even on the web. There is simply no substitute for learning how to decipher citations. Two, legal citation—for long a constant in the legal information universe—is slowly changing. For several decades a movement has been building to create a "vendor neutral" system of citation, one that does not depend on citing to a particular publisher's set of materials. To date, only about 13 states have adopted this system, but it is something to keep an eye on if planning to spend time doing legal research.

Keyword and Subject Searching for Case Law

Much of the time legal information needs are satisfied by a "known item" search; it is simply a question of knowing which resource will have that item. You begin with a citation to a statute or case (e.g., 86 N.J. 308) and determine where to go to do a direct lookup; this known item search process was covered in the previous section.

The second type of legal information need—and often the more challenging—arises when you do not know the item (e.g., the case or statute or other document) that will answer your question. Generally, finding the answer to this type of question begins with a subject word or keyword search and requires deciding the appropriate words to use in a legal database. This can be a showstopper for laypersons when dealing with "legalese" that is unfamiliar or confusing. In addition, legal publishers use standardized subject terms or classification numbers when indexing case law so that similar cases will be retrieved together; this means that figuring out the appropriate terms from the publisher's vocabulary is part of the process of a successful search.

In the following section, tips for successful subject searching for case law are described and illustrated. Two approaches are covered: using hard copy print tools and searching in online databases.

Hard-Copy Tools for Case Law Subject Searches

Hard-copy **digests** are an excellent starting point for a case law subject search. Digests contain short summaries of points of law from court decisions, arranged by topic. The topic headings used by digest publishers, however, can be difficult to understand for a layperson, and topics also have corresponding—and somewhat cryptic—topic numbers. For example, the Westlaw topic heading for cases involving attorney fees in divorce cases is "Divorce—Allowance for Counsel Fees and Expenses" and the topic number is 134k220. Fortunately, digests include separate indexes for keywords and descriptive phrases that direct you to appropriate topics. Figure 5.4 shows an excerpt from a state digest descriptive word index; this is followed by the corresponding digest entry for the topic in Figure 5.5.

After reviewing the case summaries in the digest, you can use the case citation to look up the full text of the court opinion in a case reporter. For example, in Figure 5.5, the highlighted case has the citation *Bennett v. Bennett*, 387 P.2d 517, 63 Wash.2d 404. For instructions on how to look up a specific case such as this one, see the Citations: Known Item Searching section earlier in this chapter.

Digests are a powerful lookup tool for finding relevant cases but, unfortunately, they are expensive hard-copy publications, and only larger law libraries typically have them in their collections. The other approach to a subject search is by using an online database.

Online Databases for Case Law Subject Searches

The Internet is a great source of free legal information but, as discussed earlier, many free online sources for legal information are neither comprehensive nor do they provide the kind of powerful search options

---

Figure 5.4. Excerpt from Descriptive Word Index, *Washington Digest*

APPEARANCE, **Divorce** ☞ 81

ARMED services,
   Servicemembers' relief from civil liability,
     Generally, **Armed S** ☞ 34.4(4)
     Stay, **Armed S** ☞ 34.9(2)

ARREST, **Divorce** ☞ 84

ATTORNEY fees, **Divorce** ☞ 196-198, 220-229
On appeal, **Divorce** ☞ 182

BESTIALITY, acts of bestiality as ground for divorce, **Divorce** ☞ 27(16)

BIGAMY,
   Ground for divorce, **Divorce** ☞ 18.5

BILL,
   For divorce, **Divorce** ☞ 89-95

CONCURRENT and conflicting jurisdiction,
   Courts of same state, **Courts** ☞ 475(15)
   State and federal courts, **Courts** ☞ 489(1)

CONDONATION, defense, **Divorce** ☞ 48-51

CONDUCT,
   Making condition intolerable or life burdensome, indignities, **Divorce** ☞ 29(4)
   Rendering cohabitation unsafe as ground for divorce, **Divorce** ☞ 28

CONFESSION, adultery, **Divorce** ☞ 125, 129(11)

CONFESSION of judgment, **Divorce** ☞ 159-161

CONFLICT of laws, **Divorce** ☞ 2
   Alimony, **Divorce** ☞ 199.5(1-3)

Source: Washington Digest. 2010. St. Paul, MN: West Publishing. Reprinted with permission of Thomson Reuters.

Figure 5.5. Excerpt Showing Topic Entry in *Washington Digest*

⟜182. Effect of appeal.

Library references

C.J.S. Divorce § 283.

Wash. 1963. In absence of showing of need, wife would not be allowed attorneys' fees on unsuccessful appeal by husband in divorce case.

Mumm v. Mumm, 387 P.2d 547, 63 Wash.2d 349.

Wash. 1963. Superior court had jurisdiction to consider motion of wife for an allowance from community funds for attorney's fees and costs on appeal, even though her notice of appeal from judgment in divorce action had already been filed. Rules on Appeal, rules 15, 65; RCWA 26.08.090.

Bennett v. Bennett, 387 P.2d 517, 63 Wash.2d 404.

Wash. 1962. Wife was entitled to $500 attorneys' fees plus her costs on appeal from during 29 years of marriage had value considerably in excess of one million dollars and perhaps close to two million dollars, and wife was awarded divorce and property settlement of value of about $900,000, including certain operating corporations, and, because of size of property settlement, she was awarded no alimony and no attorney's fees, and husband appealed and, by virtue of supersedeas bond, kept control and management of community assets including those awarded to wife, other than home, automobile, and personal effects, trial court should have granted wife's application for support money, suit money, and partial payment of attorney's fees pending appeal by husband.

Stringfellow v. Stringfellow, 333 P.2d 936, 53 Wash.2d 359.

Wash. 1958. In divorce action, in view of attorney's fees previously assessed and due to husband's present inability to pay, wife, although prevailing in part on appeal, would not

Source: Washington Digest. 2010. St. Paul, MN: West Publishing. Reprinted with permission of Thomson Reuters.

required for reliable legal research. Effective methods for subject searching in free case law sources are limited. Most, however, do allow for "natural language" searching, the type of search you do on Google, Yahoo!, or Bing when simply entering words that come first to mind.

While it is true that popular search engines have become increasingly effective at producing on-topic results from a basic "white box" search—and it can be tempting to stop there even when seeking legal information—trusting entirely in natural language searching surrenders control to the search engine's own determination of what is relevant. Equally important is that it is nearly impossible to know what you might have missed. For these reasons, a subject search for case law first requires determining the appropriate terminology for the legal topic, whether searching in print indexes, as illustrated in the previous section, or in free online sources.

Fortunately, online databases make it easy to do a two-step subject search for case law that will provide relevant answers for most legal questions. First, do a simple natural language search and retrieve a few cases. Browse them to view appropriate terms. Next, incorporate those terms in the second stage of the search.

Here is a very simple illustration of this "one-two punch" approach to searching. The question to be answered is about how to change child support after a divorce. Because divorce is governed by state law, the search is conducted in the state's own free online database for state case law, which allows for natural language searching. (Coverage of state case law in free online databases will vary depending on the state. Refer to Chapter 4 and Appendix 3.)

- **Step 1**: Enter a simple natural language search: *change child support after divorce.*

  Browse the documents, noting the legal terms that appear in the most relevant cases. Pay attention to terms that are exact phrases, too, and enclose these in quotation marks in the second stage of the search. Use "and" between every term that you absolutely want to have appear in your results. (There are many more search options possible, but these two—quotation marks for phrases and using "and" between required terms—are all you need for most topics.)

- **Step 2**: Use these preferred terms in a new search: *modification and "child support" and dissolution.* The results of this search will be more relevant and comprehensive.

Obviously, you can repeat this "one-two punch" approach to searching by browsing the latest results and using what you see to refine the search words further. It may take several "one-two" cycles of browsing and refining your search words before the results are satisfactory.

Keyword Subject Searching for Statutes and Regulations

The search method described for finding cases can also be used to find statutes, but with a few adjustments. Most important is that there is a big difference between searching the annotated version of statutes and the unannotated version. As explained in Part I, annotations can be lengthy, including the legislative history of the statute, summaries of court decisions interpreting the statutes, references to secondary sources that relate to the statute, and more. If you are seeking a specific statute but do not know its citation for direct lookup (leaving you unable to do a "known item" search), it is best to search only the text of the statutes themselves and not the text of the statutes and their annotations. The free online versions of most state statutes do not include annotations, so this means a simple keyword search here can be very effective. If searching on a pay-for-view service you usually have two choices: you can run the search in the unannotated version of the statute or in the annotated version. If you choose the latter method, it is necessary to use "field" or "segment" delimiters to search only the text of the statute itself.

Another effective technique when keyword searching for statutes or regulations is restricting the search to a particular section (often called a "title" or chapter in some states or the federal code) before proceeding to enter your keywords. For example, it may be possible to search only in the criminal or penal code of the state statutes or only in the employment law or motor vehicle law section. In this way you retrieve more relevant results quickly because all results are from the section of the statutes you are interested in. Figure 5.6 is an illustration using the Cornell Legal Information Institute website to search the Internal Revenue Service Code, which is Title 26 in the USC.

Figure 5.6. Cornell's Legal Information Institute, U.S. Code Title 26

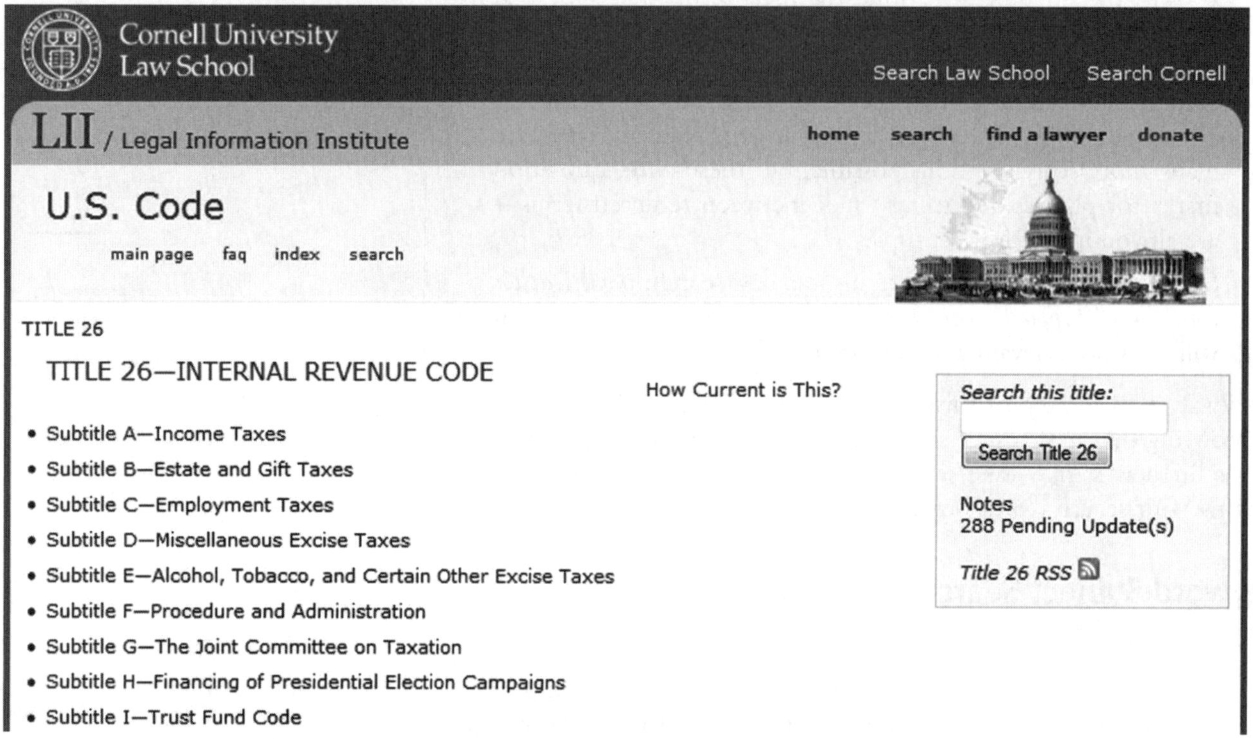

Cornell University
Law School

Search Law School   Search Cornell

LII / Legal Information Institute

home   search   find a lawyer   donate

U.S. Code

main page   faq   index   search

TITLE 26

TITLE 26—INTERNAL REVENUE CODE

How Current is This?

Search this title:

[Search Title 26]

Notes
288 Pending Update(s)

Title 26 RSS

- Subtitle A—Income Taxes
- Subtitle B—Estate and Gift Taxes
- Subtitle C—Employment Taxes
- Subtitle D—Miscellaneous Excise Taxes
- Subtitle E—Alcohol, Tobacco, and Certain Other Excise Taxes
- Subtitle F—Procedure and Administration
- Subtitle G—The Joint Committee on Taxation
- Subtitle H—Financing of Presidential Election Campaigns
- Subtitle I—Trust Fund Code

For resource updates, visit this book's companion website at

▶ **www.GetLaw.net**

RESOURCES RECAP

Finding Legal Information

	Resource	Notes
Interpreting Legal Citations: Online Sources	▶ Sonoma State University Library, "How to Read a Legal Citation": libweb.sonoma.edu/research/subject/legalcitation.html ▶ University of Wisconsin Law Library, "Interpreting Legal Citations": library.law.wisc.edu/services/find/guides/subject/legalcitations.html ▶ West Texas A&M, "Interpreting Legal Citations": www.wtamu.edu/library/govt/casecite.shtml	

Building on What Is Found

"Pearl Growing": Finding One Good Case, Then More Like It

One effective method frequently used by experienced searchers to find relevant documents is called "pearl growing." In legal research, this approach involves locating one case or a few cases that are precisely on point; this is the "pearl." Often a person already has a relevant case from looking at the annotations on a statute or a case cited in a secondary source such as a practice guide or legal encyclopedia. Figure 5.7 shows an Alaskan statute, and Annotation #19 is a summary of the court decision in the case *Vezey v. Green* (2001) Alaska, 35 P.3d 14. Otherwise, a search in a digest is an efficient way to isolate cases on a particular legal issue. (See section titled Hard-Copy Tools for Case Law Subject Searches.)

Once you have a relevant case—the pearl—it is possible to find more cases like it by (1) looking at the topic and key numbers assigned to the case and then searching on these topic numbers to find similar cases or by (2) using a **citatory** to locate more recent cases that cite this case. This second method also helps you find out if the case is "still good law," e.g., determining if later court decisions have overturned one or more points of law in the case.

Pay-for-View Services: Lexis and Westlaw

If you are fortunate enough to have access to one of the leading commercial—or "pay-for-view"—legal search engines, your options for subject searching are greatly expanded. These search engines are available

---

Figure 5.7. Annotated Statute from *West's Alaska Statutes Annotated*

AS § 09.45.052 Adverse possession

(a) The uninterrupted adverse notorious possession of real property under color and claim of title for seven years or more, or the uninterrupted adverse notorious possession of real property for 10 years or more because of a good faith but mistaken belief that the real property lies within the boundaries of adjacent real property owned by the adverse claimant, is conclusively presumed to give title to the property except as against the state or the United States. For the purpose of this section, land that is in the trust established by the Alaska Mental Health Enabling Act of 1956, P. L. 84-830, 70 Stat. 709, is land owned by the state.

(b) Except for an easement created by Public Land Order 1613, adverse possession will lie against property that is held by a person who holds equitable title from the United States under paragraphs 7 and 8 of Public Land Order 1613 of the Secretary of the Interior (April 7, 1958).

(c) Notwithstanding AS 09.10.030, the uninterrupted adverse notorious use of real property by a public utility for utility purposes for a period of 10 years or more vests in that utility an easement in that property for that purpose.

(d) Notwithstanding AS 09.10.030, the uninterrupted adverse notorious use, including construction, management, operation, or maintenance, of private land for public transportation or public access purposes, including highways, streets, roads, or trails, by the public, the state, or a political subdivision of the state, for a period of 10 years or more, vests an appropriate interest in that land in the state or a political subdivision of the state. This subsection does not limit or expand the rights of a state or political subdivision under adverse possession or prescription as the law existed on July 17, 2003.

[text omitted]

19. Notoriety of possession, visible and notorious possession

Because the notice requirement of establishing title by adverse possession pertains only to the record owner, the adverse possessor's title does not directly depend on whether parties other than the record owner are on notice of the adverse possession. Vezey v. Green (2001) Alaska, 35 P.3d 14.

Source: West's Alaska Statutes Annotated. 2010. St. Paul, MN: West Publishing. Reprinted with permission of Thomson Reuters.

only by subscription and do not come cheap; they are most likely to be accessible to the public at larger public law libraries and county law libraries and at law school libraries at publicly funded universities.

The two dominant pay-for-view legal search engines and publishers, Westlaw and Lexis, do extensive analysis of case law, assigning subject keywords and **headnotes** that describe the important legal issues in the case. Headnotes (see Figure 5.8) are short paragraphs at the beginning of a case report that summarize each point of law in the case; headnotes are added by the publisher, not the court, and should not be cited or quoted.

As explained, digests serve as subject indexes to case law. Publishers also index the cases cited by one case so that it is easy, for example, to view a case from 1986 and retrieve all cases that have cited it since 1986. Both systems analyze the nature of the citation and provide flags to indicate if the case has been cited positively, negatively, or overturned by a later court decision. On Lexis this feature is called Shepard's; on Westlaw it is called KeyCite.

Searching on either of these services can be done in two ways. Most nonprofessional searchers are likely to use natural language mode, whether they are aware of it or not. This search mode is much like running a search on Google or Yahoo! and does not require any particular knowledge of the commands and features on the search engine. While the natural language method seems the easiest, it is not the best method. For more control over search results and options like Boolean, restricting to certain fields or segments (like the case title), or date restrictions, there is a "power search," or "terms and connectors," mode.

Figure 5.8. Headnote from a Case Record on Westlaw

[21] KeyCite Citing References for this Headnote ⟸134 Divorce

⟸134V Alimony, Allowances, and Disposition of Property

⟸134k220 Allowance for Counsel Fees and Expenses

⟸134k221 k. In General. Most Cited Cases

There is difference between allowance of attorney's fees in original divorce proceeding and in divorce modification proceeding.

Source: Westlaw. Available: directory.westlaw.com/ (accessed 2010). Reprinted with permission of Thomson Reuters.

CLOSER LOOK

Power Searching on Westlaw and Lexis

Here are the key searching options available when in the "power" or "terms and connectors" search mode. This search mode makes it possible to finesse search results and have more control over which documents are retrieved.

Search Method	Lexis	Westlaw
Exact phrase	*adverse possession* [No quotes needed; a space between words means an exact phrase.]	*"adverse possession"* [Enclose phrase in quotes.]
Both words must appear (Boolean AND)	*adverse and possession*	*adverse & possession*
Either word must appear (Boolean OR)	*possession or possessor* [Use the word OR between words.]	*possession possessor* [A space between words means OR.]
All words starting with [word] ("wildcard")	*possess!* [Retrieves possess, possesses, possessing, possession, possessor, etc.]	
Words in same sentence	*search /s seizure*	
Words in same paragraph	*search /p seizure*	
Words within "n" words of one another, in either order	*search /2 seizure*	
Words within "n" words of one another, in specified order	*search pre/2 seizure*	*search +2 seizure*
Words must appear at least "n" times	atleast5(adverse possession)	atleast5("adverse possession") [Not available in all Westlaw databases]
Exclude a word *Note*: Use this feature with care. It's easy to exclude documents you *do* want.	*trust! and not testamentary*	*trust! but not testamentary* *trust! % testamentary*
Restrict by date	Easiest method: Use the "Specify Date" feature and choose dates from dropdown lists.	Easiest method: Click the "Dates" link and use the template to enter desired dates.
Restrict to a specific part of a document	Called "segment" on Lexis. Example: to search only in the case name *name(roe and wade)*	Called "field" on Westlaw. Example: to search only in the case name *ti(roe and wade)*

Updating

The law changes constantly. While stability and predictability are important to the legal system, so is change. If this were not true, our legal system would still consider women property, slavery humane, and the landless ineligible to vote. Thankfully, then, change is "built in" to the legal system and so it is built in to legal research sources as well. The legal researcher must always check whether the material in hand is up to date. "Updating" primary sources (and some secondary sources) in the print universe is done through at least five different methods:

- slip laws or slip opinions;
- pocket parts;
- advance sheets, pamphlets, or legislative services;
- replacement volumes; and
- case citators.

Slip laws are usually loose-leaf collections of pages that print a newly enacted statute. **Slip opinions** are similar but are newly announced decisions from a particular court. These publications are collected only by some libraries, called **depository libraries**. Large law libraries but few public libraries are likely to collect these.

Pocket parts are paper pamphlets designed to be inserted in the back of hardbound volumes of books. These pocket parts contain changes in the law and other updates that have occurred since the publishing of the material in the hardbound volume. Most often these pocket parts are found in annotated statutory codes. Always check for pocket parts when working in annotated statutory codes, and if there is not one in the volume, find out why. Pocket parts may also be found in court rules, regulations, legal treatises, most encyclopedias, the newer series of the *American Law Reports*, and other legal publications. Always check for pocket parts when using hard copy materials.

When the pocket part grows too large to be inserted in the back of a hardbound volume, and in other circumstances, a set of books may be updated by what are often called advance sheets, pamphlets, supplements, or "legislative services." Again, these are most characteristic of annotated statutory codes. Advance pamphlets may be independent of specific hardbound volumes, however, and may contain the most recent legislation—the session laws of a legislature or newly codified statutes. Always look for advance pamphlets, especially when doing statutory, and sometimes administrative, law research.

Advance pamphlets also are published for case reporters. They contain the most recent decisions from the courts. Except in rare instances, these advance pamphlets for the courts will not "update" a specific case in an earlier hardbound volume. The thorough researcher will glance through the advance sheets containing recent decisions from a specific court to determine if the court has recently announced a decision pertaining to an issue of interest to the researcher.

Replacement volumes pose little cause for confusion. It is best to be aware that hardbound volumes, especially volumes of the annotated statutory codes, may often be entirely replaced by updated hardbound or sometimes paperbound volumes. The volumes of the Internal Revenue Code portion of the U.S. Code, for instance, are replaced every year. Many states now publish unannotated statutory codes in paperbound versions, and these are often replaced every year or two. This is true also of administrative codes, both on the federal level (the *Code of Federal Regulations*) and in many states. Sections of the paperbound *CFR* are updated throughout the year and gradually change color.

Citators are an entirely different and strange animal. Few disciplines have such a beast. The first clue to how to use a citator is in its name: citator. The focus is on citations. The researcher wanting to make sure a specific piece of law—say, a case opinion—is still "good law" and has not been changed by later developments will use the citation to that piece of "found law" and check in the appropriate citator for citations to other, later pieces of law that have cited the prior piece of found law. Let us look at this more concretely.

The citator system began in relation to case opinions. Court opinions can be cited by later court opinions for a wide variety of reasons. The most important, initial reason the researcher will want to use a citator for cases is to be sure that later case opinions have not reversed or overruled the earlier case opinion. The researcher will also use the citator to find later court opinions on the same issue as the earlier opinion. Every case that has ever cited the earlier opinion will be cited in the citator, and these later cases are often likely to be relevant to the issue that was the subject of the earlier opinion.

The citator system was later extended to statutory citations and administrative code (i.e., regulatory citations). In other words, if you are relying on a specific statutory section you should go to the statutory citator with that section's citation to make sure the statute has not been repealed or amended and to find cites to every case opinion that has ever cited that statute. The same is true of regulations in administrative codes. You should see again that this process not only assures the researcher that the statute or regulation is still "good law" but also helps the researcher find other relevant law likely pertaining to that statute or regulation.

Using citators in print is difficult at first. Ask for help. Read the documentation in the volumes closely. And persevere. The process is also complicated because only the largest law libraries carry citators and even those libraries are cutting back their subscriptions to these very expensive services.

But the slow disappearance of print citators may be a blessing because many county or governmental law libraries now provide this "citator" service for free in an online format. This service alone is worth the trip to the law library, no matter how far away it may be from home. Ask for help once you are there.

The online world has not only changed the citator process drastically, it has changed the updating process for all materials. In the online world, pocket parts, advance sheets, and replacement volumes are obviously obsolete. This sometimes makes "updating" the law one finds on the web more challenging. Most important, you must always be aware that change is likely to have occurred and that you should therefore look for updates. There is no uniform way of updating online legal information sources. Here are some guidelines:

WORTH WATCHING

Google Legal

In November 2009 Google launched a legal information service within its Google Scholar product. Coverage includes selected state appellate cases since 1950; federal district, appellate, tax, and bankruptcy courts since 1923; and U.S. Supreme Court cases since 1791. There is also selected coverage of legal journal articles. Go to scholar.google.com and click the option for "Legal opinions and journals."

Options have certainly come a long way in the very short time since legal information was to be found only in books. As recently as 1996 the CEO of LexisNexis was quoted saying, "The Internet is over-hyped and unlikely to be the standard for information delivery" (Blake, 1996). Google's entry in the legal information market means more access to legal information and a familiar search interface for consumers. Industry reviewers have welcomed the move as furthering government transparency, too, predicting that "freeing the law from behind the Westlaw and LexisNexis paywall will help improve the health of our democracy" (Tsai, 2009). Tsai adds that it also benefits attorneys, stating, "While it may not break up the LexisNexis and Westlaw duopoly right away, it does increase competition and foster innovation." Interestingly, both Lexis and Westlaw are launching new "easy" search products in 2010 with Google-like interfaces, which are also worth watching.

- To check to see if a state or federal case has been overruled, reversed, or cited in later opinions, find a library that provides free access to online citators or consider a per-access charge for the privilege.

- To check to see if a federal statute has been repealed, amended, or otherwise impacted, use the online U.S. Code and use Thomas (thomas.loc.gov/). For state statutes, look for hyperlinks on the pages that display the statute with which you are concerned. Often a link to updates is available. Also, check the websites for the legislative houses or bodies in your state.

- For changes to sections of the *Code of Federal Regulations*, check the "List of CFR Sections Affected" (www.gpoaccess .gov/lsa/index.html). Also check the online *Federal Register* (www.gpoaccess.gov/fr/).

- For changes to state regulations, access the online administrative code and follow the advice pertaining to state statutes. Also, check the online administrative register or its equivalent for the state with which you are concerned.

Assuming you have followed all the advice in this chapter, you should have a very thorough and up-to-date grasp of the area of law you are researching—and it is very likely you are exhausted as well. You might well be asking, "When can I stop? When do I have enough?"

How Much Is Enough? Who Can Help Me Further?

When doing a subject search, how do you know when you have searched "enough"? How can you feel confident that you have found the relevant cases? The guideline used by legal researchers is this: you know you are "done" when you keep finding the same cases. However, if you are an amateur searcher, it is strongly recommended that you consult with a law librarian when faced with a legal information need that requires using a digest, topic numbers, keywords, and citation searching. Law librarians have special training in advanced search techniques and in legal information and can be of invaluable assistance in finding information even though they cannot provide legal advice.

For resource updates, visit this book's companion website at

▶ *www.GetLaw.net*

RESOURCES RECAP		
Researching the Law and Updating		
	Resource	**Notes**
Researching Federal Law	Refer to Chapters 1, 2, and 3 of this book.	
Researching State Law	Refer to Chapters 1, 2, 4, and Appendix 3 of this book.	
Updating Federal Statutes Online	▶ Thomas: thomas.loc.gov/	
Updating Federal Regulations Online	▶ *Federal Register*: www.gpoaccess.gov/fr/	The official daily publication for rules, proposed rules, and notices of federal agencies and organizations as well as for executive orders and other presidential documents
List of Sections Affected	▶ GPO Access, "List of CFR Sections Affected (LSA): Main Page": www.gpoaccess.gov/lsa/index.html	For proposed, new, and amended federal regulations published in the *Federal Register* since the most recent revision date of a *CFR* title
Do-It-Yourself Publications	▶ American Association of Law Libraries. 2009. "Public Library Toolkit." Available: www.aallnet.org/sis/lisp/toolkit.htm. ▶ Elias, S. 2009. *Legal Research: How to Find and Understand the Law*. Berkeley, CA: Nolo.	

References

Blake, P. 1996. "Online Services Race to Embrace the Web: Major Players Move to the Web, but Their Views on the Medium Differ." *Information Today* 13, no. 7: 41–42.

Garner, Bryan A. ed. 2009. *Black's Law Dictionary*. St. Paul, MN: West.

Nyberg, C. 2004. "Legal Reference for Non-law Librarians." *Pacific Northwest Library Association Quarterly* 69, no. 1: 6, 25–27. Available: www.pnla.org/quarterly/Fall2004/PNLA_Fall04.pdf (accessed August 10, 2010).

Prince, Mary Miles. 2001. *Bieber's Dictionary of Legal Abbreviation: A Reference Guide for Attorneys, Legal Secretaries, Paralegals, and Law Students*. Buffalo, NY: W. S. Hein.

Ross, C. S., K. Nilsen, and M. L. Radford. 2009. *Conducting the Reference Interview*. 2nd ed. New York: Neal-Schuman.

Tsai, D. 2009. "Google Scholar: A New Way to Search for Cases and Related Legal Publications." *LLRX*, December 30. Available: www.llrx.com/features/googlescholar.htm (accessed August 10, 2010).

Resources Beyond the Public Library

This chapter is about the frontline decisions that public librarians make when a patron has a legal information need that cannot be met by the library's own collection. In these situations the best response is often to refer the person to other resources. Depending on the local community, these may include law libraries, free legal services and legal aid organizations, and alternative dispute methods such as mediation services. Sometimes it is simply wise for a person to consult with a lawyer; this chapter provides resources and recommendations for how to go about choosing one.

Law Libraries

Law libraries are often the first place to go for help for two principal reasons: (1) they have legal materials and reference sources not available at most public libraries and (2) they are staffed by law librarians experienced in legal research. There are several kinds of law libraries providing access to legal materials to the public: county law libraries, court libraries, public university libraries, law school libraries, and public libraries in large cities or metropolitan areas.

Most counties have law libraries open to the public. Not surprisingly, the size and breadth of each library's collection and the online databases offered will generally depend on the size of the community served and its funding sources. A typical county law library will have the following basic legal research publications: a set of annotated state statutes, state administrative regulations, state appellate court decisions, a state case law digest, state practice materials, and local, state, and federal court rules. County law libraries are frequently depository libraries for state case reporters and possibly other state materials, meaning that they automatically receive these publications free of charge and must make them available to the public. Although it is less predictable which additional secondary sources a county law library will have, as funding sources and budgets are driving factors, it is common to find a legal encyclopedia, additional practice materials, legal forms, and perhaps a selection of treatises. Some states have a network of trial court law libraries (e.g., Massachusetts) instead of county law libraries, although these provide similar legal research services.

Larger county and court libraries will have additional materials, such as regional case reporters (e.g., *Atlantic Reporter*) as well as more extensive secondary source collections, including treatises and a range of practice materials. Reference services are also more extensive, and some even offer free or low-cost workshops on common legal matters, particularly those in which laypersons often represent themselves. These may be provided in partnership with local bar associations, public libraries, or legal aid groups. (For more on legal aid groups, see the following section in this chapter.) In addition to county law libraries, larger metropolitan areas with extensive public library systems may have a law library or a legal reference collection staffed by law librarians.

Another excellent institution for more extended legal research can be the library of a public university. Publicly funded universities typically have some arrangement for public access to the library's collection, although this will rarely be the same privileges as those for students. If there is a nearby university with a law school, this can be a particularly great place for legal research. Not only is the library's collection vast but librarians at law school libraries usually have both a graduate degree in library and information science (the MLS or MLIS), a JD (Juris Doctor), and broad experience in legal research. They may be limited in how much assistance they can provide to members of the public but are usually very helpful in addressing questions about using the library's materials. Keep in mind that the library's primary purpose is serving the information needs of the students and faculty of the university.

Another way law school libraries can be enormously helpful is through the use of their websites. These are typically full of links to research guides (sometimes called library guides or "pathfinders") on a wide range of legal topics. For example, WashLaw, the Washburn University School of Law website (www.washlaw.edu) mentioned throughout this book as a key resource, is maintained by the law school's library staff. Research guides may also be found on websites of larger county law libraries and metropolitan public libraries. For an example, see the San Diego County Public Law Library website (www.sdcll.org/resources/guides.htm).

Law library consortiums also provide valuable legal resources. For example, the Council of California County Law Librarians has a website with short tutorials about legal research generally and California law specifically (see www.publiclawlibrary.org/research.html). Finally, each state capital has a law library that typically has a website with state resources and links. Refer to the law library directories in this section's Resources Recap.

The professional organization for law librarians is the American Association of Law Librarians (AALL). AALL currently has over 5,000 members who work in law libraries in law firms, corporations, the courts, public law libraries, government agencies, and other settings. Its

QUICK TIP

Finding the Nearest Law Library

The most straightforward and effortless way to find the law library that is both nearby and open to the public is often to contact the clerk's office at the local courthouse. Court clerks field many requests for legal information—and, of course, requests for legal advice, too—that they are not permitted to answer. They are happy to redirect people to the closest law library, whether it is within the courthouse or elsewhere. The local court's website may also include contact information for law libraries in the community.

website includes an array of information about the profession of law librarianship, including a directory of graduate study programs and standards for public county law libraries.

LLRX, Law Librarians Resource Xchange (www.lllrx.com), is a resource with an assortment of materials related to law libraries, new

For resource updates, visit this book's companion website at

▶ *www.GetLaw.net*

RESOURCES RECAP

Law Libraries

	Resource	Notes
Law Library Directories	▶ American Bar Association (ABA), "ABA Approved Law Schools": www.abanet.org/legaled/approved lawschools/approved.html	Provides alphabetical and geographic region lists
	▶ Law School Admission Council (LSAC), "Official Guide to ABA-Approved Law Schools": officialguide.lsac.org/	Provides lists that are searchable by location and description
	▶ WashLaw, "Law School Library and State Law Library Catalogs": www.washlaw.edu/lawcat/	Has fewer search options than the two previous directories
	▶ WashLaw, "State, Court, and County Law Libraries": www.washlaw.edu/statecourtcounty/	Contains very selected listings of county law libraries
		To locate a more complete list for a particular state, go to your favorite website search engine (Google, Yahoo!, Bing) and enter, for example, *oregon county law libraries* or *louisiana parish law libraries.*
Law Librarianship and Standards	▶ American Association of Law Librarians (AALL): www.aall.org	
	▶ American Association of Law Libraries, "ALA-Accredited Graduate Programs in Library Science with Law Library Classes or Joint MLS/JD Classes": www.aallnet.org/committee/rllc/resources/lawlib-state.asp	
	▶ American Association of Law Libraries, "Careers in Law Librarianship": www.lawlibrarycareers.org/	
	▶ American Association of Law Libraries, "County Public Law Libraries Standards" (2009): www.aall.org/about/policy_county_standards.asp	
Listserv Directories	▶ CataList—Official Directory of Listservs: www.lsoft.com/lists/list_q.html	
	▶ Library of Congress, "Library Listservs": www.loc.gov/rr/program/bib/libsci/guides.html#listservs	
Sample Public Law Library Websites	▶ Massachusetts Trial Court Law Libraries: www.lawlib.state.ma.us/index.html	Trial court libraries—Massachusetts
	▶ Oregon Council of County Libraries: www.occll.org	Consortium of county law libraries—Oregon
	▶ San Diego County Public Law Library: www.sdcpll.org/	Large county library—San Diego County Law Library
	▶ Your Public Law Library: www.publiclawlibrary.org	Consortium of county law libraries—California

technologies for librarians and lawyers, and articles on a wide variety of law-related and library topics. It is updated daily with news of interest to those doing legal research, law librarians, and other legal professionals.

Listservs are another resource to consider. Law-lib is the leading listserv for law libraries, and there may also be regional and local listservs in your area. The largest directory of listservs is CataList, www.lsoft .com/lists/list_q.html, maintained by the company that created the listserv software. The Library of Congress also maintains a list of recommended listservs for libraries at www.loc.gov/rr/program/bib/ libsci/guides.html.

Libraries and targeted online legal resources are excellent for legal research and learning about the law. However, there are many situations that require legal advice. The following sections in this chapter discuss options for finding organizations that provide free legal assistance, alternatives to settling a dispute in court, and how to go about finding an attorney.

Free Legal Help

Lawyers sometimes work for free. Civil legal aid, or legal service offices as they are sometimes called, will represent some people in some cases for free. Usually the client will have to meet monetary requirements of not earning over a specific amount. These offices often will handle only very specific types of cases, or there may be other civil legal aid offices that specialize in one type of law, such as social security, unemployment, immigrant rights. Two great starting places for finding free legal aid in your area are:

▶ LawHelp.org: www.LawHelp.org
  LawHelp.org is a gateway to nonprofit legal aid providers in the United States, with the mission of helping low and moderate income people find free legal aid programs in their communities.

▶ FindLegalHelp: www.FindLegalHelp.org
  FindLegalHelp is a service of the American Bar Association (ABA), with links to legal aid resources in all 50 states and Canada.

In addition to legal aid organizations that may represent people for free (called **pro bono**) in civil cases, when a person is charged with a felony and found to be **indigent**—that is, with few financial assets—that person will be eligible for free, court-appointed legal representation. Those providing this type of representation are most often called **public defenders**, either formally or informally. A Google search of this phrase followed by the name of your state is likely to yield a list of public defender offices in your state.

Finally, a person may need some legal advice without actually being involved in a lawsuit or without actually needing full representation. Many times bar associations will run free "legal clinics" in their communities. These clinics may be in various locations and are often open only one evening a week. Attorneys volunteer their time to come to these clinics and provide people with free legal advice. The place to start to find out if such a clinic exists in your community is, again, the bar associations themselves or the web.

For resource updates, visit this book's companion website at

▶ *www.GetLaw.net*

RESOURCES RECAP		
Free Legal Aid Resources		
	Resource	**Notes**
Online	▶ LawHelp.org: www.LawHelp.org	This gateway to nonprofit legal aid providers in the United States has the mission of helping low- and moderate-income people find free legal aid referrals, programs, and information in their communities.
	▶ FindLegalHelp.org: www.FindLegalHelp.org	This service of the American Bar Association (ABA) provides links to legal aid resources in all 50 states, the District of Columbia, Puerto Rico, the Virgin Islands, and Canada.

Alternative Dispute Resolution

Alternative dispute resolution—also called **ADR**—has been rapidly on the rise in recent years. What is alternative dispute resolution exactly? In short, it is a process for settling a dispute outside of the courtroom with the help of a neutral trained professional. The most common type of ADR is **mediation**, but other alternatives to litigation exist, including arbitration, negotiation, and facilitation as well as other forms. A recent development is **collaborative law**, most commonly practiced currently in divorce cases. In collaborative law the parties agree that they will not go to court to resolve differences, and their respective attorneys agree to withdraw if their clients change their minds and decide to litigate the matter. **Arbitration** differs from mediation in that the arbitrator is the decision maker and not the parties: after hearing from both sides, the arbitrator renders a decision that is binding and as enforceable as a court judgment. In this type of dispute resolution, an arbitrator (or a panel of arbitrators) conducts a kind of simplified trial. Almost all states have adopted the Uniform Arbitration Act and are guided by its rules and standards.

About Mediation

Because mediation is most often the type of ADR used as an alternative to litigation, its key characteristics are worth noting:

- Mediation is a process. Different styles of mediation exist, but all involve specific stages facilitated by the mediator. Typically these include ensuring that both sides fully express their concerns, confirming that each side has heard the other, brainstorming on possible solutions, and agreement on the settlement terms.

- Decision-making authority rests with the parties, not the mediator. This is based on research showing that the most durable and satisfactory agreements are those the parties have collaboratively created themselves.

- The settlement agreement is not binding unless all parties agree (unlike "binding arbitration"). If no agreement can be arrived at, the parties may choose to leave the mediation.

- Mediation is not recommended in situations in which there is an extreme difference in power between the disputing parties or in which domestic violence has occurred.

What are the reasons people try mediation? In some situations, the court may order a matter to mediation but most often the parties attempt mediation voluntarily. The most common reasons are these: in mediation the individuals are fully engaged in the decision-making process (instead of waiting for a decision that is handed down), the cost for mediation is usually much lower than that of litigation, and the person is more likely to be paid the agreed-on settlement amount than if there had been a court judgment. Often each party ends up compromising to some extent, but the advantages in cost and closure can be significant to people who opt for mediation. In addition, mediation can work particularly well when both parties are interested in restoring communication and continuing on good terms, such as neighbors or family members.

As mentioned, some jurisdictions require that mediation be attempted before the court will hear certain types of cases. This sort of prelitigation mediation may include small claims matters or divorces, for example. In addition, there may be a contract between the parties that requires them to take their dispute to arbitration, mediation, or other type of dispute resolution forum. Refer also to the information in Chapter 7.

ADR Organizations and Resources

▶ American Arbitration Association (AAA): www.adr.org/
The AAA maintains a directory of about 8,000 arbitrators who are independent contractors. The organization has five divisions: Commercial, Construction, International, Labor/Employment, and Insurance.

▶ Association for Conflict Resolution (ACR): www.acrnet.org/
The ACR promotes the practice and public understanding of conflict resolution. The organization represents an international group of over 6,000 mediators, arbitrators, facilitators, educators, and others involved in the field of conflict resolution and collaborative decision making. ACR has a Directory of Mediators for family and workplace matters (www.acrnet.org/referrals/mediators.htm).

▶ Mediate.com Newsletter: www.mediate.com/Newsletter/
Mediate.com provides newsletter articles to the public and promotional services to mediation professionals. The website has several helpful articles on frequently asked questions about mediation.

▶ National Association for Community Mediation (NAFCM): www
.nafcm.org/
NAFCM promotes community mediation services that are designed to
resolve differences and conflicts between individuals, groups, and
organizations.

For resource updates, visit this book's
companion website at

▶ **www.GetLaw.net**

RESOURCES RECAP

Alternative Dispute Resolution

	Resource	Notes
Federal and Uniform Acts	▶ Cornell's Legal Information Institute, "Uniform Arbitration Act": www.law.cornell.edu/uniform/vol7.html#arbit	
	▶ Cornell's Legal Information Institute, "U.S. Code: Title 9—Arbitration": www.law.cornell.edu/uscode/html/uscode09/	Federal Arbitration Act
	▶ National Conference of Commissioners on Uniform State Laws, "Uniform Collaborative Law Act": www.law.upenn.edu/bll/archives/ulc/ucla/2009am_approved.htm	Pending approval as of July 2009
State Statutes	▶ Cornell's Legal Information Institute, "Alternative Dispute Resolution: State Statutes": topics.law.cornell.edu/wex/table_alternative_dispute_resolution	
Associations	▶ American Arbitration Association (AAA): www.adr.org	The AAA maintains a directory of about 8,000 arbitrators who are independent contractors. The organization has five divisions: Commercial, Construction, International, Labor/Employment, and Insurance.
	▶ American Bar Association Section of Dispute Resolution: www.abanet.org/dispute/	The section's website includes ADR policies, publications, a free brochure, and a number of free ADR resources.
	▶ Association for Conflict Resolution (ACR): www.acrnet.org; "Directory of Mediators" (for family and workplace matters): www.acrnet.org/referrals/mediators.htm	The ACR promotes the practice and public understanding of conflict resolution. The organization represents an international group of over 6,000 mediators, arbitrators, facilitators, educators, and others involved in the field of conflict resolution and collaborative decision making.
	▶ Mediate.com: www.mediate.com	Mediate.com provides newsletter articles to the public and promotional services to mediation professionals. The website has several helpful articles on frequently asked questions about mediation.
	▶ National Association for Community Mediation (NAFCM): www.nafcm.org	NAFCM promotes community mediation services designed to resolve differences and conflicts between individuals, groups, and organizations.
Self-Help Publications	▶ American Bar Association. 2006. *Brief Guide to Dispute Resolution Process.* Available: www.abanet.org/dispute/draftbrochure.pdf.	
	▶ Lovenheim, Peter, and Lisa Guerin. 2004. *Mediate, Don't Litigate.* Berkeley, CA: Nolo.	

Choosing a Lawyer

This book frequently states that a person facing an actual court case, especially criminal charges but serious civil suits as well, should retain an attorney. In addition, in other types of litigation, consulting with a lawyer—even if one is not retained—can be advisable. But how does a person go about finding a good lawyer?

First, asking one's friends and acquaintances if they know of a good attorney is often the best resource. As in many things, personal experience can be the best guide. However, friends may not know of an attorney, or a friend involved in a court case might not feel comfortable discussing it with others. Another way to get reliable leads through personal experience is by asking a good attorney in one practice area to recommend someone for the legal matter currently of concern. Lawyers in a community typically know who specializes and has experience in specific areas of the law and who is likely to be a good fit for your legal need.

A second way to find an attorney is to look for professional associations that may have a referral service. One can usually locate bar associations in the phone book or on the Internet simply by searching for "X bar association," which could be a state bar association, a county bar association, or even a city bar association in many of the largest cities. Additionally, three FindLaw websites can be good starting points:

- ▶ "Legal Associations and Organizations," for legal and law-related associations, generally: www.findlaw.com/06associations/index.html

- ▶ "National and Specialty Legal Associations": www.findlaw.com/06associations/national.html

- ▶ "State and Local Legal Associations": www.findlaw.com/06associations/state.html

State and county bar associations frequently provide a referral service, which represents a service to the bar association's members and to the general public. Sometimes these services may charge a small fee, or the attorney to whom one is referred may charge a fee. Usually these fees are fairly low and the attorneys may charge a lower than normal rate, or they may take some cases for no fee at all. A person consulting an attorney, however, should not assume anything about fees and costs: a potential client will always want to clarify with the attorney the specifics about fees and costs.

Fees and costs are often a source of confusion—and sometimes acrimony—between clients and attorneys. A potential client should be very clear about whether fees will be charged, on what occasions or for what services they will be charged, when they will be billed, if they will ever be waived, and all of the other details. It is also important to remember that fees are different from "costs," which may include filing fees, copying, mailing, expert witnesses, and the like. In general, the law requires that the client remain responsible for all costs, even if there will be no fee charged. For instance, in some cases such as personal injury suits, the lawyer will not charge a fee if the case is not successful, but the client will still be responsible for all of the costs that are involved in litigation. These costs can be sizable. Because much confusion can arise around the issue of fees and costs, it is usually preferable, and sometimes required, that there be a written fee agreement signed by the attorney and the client.

Here are a few additional websites that discuss strategies for choosing an attorney:

▶ Georgia Bar Association, "How to Choose a Lawyer," Consumer Pamphlet Series: www.gabar.org/public/pdf/cps/chooselawyer.pdf

▶ Massachusetts Bar Association, "Tips on Choosing a Lawyer," an entire page dedicated to this question: www.massbar.org/for-the-public/need-a-lawyer/tips-on-choosing-a-lawyer

▶ South Carolina Bar Association, "Choosing a Lawyer," a similar page that is particularly helpful in discussing the issue of fees: www.scbar.org/public_services/lawline/choosing_a_lawyer/

Finally, if none of these methods work in finding an attorney, there is the method of last resort: the yellow pages of the local phone book (or its equivalent on the Internet). Often the yellow pages arrange the entries by two methods: alphabetically by name and by legal specialty. The legal specialization entries provide at least a clue of where to begin. Remember that you should assess advertisements, whether in the yellow pages or elsewhere, with caution: lawyers are allowed to advertise, and many perfectly reputable firms and attorneys do so. When making a choice, be guided by the advice given here and in the sources suggested here. Make sure you know whether you will be charged for the initial consultation. Not every attorney charges by the hour for an initial consultation, but many do, and it is best to be prepared.

For resource updates, visit this book's companion website at

▶ *www.GetLaw.net*

RESOURCES RECAP		
Choosing a Lawyer		
	Resource	**Notes**
Online Directories	▶ FindLaw, "Legal Associations and Organizations": www.findlaw.com/06associations/index.html ▶ FindLaw, "National and Specialty Legal Associations": www.findlaw.com/06associations/national.html ▶ FindLaw, "State and Local Legal Associations": www.findlaw.com/06associations/state.html	
Online Information	▶ Georgia Bar Association, "How to Choose a Lawyer," Consumer Pamphlet Series: www.gabar.org/public/pdf/cps/chooselawyer.pdf ▶ Massachusetts Bar Association, "Tips on Choosing a Lawyer": www.massbar.org/for-the-public/need-a-lawyer/tips-on-choosing-a-lawyer ▶ South Carolina Bar Association, "Choosing a Lawyer": www.scbar.org/public_services/lawline/choosing_a_lawyer/	Particularly helpful in discussing fee issues

Conclusion: Knowing the Community

This chapter has been about finding legal help beyond the public library. The resources available will be different with every community, so the more you can find out about your community along the lines suggested in this chapter the more help you will be able to find. Your community most likely has a law library, and if you are lucky it has one or more agencies that provide some sort of free legal advice. Your community likely has lawyers, and it may have a court system or other agencies that provide a way to settle legal problems without litigation. If you are a librarian helping someone with a legal problem, a productive and insightful reference interview is always at the center of a helpful referral. If you yourself are in need of legal help that requires information or resources beyond your library, this chapter has addressed considerations to keep in mind and starting points to use in the process of finding that help.

Information: Specific Legal Questions

Part III contains eight chapters, each covering an area of law that generates the questions most frequently asked by people trying to do their own legal work. Each chapter typically includes: the framework for the area of law (whether it is governed by state or federal law, for example, or a combination), a "getting started" section (what a person needs to know to begin finding answers in that area of law), frequently asked questions and helpful ideas for finding answers, and "resources recaps," summarizing important print and online sources covered in the chapter. The questions in these chapters were determined through a combination of the authors' experiences and an informal survey of reference librarians at public libraries.

Lawsuits

Framework for Questions in This Area of Law

Lawsuits can come in all shapes and sizes. They can be simple and quick or they can be extraordinarily complex and span many years. They can take place in small claims court or in towering federal courthouses. Lawsuits do not always end up in court in a full trial. In fact there are those who say that a lawsuit is a failure if it *does* go to trial because the system is designed to get the parties to settle their lawsuits without the enormous time and expense of a trial. Lawsuits can also end in arbitration or mediation without a trial. The lawsuit process is largely governed by court rules, so the "area of law" is really *procedural* law—the rules concerning the procedures or processes of carrying out a lawsuit.

This chapter is a bibliography of materials, mostly in hard copy, that have been written to help nonlawyers and lawyers in carrying out a civil lawsuit or in carrying out a successful defense to a civil lawsuit. Sources about criminal trials are not included. This chapter does not tell you how to conduct a lawsuit but provides citations to materials that do tell you how. Most of the materials listed here will be available only in a well-stocked law library. A few of the self-help resources, however, will be available to buy online or from a good bookstore. The chapter begins with some general books that encompass all phases of a lawsuit and then continues with references to books or treatises that focus on specific aspects of lawsuits. This chapter does not advise you about materials related to specific types of lawsuits, such as dissolutions, bankruptcy proceedings, or criminal prosecutions. Materials on those specific areas are the subject of other chapters in this book.

Getting Started

The legal profession refers to individuals who are carrying out lawsuits without counsel as **pro se** or pro se litigants. The phrase "pro se" means, roughly, "on one's own behalf." Thus, for the pro se litigant, the person attempting to bring or defend a lawsuit without assistance of counsel, Nolo has at least two books for this purpose that are easily available, one in print and one an e-book.

> ▶ Berman, Sara, and Paul Bergman. 2008. *Represent Yourself in Court: How to Prepare and Try a Winning Case.* 6th ed. Berkeley, CA: Nolo.

The publisher states that the book "breaks down the trial process into easy-to-understand steps so that you can act as your own lawyer—safely and efficiently." The book is indeed a very practical step-by-step guide and would be very helpful if you choose to go it alone in court. It covers everything from filing court documents, to choosing a jury, to hiring experts. It can also be used even if you are working with an attorney either in a limited way or with full representation but want to know more about the litigation process.

A second general book from Nolo is actually available from the publisher's website (www.nolo.com) as an e-book, downloadable directly from the website as a PDF document:

> ▶ Matthews, Joseph. 2001. *The Lawsuit Survival Guide: A Client's Companion to Litigation.* 1st ed. Berkeley, CA: Nolo.

This book provides explanations of many aspects of the legal process and has the advantage of being easily available online. It answers questions such as "How do I find the right lawyer?" and "Can I cut costs by helping my lawyer?" and many more. It is arranged in the typical chronology of a lawsuit. It can be helpful for anyone, pro se or not, who has an interest in civil court cases.

For resource updates, visit this book's companion website at

▶ **www.GetLaw.net**

RESOURCES RECAP		
Getting Started		
	Resource	**Notes**
Do-It-Yourself Publications	▶ Berman, Sara, and Paul Bergman. 2008. *Represent Yourself in Court: How to Prepare and Try a Winning Case.* 6th ed. Berkeley: Nolo. ▶ Matthews, Joseph. 2001. *The Lawsuit Survival Guide: A Client's Companion to Litigation.* 1st ed. Berkeley: Nolo.	
Specific Types of Litigation	▶ Cook, Joseph G., and John L. Sobieski. 1983/2009. *Civil Rights Actions.* New York: Mathew Bender. ▶ Frumer, Louis R., et al., eds. 1957. *Personal Injury: Actions, Defenses, Damages.* New York: Mathew Bender. ▶ Matthews, Joseph. 2009. *How to Win Your Personal Injury Claim.* 7th ed. Berkeley, CA: Nolo. ▶ Rosenhouse, Michael A., ed. 1987. *Social Security Law and Practice.* Deerfield, IL: Clark Boardman Callaghan. ▶ Warner, Ralph E., and Emily Doskow. 2010. *Everybody's Guide to Small Claims Court.* 13th ed. Berkeley, CA: Nolo.	

Aside from the two books just discussed, a few others may be useful. These sources concern specialized litigation on topics not covered in the present book:

- ▶ Cook, Joseph G., and John L. Sobieski. 1983/2009. *Civil Rights Actions.* New York: Mathew Bender.
- ▶ Frumer, Louis R., et al. eds. 1957. *Personal Injury: Actions, Defenses, Damages.* New York: Mathew Bender.
- ▶ Matthews, Joseph. 2009. *How to Win Your Personal Injury Claim.* 7th ed. Berkeley, CA: Nolo.
- ▶ Rosenhouse, Michael A., ed. 1987. *Social Security Law and Practice.* Deerfield, IL: Clark Boardman Callaghan.
- ▶ Warner, Ralph E., and Emily Doskow. 2010. *Everybody's Guide to Small Claims Court.* 13th ed. Berkeley, CA: Nolo.

Finding Answers to Frequent Questions

Process of a Lawsuit

QUESTION: I want to sue the general contractor for the kitchen remodeling project that has turned into a disaster. Where do I start?

QUESTION: I've been sued by a homeowner who claims my remodeling business botched her kitchen remodeling project. How do I respond?

For the pro se litigant with access to a law library and lots of time, there are treatises, which are multivolumed works written by legal scholars that are designed for legal professionals to advise them about bringing or defending against lawsuits. These sources can be very helpful but also can be very time-consuming and frustrating.

The first such treatise helps a person decide what type of lawsuit might be possible in a given situation.

- ▶ West Group's Editorial Staff. 1993/2009. *Causes of Action, Second.* St. Paul, MN: West Group.

A second treatise goes beyond choosing a cause of action and into moving the case forward:

- ▶ Shepard's Editorial Staff. 1985/2009. *Shepard's Preparing for Settlement and Trial.* Colorado Springs, CO: Shepard's/McGraw-Hill.

A third treatise helps you figure out all of the different aspects of a lawsuit, from filing a complaint or answering a complaint through to the end.

- ▶ *American Jurisprudence Trials: An Encyclopedic Guide to the Modern Practices, Techniques, and Tactics Used in Preparing and Trying Cases, with Model Programs for the Handling of All Types of Litigation.* 1964/2009. St. Paul, MN: West Group.

What one seeks in a lawsuit is often called "damages," and those are usually given in monetary terms. If you are a plaintiff in a lawsuit seeking damages, you often need to know at the beginning of the lawsuit how much you are seeking in money damages. You must also know this for seeking settlement. If you are a defendant, you must be ready to dispute the amount and types of damages the plaintiff seeks. Resources differ in each state regarding damages, but here is an example:

▶ Martin, Gerald D. 1988/2009. *Determining Economic Damages*. Santa Ana, CA: James Pub. Group.

A treatise that can help the pro se litigant decide what evidence needs to be produced in a lawsuit is another large set:

▶ *American Jurisprudence Proof of Facts, 3d series: Fact Book*. 2003/2009. Eagan, MN: Thomson West.

Legal Procedures and Forms

QUESTION: Someone told me to start my lawsuit I need to file a "complaint." What's that? Where do I find one?

QUESTION: The complaint with which I was served said I needed to file an "answer" within 30 days. Is that like a letter or what? What is an "answer"?

Civil lawsuits proceed along a fairly consistent path governed by court rules of procedure. "Practice and procedure" treatises explain the rules and the process of litigation fully. Lawsuits are also heavily dependent on legal forms. A sample form, used and modified with care, can save the pro se litigant time and avoid errors. Often practice and procedure books include forms, but there are also sets that are nothing but forms. Chapters 3 and 4 provide you specific advice on finding court rules. The following sources, however, will tell you how those rules are applied in the "real world" of litigation. Practice and procedure sets include the following:

▶ *Federal Procedure: Lawyers Edition*. 1981/2009. St. Paul, MN: West Group.

▶ Moore, James William, and Daniel R. Coquillette, et al. 1997/2009. *Moore's Federal Practice*. New York: Mathew Bender.

▶ Wright, Charles Alan, Arthur R. Miller, and Mary Kay Kane. 1998/2009. *Federal Practice and Procedure*. St. Paul, MN: West Group.

These sets, particularly the Wright and Miller and Moore, are very well-respected resources. They are dense, deep scholarly works that discuss the intricacies of court rules, procedures, jurisdiction, and other aspects of litigation. It will take you a good deal of time to become familiar with these sets and to work with them, but with patience and perseverance they can be very helpful in figuring out the more complex aspects of carrying out litigation on your own. You may be able to access these sets in Westlaw or Lexis as well.

To initiate a lawsuit in most jurisdictions, you file a "complaint." The party being sued will likely in turn file an "answer." The content and form of complaints and answers are usually set out in court rules, but it is often helpful to see samples. You can benefit from sample forms throughout litigation because the entire process is usually moved forward by the filing of specific kinds of documents that you can find samples of in "form books." Use caution with these forms though because you must modify the forms for your particular purposes, and you must make sure that it is a form that you are supposed to file in your jurisdiction or in the court in which you are working. Take it slow in working with form books and check the court rules to make sure what you need and do not need. Here is a short list of sets of form books that most law libraries will have:

▶ *American Jurisprudence Legal Forms.* 1971/2010. St. Paul, MN: West Group.

▶ *American Jurisprudence Pleading and Practice Forms Annotated.* 1956/2009. Rochester, NY: Lawyers Co-operative.

▶ *Federal Procedural Forms, Lawyers Edition.* 1975/2009. St. Paul, MN: West Group.

▶ Rabkin, Jacob, and Mark H. Johnson. 1948/2010. *Current Legal Forms, with Tax Analysis.* New York: Mathew Bender.

▶ *West's Legal Forms.* 1981/2009. St. Paul, MN: Thomson/West.

Pretrial Stages of a Lawsuit

QUESTION: I filed a complaint and the defendant has filed an answer. Now what do I do?

QUESTION: I've heard the most important part of a lawsuit is "discovery." What's that?

QUESTION: I've been subpoenaed to attend a deposition. What's that?

Once a lawsuit is initiated and has survived early challenges such as motions to dismiss—often based on jurisdictional challenges—a lawsuit then enters the "pretrial" stage, and the most important aspect is "discovery." Discovery is the name that lawyers give to the stage of a lawsuit in which parties exchange, formally or informally, willingly or unwillingly, information in each party's possession concerning the subject of the lawsuit. Most lawyers agree that discovery is the most important stage of a lawsuit because it will reveal the strengths and weaknesses of each party's case. Others say that the most important aspect of discovery are "depositions," that is, the taking of sworn testimony, outside of court but under oath, of parties and key witnesses involved in the lawsuit. For an overview of the "procedure" that governs lawsuits, here is a good, short book:

▶ Kane, Mary Kay. 2007. *Civil Procedure in a Nutshell.* St. Paul, MN: Thomson West.

If your case involves state law and state court, you will want to ask a law librarian for the best book or set of books on civil procedure and jurisdiction for your state. If your case involves, or may involve, federal law and federal court, a well-respected but brief book you might consult is this one:

▶ Currie, David P. 1999. *Federal Jurisdiction in a Nutshell.* St. Paul, MN: West Group.

To get an overview of the "pretrial" process, especially after the initial stages, a standard in the field is this book:

▶ Mauet, Thomas A. 2008. *Pretrial.* New York: Aspen Publishers.

When you reach the discovery stage of the lawsuit, refer to some of the sets discussed previously, especially *American Jurisprudence Trials* and *American Jurisprudence Proof of Facts*, but here are a few more specifically about aspects of discovery:

▶ *Bender's Forms of Discovery.* 1963/2009. New York: Mathew Bender.
▶ Danner, Douglas, and Larry L. Varn. 1998. *Pattern Deposition Checklists.* 4th ed. St. Paul, MN: West Group.

Evidence

QUESTION: What is hearsay?

QUESTION: I sued someone who hit my car when I was at a stop sign. Now they are claiming I had back problems before the accident. Can they introduce my medical records from a long time ago?

QUESTION: What is the spousal privilege?

After the discovery stage of a lawsuit, a case is more likely to be ready for settlement because each party will have a better idea of the facts in the case as they pertain to proving or disproving the basis of the lawsuit. In other words, the parties will have a better idea of the *evidence* in support of the lawsuit and in support of the defenses against the lawsuit, but not all information revealed in discovery ends up as evidence in court. What will and what will not be evidence is therefore very important both to furthering the chances of settlement and of preparing for trial. Evidence, like much of the law, is a complex subject. Two treatises have been standards in the field for many decades:

▶ McCormick, Charles Tilford, and Kenneth S. Broun, ed. 2006. *McCormick on Evidence.* St. Paul, MN: Thomson.
▶ Weinstein, Jack B., and Margaret A. Berger. 1997/2009. *Weinstein's Federal Evidence.* Edited by Joseph M. McLaughlin. New York: Mathew Bender.

Trial Process

QUESTION: The insurance company refused to settle my case and we have a trial date set for six months from now. How do I prepare?

If discovery and settlement negotiations have not ended the lawsuit, it is time to prepare for the trial itself. Many of the resources discussed previously, especially *American Jurisprudence Trials* and *American Jurisprudence Proof of Facts*, can help with continuing to get ready for an actual trial. Here are two other resources, the second one being very well-known and respected.

▶ Danner, Douglas, and John W. Toothman. 1989. *Trial Practice Checklists.* Rochester, NY: Lawyers Co-operative.

▶ Mauet, Thomas A. 2007. *Trial Techniques.* Austin: Wolters Kluwer Law & Business/Aspen Publishers.

Juries and Jury Instructions

QUESTION: What is voir dire?

QUESTION: How does a jury get chosen?

QUESTION: The judge has said we are to submit jury instructions prior to trial. How do I do that?

One of the more complex areas of trial practice is jury selection and instructing the jurors. Many people who are unfamiliar with trials do not realize that jurors do not just sit and listen to the testimony and examine the exhibits, but jurors receive written instructions about the law that is applicable to a particular lawsuit. These instructions are typically proposed by each side of the lawsuit and then the judge decides which ones will be the final instructions to be given to the jurors. If your lawsuit is in state court, ask a law librarian if there is a set or sets of books that provide sample jury instructions. Similar sets will exist if you are in federal court, a few of which are listed here. The following are a few books on jury selection and instruction:

▶ Easton, Stephen D. 1998. *How to Win Jury Trials: Building Credibility with Judges and Jurors.* Philadelphia: American Law Institute/American Bar Association.

▶ Ginger, Ann Fagan. 1984. *Jury Selection in Civil and Criminal Trials.* Tiburon, CA: Lawpress.

▶ Levine, Harvey R. 1997. *Jury Selection Deskbook.* St. Paul, MN: Thomson/West.

▶ Lieberman, Joel D., and Bruce D. Sales. 2007. *Scientific Jury Selection.* Washington, DC: American Psychological Association.

▶ O'Malley, Kevin F. 1999/2000. *Federal Jury Practice and Instructions.* 5th ed. St. Paul, MN: Thomson West.

▶ Sand, Leonard B., et al. 1984– . *Modern Federal Jury Instructions.* New York: Mathew Bender.

Appeals

QUESTION: I lost my case but I do not think I got a fair trial. What can I do?

QUESTION: I won my case but the other side has appealed. How do I respond?

Jury instructions, and sometimes jury selection or alleged juror misconduct, can often lead to appeals. Issues for appeal, however, can encompass many aspects of the litigation process. If you have lost your lawsuit, you might consider appealing your case to a higher court. Sometimes you have a "right" to do this and the court will automatically take your case to review, but you still must request review by filing a notice of appeal; in other instances, you have to request the court to do so and it can accept or decline. The time limit within which to seek review or an appeal however is very quick, often 30 days, so you have to move quickly to preserve your right to that appeal. After you have filed the appeal, the process itself may take years, but to initiate the appeal you have to be diligent. Ask local experts about books on appellate practice for your jurisdiction. The following books should also give you a good idea of the practice and procedure of appeals:

- ▶ Hornstein, Alan D. 1998. *Hornstein's Appellate Advocacy in a Nutshell*. 2nd ed. St. Paul, MN: West Group.

- ▶ Levy, Herbert Monte. 1999. *How to Handle an Appeal*. New York: Practising Law Institute.

- ▶ Moskovitz, Myron. 2007. *Winning an Appeal: A Step-by-Step Explanation of How to Prepare and Present Your Case Efficiently and Effectively, with Sample Briefs*. 4th ed. New York: Mathew Bender.

For resource updates, visit this book's companion website at

▶ **www.GetLaw.net**

RESOURCES RECAP

Treatises and Authoritative Sources

	Resource	Notes
The Process of a Lawsuit	▶ *American Jurisprudence Proof of Facts, 3d series: Fact Book*. 2003/2009. Eagan, MN: Thomson West. ▶ *American Jurisprudence Trials: An Encyclopedic Guide to the Modern Practices, Techniques, and Tactics Used in Preparing and Trying Cases, with Model Programs for the Handling of All Types of Litigation*. 1964/2009. St. Paul, MN: West Group. ▶ Shepard's Editorial Staff. 1985/2009. *Shepard's Preparing for Settlement and Trial*. Colorado Springs, CO: Shepard's/McGraw-Hill. ▶ West Group's Editorial Staff. 1993/2009. *Causes of Action, Second*. St. Paul, MN: West Group.	
Legal Procedures and Forms	▶ *American Jurisprudence Legal Forms*. 1971/2010. St. Paul, MN: West Group. ▶ *American Jurisprudence Pleading and Practice Forms Annotated*. 1956/2009. Rochester, NY: Lawyers Co-operative. ▶ *Federal Procedural Forms, Lawyers Edition*. 1975/2009. St. Paul, MN: West Group. ▶ *Federal Procedure: Lawyers Edition*. 1981/2009. St. Paul, MN: West Group.	

(Cont'd.)

RESOURCES RECAP *(Continued)*		
Treatises and Authoritative Sources		
	Resource	**Notes**
Legal Procedures and Forms *(Cont'd.)*	▶ Moore, James William, Daniel R. Coquillette, et al. 1997/2009. *Moore's Federal Practice*. New York: Mathew Bender. ▶ Rabkin, Jacob, and Mark H. Johnson. 1948/2010. *Current Legal Forms, with Tax Analysis*. New York: Mathew Bender. ▶ *West's Legal Forms*. 1981/2009. St. Paul, MN: Thomson/West. ▶ Wright, Charles Alan, Arthur R. Miller, and Mary Kay Kane. 1998/2009. *Federal Practice and Procedure*. St. Paul, MN: West Group.	
Pretrial Stages of a Lawsuit	▶ *Bender's Forms of Discovery*. 1963/2009. New York: Mathew Bender. ▶ Currie, David P. 1999. *Federal Jurisdiction in a Nutshell*. St. Paul, MN: West Group. ▶ Danner, Douglas, and Larry L. Varn. 1998. *Pattern Deposition Checklists*. 4th ed. St. Paul, MN: West Group. ▶ Kane, Mary Kay. 2007. *Civil Procedure in a Nutshell*. St. Paul, MN: Thomson West. ▶ Mauet, Thomas A. 2008. *Pretrial*. New York: Aspen Publishers.	
Evidence	▶ McCormick, Charles Tilford, and Kenneth S. Broun, ed. 2006. *McCormick on Evidence*. St. Paul, MN: Thomson. ▶ Weinstein, Jack B., and Margaret A. Berger. 1997/2009. *Weinstein's Federal Evidence*. Edited by Joseph M. McLaughlin. New York: Mathew Bender.	
Trial Process	▶ Danner, Douglas, and John W. Toothman. 1989. *Trial Practice Checklists*. Rochester, NY: Lawyers Co-operative. ▶ Mauet, Thomas A. 2007. *Trial Techniques*. Austin: Wolters Kluwer Law and Business/Aspen Publishers.	
Juries and Jury Instructions	▶ Ginger, Ann Fagan. 1984. *Jury Selection in Civil and Criminal Trials*. Tiburon, CA: Lawpress. ▶ O'Malley, Kevin F. 2006/2009. *Federal Jury Practice and Instructions*. St. Paul, MN: Thomson West.	
Appeals	▶ Hornstein, Alan D. 1998. *Hornstein's Appellate Advocacy in a Nutshell*. 2nd ed. St. Paul, MN: West Group. ▶ Levy, Herbert Monte. 1999. *How to Handle an Appeal*. New York: Practising Law Institute. ▶ Moskovitz, Myron. 2007. *Winning an Appeal: A Step-By-Step Explanation of How to Prepare and Present Your Case Efficiently and Effectively, with Sample Briefs*. 4th ed. New York: Mathew Bender.	

Family Law

QUESTION: Can I do my own divorce? I found some forms on the Internet and it looks pretty easy. I really don't have the money for a lawyer and my husband and I don't have a lot to divide up anyway.

QUESTION: My ex-wife wants to move out of state because she got a better job offer. But that really changes how often I get to see our children. Can she do that? What about the parenting plan we agreed to?

QUESTION: I've been remarried for a long time now and my husband would like to adopt my son. I don't even know where his father is. What do we need to do?

Family law is very likely the area of law that generates the most **pro se** representation in the courts, the most questions at the public library, and the most do-it-yourself websites. It also generates the most anguish and upheaval when it touches a person's life or their children's lives. Finding answers to questions that point the way toward resolution in this very personal area of law—one that abounds with urgent and distressing questions—is extremely challenging. This chapter addresses finding legal information in areas of family law, including divorce, domestic partnership, parenting plans, child support, domestic violence, and adoption.

Because family law is such a far-reaching area, this chapter is divided into four sections: relationships, children, domestic violence, and adoption. Even these broad categories overlap in some matters, of course, but this general organization is intended to help make figuring out an approach to family law questions and the available resources easier to navigate for both pro se litigants and the public librarians assisting them.

Framework for Questions in This Area of Law

Family law matters are governed almost entirely by state law, and these laws can vary widely from state to state. It is essential to work with the state statutes as well as with the reference materials and forms intended for use within the state with jurisdiction. Particularly in family law matters like divorce the Internet abounds with free advice and sample forms, so caution is necessary. Many of these websites appear at the top of the list of "hits" on a general search engine like Yahoo!, Google, or Bing because they have paid for preferred placement in the search results as "sponsored sites." All too often they may not have trustworthy or state-appropriate information or forms. Fortunately, because so many people represent themselves in family law cases, most states provide the necessary forms and instructions—these are the ones to use and not forms from websites that may or may not be appropriate for your state and local jurisdiction. Supplementing these materials with a current edition of a do-it-yourself publication, such as the free guides from the American Bar Association, can help with understanding the overall process too. Refer to the recommended sources included with the questions that follow and in the different sections' Resources Recaps.

Federal law applies in a few areas of family law, such as when adopting a child from another country or when a child from one state is adopted by a family in a different state. There are also interstate agreements for matters such as enforcement of court orders for child support. These are addressed as appropriate within the Finding Answers to Frequent Questions sections that follow the Getting Started section.

Getting Started: A Checklist

Getting started in any matter involving family law is a lot like preparing for a homework assignment. This means the public library reference desk is frequently the go-to place for the most urgent questions. It also means that a checklist for preparing to do that assignment is a sensible starting point. Consider beginning with the following:

- ✓ **Research the state statutes** that are relevant for the area of law. As discussed, most areas of family law are governed by state law.

- ✓ **Locate legal forms provided by the courts**. It is always better to use the forms provided by the appropriate court than to download forms from an unofficial source on the Internet or to pay for forms from a stationery store. For family law matters, most state courts provide the legal forms needed, either as free downloads online or low-cost packets from the court clerk or law library.

- ✓ **Look for workshops** offered by local law libraries or legal aid organizations. Particularly for divorce and matters involving parenting plans (whether married or unmarried) this can be extremely helpful for those representing themselves in court. In fact, in some states, attendance at a workshop is required by those who are self-represented in family court cases such as divorces.

✓ **Invest in a do-it-yourself book from a reputable publisher**, if desired. Review the do-it-yourself publications described in this chapter. Most of these are low-cost (around 20 dollars), and those from the American Bar Association (ABA) are free to download.

✓ **Consult with an attorney**, if appropriate. It may well be that representation by an attorney is needed for particular cases. A consultation may also help in deciding whether or not an attorney is needed. Refer to the general guidelines in Chapter 6.

After the basic groundwork is reviewed, it is easier to move forward to specific questions. The frequently asked questions within this chapter are organized into the following four sections:

- Questions about relationships: marriage, living together, and divorce
- Questions about children
- Questions about domestic violence
- Questions about adoption

Finding Answers to Frequent Questions about Relationships

Questions about Marriage

Most questions about marriage and the law arise during the period just before marriage or soon after. Some of the most frequently asked questions follow.

QUESTION: What's required to be able to get married? I'm wondering about things like a waiting period. Do you have to take any tests?

Marriage is governed by state law so this question can be answered by looking at the state statutes, but an easier way is often to look at the state government's main website where basic facts about how to get a marriage license are summarized in practical language. Try searching on Google or Yahoo! with keywords like the state name and *marriage license requirements*. Then be sure to look for websites that end in .gov, which indicates a government agency. For example: *missouri marriage license requirements* retrieves many websites for vendors of marriage services, but also included is the listing for www.mo.gov/Family/Marriage, the official State of Missouri website about how to obtain a marriage license.

For a chart of all the states and an abbreviated description of each state's requirements for marriage, refer to "Marriage Laws of the Fifty States, District of Columbia and Puerto Rico" at topics.law.cornell.edu/wex/table_marriage.

QUESTION: My girlfriend and I have been living together for a long time. Aren't we considered the same as married in the eyes of the law after a certain number of years?

A few states still recognize **common law marriage** (see Closer Look, p. 109), meaning that state law recognizes the relationship between a couple as to certain legal rights, duties and responsibilities, and/or community property if they have held themselves out as being married for a certain number of years.

QUESTION: What makes a marriage invalid or void? And isn't there a way to annul a marriage? What are the differences anyway?

To **annul** a marriage means it is as if the marriage never happened. This requires some reason provided for in state law such as a serious misrepresentation or fraud by one of the parties. A marriage also might be void based on reasons set by state law that would apply to everyone. This might be if the parties are too closely related, for example, below the legal age to marry, or still married to someone else. Look at the state statutes to find out reasons that a marriage may be considered either invalid or void.

QUESTION: How can I find out what states currently allow same-sex marriage?

Several organizations maintain information on the status of same-sex marriage laws and legislation. One resource from Freedom to Marry, a nonprofit, nonpartisan group, is a list and map of the United States indicating which states allow same-sex marriage, civil unions, or domestic partnerships. Each state name links to a page with further information about that state. See www.freedomtomarry.org/states.

QUESTION: I'm getting married and need to know how to arrange for a prenuptial agreement. Where can I find out about this?

QUESTION: I recently got married and I've heard I should do a postnuptial agreement because I own rental property and want to keep it separate. Can I do that?

Because marriage is governed by state law, answers to these questions need to be researched in state statutes and case law. Some states have secondary sources and/or practice materials to help you get started thinking about all of the different considerations that should go into creating a **prenuptial** or **postnuptial** agreement. There may also be state-specific form books with sample agreements (for example, *Forms for New Jersey Divorce Practice*). However, concerns over such agreements arise often, so there may well be sample forms available from court websites—check here first because these forms are free (or low cost) and in compliance with local court requirements. (See the court listings in Appendix 3.) If there are no state-specific forms to use as models, you can try resources such as *American Jurisprudence Legal Forms*, which may be available from a law library or online from a pay-per-view service. There are also several do-it-yourself books on the topic of prenuptial agreements (see for example Stoner and Irving, 2008). It should also be said, however, that, depending on the nature of your assets, specific concerns, and whether you have children from previous relationships, you may want to consult with an attorney on this type of matter.

Questions When Unmarried and Living Together

In 2008, the United States Census Bureau reported that there were 66.9 million opposite-sex couples living together. Of these, 60.1 million were married and 6.8 million—just over 11 percent—were not (U.S. Census, 2008). In addition, the census reported a half million same-sex couples living together. This represents a huge demographic, and the kinds of questions that arise as to legal matters related to the relationships are vast and varied. Some of the most common questions are covered here.

> QUESTION: My girlfriend and I have been living together for a while now and don't plan on getting married. Should we have a written agreement about who owns what? Are there other things we should think about?

As with most relationship questions, state law needs to be researched to understand the considerations related to these questions. Common considerations include (but are not limited to) the nature and amount of what each person owned when the relationship began and what each person earns, so this is a highly individualized situation, and a complicated one. In addition, there may be other issues, such as when a relationship lasts for a long time, there may be **commingling** of assets and, in a few states, there is recognition of common law marriage. Commingling happens when separate property of one person is mixed or combined with the separate property of the other; doing so opens up the possibility of turning separate property into community property. Drawing up an agreement, its particulars and execution, may call for the advice of an attorney. If you have children together, this question is quite different, and finding the answer includes learning about making plans for their care, education, and future well-being.

> QUESTION: My significant other and I are starting to think about long-term plans and both of us have some health problems. Is there some kind of agreement we can make about what happens if one of us dies?

If you are unmarried and one of you becomes seriously ill or injured you will not be able to make decisions for the other without having executed a health care power of attorney or other type of **advance directive**. You will also not be able to leave property to your significant other without a will or other estate planning document instructing this. Refer to Chapter 10.

> QUESTION: Where can my partner and I become legal domestic partners? Is this just for same-sex couples or for opposite-sex couples, too?

Some states do allow for opposite-sex couples to register as legal domestic partners. In fact, even if a state does not provide for registering a domestic partnership, it may be allowed in local municipalities, such as the county or city. The Human Rights Campaign (HRC) maintains a listing of

---

CLOSER LOOK

Common Law Marriage

A variety of frequent questions arise that relate to the issue of **common law marriage**, what this means, and how it differs from state to state. Common law marriage means that state law recognizes the relationship between a couple as to certain legal rights, duties and responsibilities, or community property. In the early days of the United States, many states and territories recognized common law marriages, with the most important requirements typically being that the man and woman held themselves out as being married and had lived together a certain number of years. Today, only 12 states have laws recognizing common law marriage, and most with much stricter requirements than in the past.

For further information, including topics such as what happens when a couple moves from a state that has common law marriage to a state that does not, see the "ABA Guide to Family Law," available for free from www.abanet.org/publiced/practical/books/family/. For a list of states that currently recognize some form of common law marriage, refer to "Common Law Marriage States" from FindLaw.com (family.findlaw.com/living-together/living-together-common-law-marriage/).

jurisdictions that have domestic partnership registries and whether these are for same-sex and/or opposite-sex couples:

▶ City and County Domestic Partner Registries: www.hrc.org/issues/ marriage/domestic_partners/9133.htm

Questions about Divorce

In some societies and cultures divorce is difficult to do, and yet throughout history there have been many traditions and ways to end a marriage. The practice in some Pueblo Indian tribes of allowing a woman to divorce her husband by placing his moccasins outside their home is often mentioned (American Bar Association, 2004: 1). As discussed earlier in this chapter, divorce in the United States is governed by state law and is more commonly called **dissolution**. Likewise, other terminology related to divorce has been updated in recent years. "Alimony" is usually referred to as **spousal support** or "maintenance," for example.

There are so many questions surrounding divorce that only a sampling can be included here. Throughout this section, state statutes, state court forms or information packets, and self-help materials are strongly recommended for those wishing to pursue a divorce without aid of an attorney as well as for those wishing to understand the process more fully even if an attorney will be engaged. Reviewing the tips in the Getting Started section at the start of this chapter is strongly recommended.

More and more, the trend in divorces, even the more difficult ones, is to use mediation to resolve issues and disputes over plans for children and the division of assets. Some states require that mediation be attempted before a divorce will be allowed to go to trial. Refer to the section in Chapter 6 on alternative dispute resolution for information about mediation and other alternative forms of dispute resolution ranging from collaborative law to arbitration.

The two areas of concern related to divorce that generate the most questions are arrangements for children and determining how to divide assets and debts. Naturally, the questions posed by people contemplating divorce are dramatically different when children are involved than when they are not. Because of this, this chapter includes a separate section on questions about children.

QUESTION: Can I do my own divorce? I found some forms on the Internet and it looks pretty easy. I really don't have the money for a lawyer and my husband and I don't have a lot to divide up anyway.

Many people successfully represent themselves in divorce matters. In fact, in California, just over 80 percent of divorcing couples do so without attorneys (McDonough, 2008). That said, many of the free divorce forms on the Internet that appear at the top of a page of results from a search engine like Google or Yahoo! do so because they have paid for preferred placement. Unfortunately, although they are listed first, they are often not the first ones to consult: they may not contain state-specific information or forms and also may charge for forms that can be gotten for free from state court websites. For family law matters like divorce, most state courts provide the legal forms needed, either as free downloads online or low-cost packets from the court clerk or law library. The American Bar Association provides a free guide for laypersons covering legal issues related to divorce:

▶ American Bar Association. 2006. *American Bar Association Guide to Marriage, Divorce, and Families.* Chicago: ABA Division for Public Education.

Purchasing a do-it-yourself book from a reputable publisher is also recommended to help with navigating the divorce process. A few to consider are:

▶ Doskow, Emily. 2010. *Nolo's Essential Guide to Divorce.* 3rd ed. Berkeley, CA: Nolo.

▶ Woodhouse, Violet, and Dale Fetherling. 2009. *Divorce & Money: How to Make the Best Financial Decisions During Divorce.* 9th ed. Berkeley, CA: Nolo.

Additional do-it-yourself publications are included in the Resources Recap.

QUESTION: My wife and I have filed for divorce and we're not using lawyers, but it's going to take some time before it's final. Meanwhile we need to make some arrangements for things like paying bills and agreeing on a schedule for the kids. How do we do that?

Check the state statutes for provisions regarding **temporary orders**. Frequently temporary orders can cover concerns such as residential schedules for the children, child support, and payment of bills. There may be state court forms for this purpose, too, that you can download or get from a law library. Also consider getting a current and trustworthy do-it-yourself publication that covers the divorce process from start to finish and on to postdivorce issues that may arise, such as the general divorce resources listed previously as well as:

▶ Zemmelman, Mimi Lyster. 2010. *Building a Parenting Agreement That Works: How to Put Your Kids First When Your Marriage Doesn't Last.* 7th ed. Berkeley, CA: Nolo.

QUESTION: My husband and I need to get a divorce fast. I heard we can go to another state where it won't take as long. How does that work?

This is a question of which state has jurisdiction. State statutes typically require being a resident for a certain period of time in order to petition for a divorce in the state, but a few states do not have a residency requirement. The American Bar Association Section of Family Law publishes a table showing requirements for all 50 states:

▶ "Family Law in the Fifty States—Chart 4: Grounds for Divorce and Residency Requirements": www.abanet.org/family/familylaw/tables .html

QUESTION: My wife had me served with a dissolution petition, but I don't think I've done anything to deserve it. Should I just ignore it so she can't get a divorce?

Dissolution of a marriage (divorce) begins with filing a petition with the court and then serving it on your spouse. Responding to the petition is a lot like answering any other legal petition or summons—and not responding may mean having less say in the outcome. As most states have **no fault divorce**, meaning that neither spouse needs to prove wrongdoing or fault on the part of the other, it is difficult to stop a divorce from proceeding by being nonresponsive. Check the state statutes, court forms for divorce proceedings, or get advice from an attorney for help in responding to a divorce petition. The resource mentioned in the previous question, "Family Law in the Fifty States," also provides information on states that have no-fault divorce laws. See www.abanet.org/family/familylaw/tables.html.

QUESTION: Is a divorce the only way? I've heard there's something called a legal separation. Can I do that instead?

A **legal separation** is an alternative to dissolution (divorce) in almost all states and is typically chosen by couples due to reasons of religious beliefs or needing to retain spousal benefits. Some states also provide for petitioning the court to change a legal separation to a dissolution later on. The state statutes need to be consulted to know what is possible in your jurisdiction. For an overview of legal separation, refer to the following American Bar Association publication:

▶ *ABA Guide to Family Law*, Chapter 8: www.abanet.org/publiced/ practical/books/family/

For resource updates, visit this book's companion website at

▶ **www.GetLaw.net**

RESOURCES RECAP		
Relationships		
	Resource	**Notes**
Primary Sources	▶ American Bar Association, "Family Law in the Fifty States": www.abanet.org/family/familylaw/tables.html	The American Bar Association Section of Family Law publishes tables and charts summarizing state laws for child support, custody, divorce residency requirements, and several other areas of family law. The data are updated yearly.
	▶ Cornell's Legal Information Institute (LII), "Divorce Laws of the 50 States, District of Columbia, and Puerto Rico": topics.law.cornell.edu/wex/table_divorce	LII provides a table summarizing divorce laws in each state, with links to the divorce laws of individual states.
	▶ Cornell's Legal Information Institute (LII), "Marriage Laws of the 50 States, District of Columbia, and Puerto Rico": topics.law.cornell.edu/wex/table_marriage	This site includes information on states with common law marriage, age of consent, and license waiting period.
	▶ Cornell's Legal Information Institute (LII), "Uniform Interstate Family Support Act (UIFSA)": www.law.cornell.edu/uniform/vol9.html#famsp	This site provides links to the original text plus related legislation for all 50 states.

(Cont'd.)

RESOURCES RECAP *(Continued)*	
Relationships	
Resource	**Notes**
Primary Sources *(Cont'd.)*	▶ Freedom to Marry: www.freedomtomarry.org/states	This site, which focuses on the progress of same-sex marriage and domestic partnerships, covers all 50 states as well as municipalities.
Do-It-Yourself Publications	▶ American Bar Association. 2004. *ABA Guide to Family Law.* Available: www.abanet.org/publiced/practical/ books/family/. ▶ American Bar Association. 2006. *American Bar Association Guide to Marriage, Divorce, and Families.* Chicago: ABA Division for Public Education. ▶ Doskow, Emily. 2010. *Nolo's Essential Guide to Divorce.* 3rd ed. Berkeley, CA: Nolo. ▶ Hertz, Frederick, Emily Doskow, and Denis Clifford. 2010. *Legal Guide for Lesbian & Gay Couples.* 15th ed. Berkeley, CA: Nolo. ▶ Stoner, Katherine. 2009. *Divorce without Court: A Guide to Mediation & Collaborative Divorce.* 2nd ed. Berkeley, CA: Nolo. ▶ Stoner, K., and S. Irving. 2008. *Prenuptial Agreements: How to Write a Fair & Lasting Contract.* 3rd ed. Berkeley, CA: Nolo. ▶ Woodhouse, Violet, and Dale Fetherling. 2009. *Divorce & Money: How to Make the Best Financial Decisions during Divorce.* 9th ed. Berkeley, CA: Nolo. ▶ Zemmelman, Mimi Lyster. 2010. *Building a Parenting Agreement That Works: How to Put Your Kids First When Your Marriage Doesn't Last.* 7th ed. Berkeley, CA: Nolo.	
Treatises and Authoritative Sources*	▶ Goldberg, B. H. 2009. *Valuation of Divorce Assets.* St. Paul, MN: Thomson West. ▶ Rutkin, A. H. 1985. *Family Law and Practice.* New York: Mathew Bender. ▶ Turner, B. R. 2009. *Equitable Distribution of Property, 3d.* St. Paul, MN: Thomson West.	

*Most treatises and authoritative sources in family law are specific to one state because this area of law is almost entirely governed by state law. Large law libraries are likely to have treatises with in-depth discussion of family law matters and **practice materials** with instructions and sample forms, such as *Vermont Family Law*, published by LexisNexis. These may be available in print form and/or through pay-per-view database services.

Finding Answers to Frequent Questions about Children

The number of legal questions about children when parents divorce, separate, or are unmarried is beyond measure. Some of the most common questions are covered in this section, divided into two parts: parenting plans and child support.

Questions about Parenting Plans

> QUESTION: My ex-wife wants to move out of state because she got a better job offer. But that really changes how often I get to see our children. Can she do that? What about the shared custody we agreed to?

Groundwork for this question includes an understanding of **child custody** and that there are two types: physical custody, involving who is responsible for caring for the child, and legal custody, involving who is responsible for making decisions affecting the child's education, religion, and medical treatment. A parent may share joint legal custody but have full physical custody of a child, for example. Most state statutes distinguish between the two, and the parenting plan filed with the court—a plan outlining school and holiday schedules and decision-making responsibilities as well as other parenting concerns—is designed to cover both. When a major life change arises, such as a job offer that would require relocating the children as in this question, the parent wanting to modify the parenting plan would need to get approval from the court unless the existing plan allows for such changes. Most state courts provide instructions and forms for this purpose.

> QUESTION: My ex-boyfriend has one idea about a parenting plan and I have a really different idea. We don't agree at all. How is the court going to decide who's right?

The legal doctrine of "best interest of child" is used in deciding on a residential schedule, child visitation, and other aspects of a parenting plan. The specifics of how this will be determined will depend on the state's statutes and how these have been interpreted in case law. The court may require that parents use mediation to try to settle their differences in coming up with a parenting plan or to agree on a temporary plan that is reviewed later. The American Bar Association Section of Family Law publishes a table summarizing the factors and guidelines used in all 50 states; see "Family Law in the Fifty States—Chart 2: Custody Criteria," available from www.abanet.org/family/familylaw/tables.html.

> QUESTION: I've decided to give up on any time with my kid because that way I think I can get out of paying any child support. Can I do that?

Generally speaking, the responsibility for supporting one's child is separate and distinct from the visitation schedule in a parenting plan. A child support order is still enforceable even if a parent has chosen not to abide by the parent's schedule of time with the child. The state statutes should be consulted for specific information. Refer to the following section for more questions about child support.

Questions about Child Support

> QUESTION: How does the court decide how much child support should be paid?

Each state has its own tables and methods for calculating the appropriate amount of child support. Typical factors include the age of the child, any medical or other special needs of the child, and the income of each parent. Check for state forms or worksheets that are used to prepare estimates for the court to use in setting child support amounts. The American Bar Association Section of Family Law publishes a table summarizing guidelines for all 50 states; see "Family Law in the Fifty States— Chart 3: Child Support Guidelines," available from www.abanet.org/ family/familylaw/tables.html.

QUESTION: Things are really different in my life since the child support order a few years ago. How do I get the child support amount changed?

It is possible to ask the court—usually by filing a motion or petition—to modify child support due to reasons of significant lifestyle changes, such as a substantial increase or decrease in income, a serious illness or disability,

For resource updates, visit this book's companion website at

▶ *www.GetLaw.net*

	RESOURCES RECAP	
	Children	
	Resource	**Notes**
Primary Sources	▶ American Bar Association, "Family Law in the Fifty States": www.abanet.org/family/familylaw/tables.html	The American Bar Association Section of Family Law publishes tables and charts summarizing state laws for child support, custody, divorce residency requirements, and several other areas of family law. The data are updated yearly.
	▶ Cornell's Legal Information Institute (LII), "Uniform Interstate Family Support Act (UIFSA)": www.law.cornell.edu/uniform/vol9.html#famsp	This site provides links to the original text plus related legislation for all 50 states.
Do-It-Yourself Publications	▶ American Bar Association. 2004. *ABA Guide to Family Law*. Available: www.abanet.org/publiced/practical/ books/family/.	
	▶ American Bar Association. 2006. *American Bar Association Guide to Marriage, Divorce, and Families*. Chicago: ABA Division for Public Education.	
	▶ Zemmelman, Mimi Lyster. 2010. *Building a Parenting Agreement That Works: How to Put Your Kids First When Your Marriage Doesn't Last*. 7th ed. Berkeley, CA: Nolo.	
Treatises and Authoritative Sources*	▶ Elrod, L. D. 2008. *Child Custody Practice and Procedure*. St. Paul, MN: Thomson West.	
	▶ Rutkin, A. H. 1985. *Family Law and Practice*. New York: Mathew Bender.	

*Most treatises and authoritative sources in family law are specific to one state because this area of law is almost entirely governed by state law. Large law libraries are likely to have treatises with in-depth discussion of family law matters and **practice materials** with instructions and sample forms, such as *Vermont Family Law*, published by LexisNexis. These may be available in print form and/or through pay-per-view database services.

or relocation. Because this happens often, the court or local law library will usually have the necessary materials for this type of matter.

> QUESTION: My ex-husband is going to move out of state to a new job. Will child support still get collected there and sent to me?

The Uniform Interstate Family Support Act (UIFSA) has been adopted by almost all 50 states and provides a system for enforcing child support and custody orders across state lines. The act was also created to help protect victims of domestic violence and child abuse. The text of the act is available from Cornell's Legal Information Institute (www.law.cornell .edu/uniform/vol9.html#famsp).

In addition, the U.S. Department of Health and Human Services Office of Child Support Enforcement operates a Federal Parent Locator Service to assist in enforcement of child support orders, collection of child support payments, and communication between states. For more information, see www.acf.hhs.gov/programs/cse.

> QUESTION: My daughter is going to graduate from high school in a year and wants to go to college. Can I make my ex-wife help pay for her college tuition?

Some states have laws allowing parents to get court orders for a child's college expenses, and others do provide for support after high school or the age of 18. Look at state statutes referencing "postsecondary" educational support. In addition, "Family Law in the Fifty States—Chart 3: Child Support Guidelines," described previously, available from American Bar Association Section of Family Law includes brief data on state statutes that provide for a child's college support. See www.abanet.org/family/familylaw/tables.html.

Finding Answers to Frequent Questions about Domestic Violence

Domestic violence cuts across all segments of American society. The Centers for Disease Control and Prevention (CDC) collects data on intimate partner violence (IPV) and reported in 2009 that IPV had resulted in 1,510 deaths in 2005. In addition, the medical care, mental health services, and lost productivity (e.g., time away from work) resulting from domestic violence was an estimated $5.8 billion in 1995 (CDC, 2009).

State statutes primarily govern this area; however, key federal laws should be noted, including the Violence Against Women Act of 2000 (VAWA 2000) and the Violence Against Women and Department of Justice Reauthorization Act of 2005 (VAWA 2005). VAWA was enacted to improve the criminal justice response to domestic violence, stalking, and sexual assault and also to expand services to crime victims. It requires coordinated community response (CCR), meaning that law enforcement, the courts, corrections, and victim advocates are to combine their efforts. VAWA 2005 reauthorized the grant programs of the original

VAWA and added programs such as improving enforcement of protection orders across state lines. Refer to www.ovw.usdoj.gov/regulations.htm. Questions about domestic violence are often motivated by a crisis so both legal information and support services are covered in this chapter.

QUESTION: What is domestic violence?

The U.S. Department of Justice (DOJ) Office on Violence Against Women provides this definition of domestic violence:

> Domestic violence can be defined as a pattern of abusive behavior in any relationship that is used by one partner to gain or maintain power and control over another intimate partner. Domestic violence can be physical, sexual, emotional, economic, or psychological actions or threats of actions that influence another person. This includes any behaviors that intimidate, manipulate, humiliate, isolate, frighten, terrorize, coerce, threaten, blame, hurt, injure, or wound someone. (U.S. Department of Justice, 2010)

Additional information and examples of domestic violence behaviors are included on the website (www.ovw.usdoj.gov/domviolence.htm).

QUESTION: Where can I go for help with domestic violence?

For resource updates, visit this book's companion website at

▶ *www.GetLaw.net*

RESOURCES RECAP		
Domestic Violence		
	Resource	**Notes**
Primary Sources	▶ U.S. Department of Justice, "Federal Legislation: Violence Against Women and Department of Justice Reauthorization Act of 2005" (VAWA 2005): www.ovw.usdoj.gov/regulations.htm ▶ WomensLaws.org, "Know the Laws": www.womenslaw.org/laws.php	Provides listings by topic and jurisdiction
Agency and Nonprofit Resources	▶ ABA Commission on Domestic Violence: www.abanet.org/domviol/ ▶ National Coalition Against Domestic Violence: www.ncadv.org ▶ National Coalition Against Domestic Violence, "State Coalition List": www.ncadv.org/resources/StateCoalitionList.php ▶ National Domestic Violence Hotline: 1-800-799-SAFE (1-800-799-7233) or 1-800-787-3224 (TDD); www.ndvh.org ▶ U.S. Department of Justice—Office on Violence Against Women: www.ovw.usdoj.gov	
Treatises and Authoritative Sources*	▶ Scott, I. 2008. *Domestic Violence: Practice and Procedure*, St. Paul, MN: Thomson West.	

*Most treatises and authoritative sources in family law are specific to one state because this area of law is almost entirely governed by state law. Large law libraries are likely to have treatises with in-depth discussion of family law matters and **practice materials** with instructions and sample forms, such as *Vermont Family Law*, published by LexisNexis. These may be available in print form and/or through pay-per-view database services.

Many communities have support services ranging from hotlines and shelters to legal advocacy. The National Coalition Against Domestic Violence maintains an online directory of resources by state:

▶ National Coalition Against Domestic Violence: www.ncadv.org/resources/StateCoalitionList.php

There is also the National Domestic Violence Hotline, a 24-hour, toll-free number available nationwide for crisis support and referrals:

▶ National Domestic Violence Hotline: 1-800-799-SAFE (1-800-799-7233) or 1-800-787-3224 (TDD); www.ndvh.org/

QUESTION: Where can I find out my local laws about domestic violence? What are the penalties for it, for example?

There may be state-specific laws as well as federal and tribal laws that govern a particular jurisdiction. The WomensLaw.org website has a resource of laws on specific domestic violence legal topics, such as restraining orders and parental kidnapping as well as links to state statutes, federal laws, and tribal laws.

▶ WomensLaws.org, to search laws by topic and jurisdiction: www.womenslaw.org/laws.php

Finding Answers to Frequent Questions about Adoption

Adoption is primarily governed by state statutes; however, there are several different types of adoptions, and some of these may involve other jurisdictions and other laws. The main types of adoption are:

- **Stepparent**, when the spouse of one of the biological parents becomes the legal parent after the other parent consents, dies, or has parental rights terminated.

- **Private**, when the biological parents voluntarily consent to the adoption and to having their parental rights legally terminated so that the adoptive parents can become the legal parents. Typically an attorney assists with a private adoption.

- **Foster care or public agency**, when a child is adopted by his or her foster parents after becoming legally free, meaning that the parental rights of the biological parents have been terminated by the court, usually for reasons of abuse or neglect. The trend is increasing and, in 2008, 55,000 children were adopted through foster care (U.S. Department of Health and Human Services, Administration for Children and Families, 2008).

- **Relative**, when a person related to the child becomes the legal parent through adoption. This may be done as a private adoption or through the foster care system.

- **International or intercountry**, when a child from another country is adopted by U.S. parents. The child may have already been adopted in proceedings in the other county; if this is the case, the adoption in the United States is referred to as a "read-option." Intercountry adoptions numbered almost 23,000 in 2004 nationwide, but there has been a steady decrease since then, and in 2009 there were approximately 17,000 (U.S. Department of State, Office of Children's Issues, 2009).

In all of these situations, the biological parents must consent to the adoption or have their parental rights legally terminated. There also may be the situation of an abandoned child, in which case abandonment must be proved before the adoption can go forward. The standards for terminating parental rights will depend on state law, as will the terms of consents and other aspects of the adoption case. If the father is unknown or cannot be found, the state laws may specify who is the **putative father**, the man presumed to be the father, for example. If a child is considered old enough—12 or 14 years of age in many states—he or she will also need to sign a consent to the adoption. For a list of links to state adoption laws, refer to one of these sources:

▶ Adoption.com: laws.adoption.com/statutes/state-adoption-laws.html

▶ Cornell's Legal Information Institute: topics.law.cornell.edu/wex/table_adoption

▶ MegaLaw-Adoption: www.megalaw.com/top/adoption.php

An important component of the adoption process in all states is that prospective adoptive parents be thoroughly investigated as to their fitness to be parents. A licensed adoption social worker prepares a "home study" that includes information on the couple's physical and mental health, criminal history, personal relationship stability, other children and extended family, and financial stability. The court reviews the home study in determining if the adoption is in the best interests of the child. In some states, the home study required for a stepparent adoption may be less extensive than for other adoptions. Federal laws that apply to adoption include the following:

▶ Adam Walsh Child Protection and Safety Act (P.L. 109-248): frwebgate.access.gpo.gov/cgi-bin/getdoc.cgi?dbname=109_cong_public_laws&docid=f:publ248.109.pdf

   Signed into law in July 2006, this act includes a wide range of provisions for protecting children from violent and sexual crimes. As it relates to adoption, it requires full background checks before any foster care or adoptive placement can be approved; this includes checking national crime information databases and state child abuse registries.

▶ Adoption Assistance Program (42 U.S.C. § 673): www.law.cornell.edu/uscode/html/uscode42/usc_sec_42_00000673----000-.html

   The Adoption Assistance Program provides federal financial support for adopted children identified as having special needs.

▶ Child Abuse Prevention and Treatment Act (CAPTA) and Adoption Reform Act of 1978 (42 U.S.C. § 5101-5119c and P.L. 95-266): www.law.cornell.edu/uscode/html/uscode42/usc_sup_01_42_10_67.html

The act's purpose is to facilitate the adoption of children with special needs, to provide for national adoption information exchange system, and to promote standards for adoptive placement and the rights of adopted children.

▶ Indian Child Welfare Act (25 U.S.C. § 1901 et seq.): www.nicwa .org/Indian_Child_Welfare_Act/ICWA.pdf (PDF, printable format); www.law.cornell.edu/uscode/25/ch21.html (searchable format)

ICWA was enacted to ensure the placement of adopted children who are Native American in homes that reflect the values of Native American culture.

In addition to federal and state law, there are agreements governing adoptions that involve multiple states, such as when a child from one state is adopted by parents in another state. The ICPC, Interstate Compact on the Placement of Children, has been enacted into law in all 50 states and applies to both adoptions and foster care placements. In accordance with the ICPC, both the originating state where the child was born and the receiving state—where the adoptive parents live and where the adoption proceeding will take place—must provide written approvals before the child can leave the originating state. The Association of Administrators of the Interstate Compact on the Placement of Children (AAICPC) is authorized by the ICPC to administer the Act. Refer to its website (icpc.aphsa.org) for further information.

International or intercountry adoptions are subject to the Hague Adoption Convention (full name: Hague Convention of 29 May 1993 on Protection of Children and Co-operation in Respect of Intercountry Adoption). The Hague Adoption Convention protects children and their families against illegal or ill-prepared adoptions abroad. The convention "seeks to ensure that intercountry adoptions are made in the best interests of the child and with respect for his or her fundamental rights, and to prevent the abduction, the sale of, or traffic in children" (Hague Conference on Private International Law, 2010).

Questions abound when it comes to adoption. The type of adoption as well as the individual concerns and family dynamics will drive the specific answers. Here are a few most frequently asked questions.

QUESTION: I've been remarried for a long time now and my husband would like to adopt my son. I don't even know where his father is. What do we need to do?

State law will usually require either getting the father's consent or proving it is not necessary before your husband can adopt your son and become his legal father. Because state law governs this type of proceeding, be sure to use legal documents that are intended for use in your state. Many states will require a background check on your husband and a home study or a report from an independent adoption counselor showing that the adoption is in the best interests of the child. A more extensive discussion of general issues related to stepparent adoption is available from Nolo Legal Encyclopedia at www.nolo.com/legal-encyclopedia/article-29643.html.

However, you will need to get information specific to your own state. Many states provide instructions and the forms necessary to do a step-parent adoption, or local law libraries may have them. Refer to the one of these sources to locate the adoption statutes for your state:

▶ Adoption.com: laws.adoption.com/statutes/state-adoption-laws.html

▶ Cornell's Legal Information Institute: topics.law.cornell.edu/wex/table_adoption

▶ MegaLaw-Adoption: www.megalaw.com/top/adoption.php

QUESTION: Our nephew has lived with us since he was a baby. Now he's older and we would like to formally adopt him. His parents are fine with it. How do we get started?

Your state's statutes will determine exactly what is needed to get started but be prepared to have a home study done and to have his parents sign written consents. Depending on his age he may need to sign a consent too. Your local court can usually provide names of local adoption social workers who are licensed to do home studies. For the legal documents, look for state-specific forms and instructions from your state court website or law library. Do not rely on adoption materials from Internet form vendors that may not be valid in your state. Even though everyone is in agreement on proceeding with the adoption, this may be a matter to handle with the assistance of an attorney.

QUESTION: I'm adopted and I want to locate my birth mother. Where should I start?

Many organizations provide guidance to adult adoptees wanting to locate their birth parents. This is a fiercely debated trend, of course, as many birth parents do not want to be found and consented to the adoption with the understanding that identifying information would be sealed. Often state statutes protect this information as well. However, some states have "mutual consent registries" so that if the adoptee and the birth parent both consent, they can exchange information. Search on Google or Yahoo! for *adoption reunion registry* to find out what is available in your area.

For resource updates, visit this book's companion website at

▶ *www.GetLaw.net*

RESOURCES RECAP		
Adoption		
	Resource	**Notes**
Primary Sources: Federal	▶ Cornell's Legal Information Institute, "U.S. Code: Adoption and Guardianship Assistance Program": www.law.cornell.edu/uscode/html/uscode42/usc_sec_42_00000673----000-.html ▶ Cornell's Legal Information Institute, "U.S. Code: Child Abuse Prevention and Treatment and Adoption Reform": www.law.cornell.edu/uscode/html/uscode42/usc_sup_01_42_10_67.html	
		(Cont'd.)

RESOURCES RECAP *(Continued)*		
Adoption		
	Resource	**Notes**
Primary Sources: Federal *(Cont'd.)*	▶ Cornell's Legal Information Institute, "U.S. Code: Indian Child Welfare": www.law.cornell.edu/uscode/25/ch21.html ▶ GPO Access, "Adam Walsh Child Protection and Safety Act of 2006" (P.L. 109-248): frwebgate.access.gpo.gov/cgi-bin/getdoc.cgi? dbname=109_cong_public_laws&docid= f:publ248.109.pdf ▶ National Indian Child Welfare Association, "Indian Child Welfare Act (ICWA) Compliance": www.nicwa.org/Indian_Child_Welfare_Act/	Also provides a list of tribal agents
Primary Sources: State	▶ Adoption.com, "State Adoption Laws": laws.adoption.com/ statutes/state-adoption-laws.html ▶ Cornell's Legal Information Institute, "Adoption Laws of the Fifty States, District of Columbia, and Puerto Rico": topics.law .cornell.edu/wex/table_adoption ▶ MegaLaw.com, "Adoption Law": www.megalaw.com/top/ adoption.php	
Primary Sources: Interstate and Intercountry	▶ HCCH, Hague Convention on Private International Law, "Convention on Protection of Children and Co-operation in Respect of Intercountry Adoption": www.hcch.net/index_en .php?act=conventions.pdf&cid=69 ▶ HCCH, Hague Convention on Private International Law, "Intercountry Adoption Section": www.hcch.net/index_en.php?act=text.display&tid=45 ▶ Interstate Compact on the Placement of Children (ICPC)— Association of Administrators: icpc.aphsa.org ▶ U.S. Department of State Adoption, "Intercountry Adoption: Country Information": adoption.state.gov/countryinformation .html	Provides the full text of the Convention
Do-It-Yourself Publications	▶ American Bar Association, *ABA Guide to Family Law*, "Chapter 6: Adoption": www.abanet.org/publiced/practical/books/family/	

References

American Bar Association. 2004. "ABA Guide to Family Law." Available: www.abanet.org/publiced/practical/books/family/ (accessed May 15, 2010).

Centers for Disease Control and Prevention. 2009. "Understanding Intimate Partner Violence." Available: www.cdc.gov/violenceprevention/pdf/IPV_ factsheet-a.pdf (accessed August 10, 2010).

Hague Conference on Private International Law. 2010. "Intercountry Adoption." Available: www.hcch.net/index_en.php?act=text.display&tid=45 (accessed August 10, 2010).

McDonough, M. 2008. "More Americans Go Pro Se, Even in Complex Matters." *ABA Journal Law News Now* (November 25). Available: www.abajournal.com/news/article/more_americans_go_pro_se_even_in_complex_matters/ (accessed May 15, 2010).

Stoner, K., and Irving, S. 2008. *Prenuptial Agreements: How to Write a Fair & Lasting Contract.* 3rd ed. Berkeley, CA: Nolo.

United States Census Bureau. 2008. "Families and Living Arrangements." Available: www.census.gov/population/www/socdemo/hh-fam.html (accessed August 10, 2010).

United States Department of Health and Human Services, Administration for Children and Families. 2008. "Trends in Foster Care and Adoption—FY 2002–FY 2008." Available: www.acf.hhs.gov/programs/cb/stats_research/afcars/trends.htm (accessed August 10, 2010).

United States Department of Justice. 2010. "About Domestic Violence." Available: www.ovw.usdoj.gov/domviolence.htm (accessed August 10, 2010).

United States Department of State, Office of Children's Issues. 2009. "Intercountry Adoptions: Total Adoptions to the United States." Available: adoption.state.gov/news/total_chart.html (accessed August 10, 2010).

Landlord–Tenant

QUESTION: I moved out a month ago and my landlord still hasn't returned my deposit. I think I should get all of it back too.

QUESTION: I rent out an apartment in my house to students and the last one left behind damages that cost a lot more to repair than the security deposit covered. I gave him the move-out statement showing he owes $350, but he hasn't paid. What should I do?

This chapter encompasses perspectives from both sides of the landlord–tenant divide, emphasizing the importance of knowing both your rights and responsibilities—whether you are the tenant or the landlord—and how to locate the applicable laws as well as resources for sample forms and handling disputes. The chapter's focus is residential landlord–tenant legal information; it does not address commercial rental property matters.

Framework for Questions in This Area of Law

In the broadest sense, the landlord–tenant relationship is governed by both **statutory law** and **common law** as well as by the specific terms of the rental (lease) agreement. As discussed in Chapter 2, common law is derived from judicial decisions. The earliest U.S. common law was taken from English common law, and this mostly concerned the "oldest" legal areas, including real property and landlord–tenant law. However, most states have codified this old common law into their statutes.

So it is state law that governs the landlord–tenant area of law—but some federal law applies as well, guiding issues such as antidiscrimination and certain potential health hazards. For example, the Federal Fair Housing Act, adopted in 1968 and amended in 1988, prohibits discrimination in housing-related transactions—including rentals—on the basis of race, color, national origin, religion, gender, familial status, and disability. (However, there are some exceptions; for example, if renting out

IN THIS CHAPTER:

✔ Framework for Questions in This Area of Law

✔ Getting Started

✔ Finding Answers to Frequent Questions
From Tenants
From Landlords

✔ Epilogue

a room in a single family residence, a landlord may restrict by gender.) Similarly, federal law governs certain safety concerns, for example, establishing strict limits on exposure to toxins like lead and asbestos (Residential Lead-Based Paint Hazard Reduction Act, P.L. 102-550). These federal laws are reflected in state statutes and local ordinances. Landlords need to be fully aware of these laws and take them seriously; courts have found landlords liable for tenant health problems even when the landlord did not create or know about the hazard.

The Federal Fair Housing Act is administered by the U.S. Department of Housing and Urban Development (HUD), and the agency provides extensive resources for both tenants and landlords, including online directories linking to state-specific information, statutes, and tenant rights groups. The HUD website (www.hud.gov/renting/local.cfm) is one of the most comprehensive resources for locating legal information related to housing for all 50 states.

Getting Started

With state law as the main framework, the first step is locating the set of state statutes for landlord–tenant matters. The HUD website discussed previously points to relevant state statutes as well as other state resources such as tenant rights groups. The Washburn Law website (washlaw.edu) is another mega-resource, with a page for each state containing a link to its statutes under the page's "Legislative Branch" subheading. There is likely to be one set of state statutes for residential rental properties and a different set for commercial properties. In addition, it may be that mobile homes or condominiums have separate statutes that apply as well.

State statutes can also be very specific and very often pertain to "habitability" requirements. For example, in Washington State (and other locales) there are laws pertaining to mold (aligned with the federal Environmental Protection Agency guidelines), and in Florida there are laws for the minimum number of electrical outlets in each room. Common requirements include smoke detectors, door and window locks, and minimum standards for plumbing and hot water. So be certain when using sample pleading forms from the Internet or do-it-yourself publications that these have been prepared for use in your state. Forms intended for use in California will not necessarily be easily adaptable for use in any state other than California. Always check first for local resources. The good news is that landlord–tenant matters (and problems) are so common that many free, reliable, and state-specific resources are readily available. Many communities have legal aid groups that provide help with landlord–tenant disputes. This might include mediation services available on a sliding scale, help hotlines, and packets of samples or templates for the most commonly used court pleadings and legal forms. A good starting point for locating these groups is the state's attorney general website or the HUD state resources directory:

▶ State Attorneys General Directory (from the National Association of Attorneys General): www.naag.org/attorneys_general.php

---

CLOSER LOOK

Model Residential Landlord–Tenant Acts

The Uniform Residential Landlord and Tenant Act (URLTA), created in 1972 by the National Conference of Commissioners on Uniform State Laws (NCCUSL), is a uniform or model act whose purpose is to clarify the responsibilities of and provide protections for both landlords and tenants.

The URLTA is based on model code originally drafted by a legal services project funded by the federal government. The American Bar Association approved the URLTA in 1974. The full text of the act is available from the University of Pennsylvania Law School Library that houses the NCCUSL archives at www.law.upenn.edu/bll/archives/ulc/ fnact99/1970s/urlta72.htm. For a list of states that have adopted the URLTA, see www.law.cornell.edu/ uniform/vol7.html#lndtn. Another model act is the Model Residential Landlord–Tenant Code (42 U.S.C. § 3604). At this time, most states have adopted one or the other of these two model acts.

▶ State Statutes and Resources for Landlord–Tenant: www.hud.gov/renting/local.cfm

In addition to state law, there may be local **ordinances** that further limit permissible conduct, such as noise restrictions. This can mean municipal (city) or county (or parish) code that applies to rental housing, and landlords may even choose to reference these in the rental agreement. Local laws may provide for further protections for tenants, too, such as rent control and additional habitability requirements. Also, if the rental property is within a condominium or other residential development it may be subject to restrictive covenants (sometimes called "CC&Rs" for covenants, conditions, and restrictions), and these are then also part of the agreed-to terms between landlord and tenant. For example, the covenants may prohibit having a home business or parking an RV in the driveway.

In addition to state statutes governing landlord–tenant matters, federal laws for safe and fair housing, local ordinances, and homeowner covenants are the terms of the rental agreement itself, also called a lease agreement or simply a lease. The landlord is limited by law as to what provisions may be included, but these can still be wide ranging. Commonly included are restrictions for no smoking or pets on the premises,

GOOD TO KNOW

Rights of Tenants in Foreclosed Homes

The steep rise in home foreclosures has meant serious consequences for renters as well as homeowners. Tenants living in foreclosed homes were often faced with sudden eviction. The Protecting Tenants At Foreclosure Act (Title VII of P.L. 111-22), signed into law in May 2009, protects tenants living in foreclosed residential properties. (It does not apply to commercial rentals.) The major provisions of the act are described in the following list; at this time, these provisions will expire on December 31, 2012.

- During the term of the lease, the tenant has a right to remain in the unit and cannot be evicted except for actions that constitute good cause.
- If the lease ends in fewer than 90 days, the new owner may not evict the tenant without giving the tenant a minimum of 90 days notice.
- At the end of the term of the lease, the new owner may terminate the tenancy if the new owner provides a 90-day notice.
- The new owner may terminate the tenancy if the owner will occupy the unit as a primary residence and has provided the tenant a notice to vacate at least 90 days before the effective date of such notice. This is the only exception to the rule that the tenant may not be evicted during the term of the lease.

It is important to know that no federal agency (such as HUD) is responsible for enforcing the act; rather it is up to legal advocates to ensure that tenants, landlords, the court, and public housing authorities are aware of these protections for tenants and abide by them. The National Low Income Housing Coalition website (www.nlihc.org) provides answers to frequently asked questions about the act, sample forms, and a list of state-specific resources.

number of occupants, or terms requiring regular maintenance of the yard and disposal of garbage. The following do-it-yourself publications include sample lease agreements:

▶ Portman, Janet. 2009. *Every Landlord's Guide to Finding Great Tenants.* 2nd ed. Berkeley, CA: Nolo.

▶ Stewart, Marcia. 2009. *Leases and Rental Agreements.* 8th ed. Berkeley, CA: Nolo.

▶ Stewart, Marcia. 2010. *Every Landlord's Legal Guide.* 10th ed. Berkeley, CA: Nolo.

Finding Answers to Frequent Questions

From Tenants

QUESTION: As a tenant, what am I responsible for? And how do I know what I'm not allowed to do?

State laws prescribe the responsibilities of tenants and landlords. In addition, the rental agreement (lease) may include specific responsibilities such as maintenance of yard or disposal of garbage or notifying landlord of suspected problems with insects or rodents within a reasonable amount of time. It's important to know what is in the lease you signed *and* know what is in the state statutes. To understand the statutes it can help to consult a tenant rights publication or webpage. Fortunately many states have these. Often these are listed on (or even available from) the website of the state's attorney general. The following directories are good places to start:

▶ State Attorneys General Directory (from the National Association of Attorneys General): www.naag.org/attorneys_general.php

▶ State Statutes and Resources for Landlord–Tenant: www.hud.gov/renting/local.cfm

QUESTION: What can I do if there are serious problems with the apartment I'm renting and the landlord refuses to fix them? I mean, we're talking plumbing that doesn't work!

When it comes to habitability problems—which are defined by state statute and may also be guided by federal laws—a tenant has various options, again depending on state statutes. It may be that the tenant can withhold rent after giving written notice to the landlord, make the repairs and deduct expenses from the rent (called "repair and deduct"), or arrange for a city or county official to inspect the premises. Check the provisions in state statutes. If the landlord is refusing to make needed repairs and the situation is contentious, contacting a local tenant advocacy group for advice can be wise. The following self-help materials may be useful as well:

▶ American Bar Association, "Renting a Home," for general information for landlords and tenants (free): www.abanet.org/publiced/practical/rentinghome.html

- Nolo Press, "Ten Tips for Tenants" (free): www.nolo.com/legal-encyclopedia/checklist-29446.html
- Portman, Janet. 2009. *Renters' Rights: The Basics.* 6th ed. Berkeley, CA: Nolo.
- Stewart, Marcia. 2010. *Every Tenant's Legal Guide.* 10th ed. Berkeley, CA: Nolo.

QUESTION: I've been renting the same house for several years with small increases every year. Suddenly the landlord wants to raise the rent 20 percent. Can she really do that?

You will want to check both state and local laws for any restrictions on the amount of rental increases as some jurisdictions do have rent control. Also, if you are still within a lease agreement that sets a fixed rental amount for the period of the lease it may be that the increase can be forestalled until the end of the lease period. Otherwise, check that proper notice has been given: for example, state or local law may require a 30- or 45-day notice before an increase may take effect.

QUESTION: I'm being evicted, but it seems for no good reason. How do I know what's allowed and how do I defend myself?

Good cause for eviction is determined by state law and by the terms of the rental agreement. There are also statutory requirements for the notices that must be given to the tenant being evicted. Some common defenses to an eviction are that the landlord's claims about violating the lease are false, that the eviction is retaliatory for actions taken by the tenant that are legal (such as withholding rent due to habitability issues), or failure to properly serve the tenant with the eviction notices. Getting advice can be wise; many states have tenant advocacy groups that can assist with an eviction matter, and most states' attorney general websites include a list of these groups. Refer to:

- State Attorneys General Directory (from National Association of Attorneys General): www.naag.org/attorneys_general.php

QUESTION: The house I've been renting just went through foreclosure. The new owner told me I have to move out in two weeks. Can he really do that?

This is covered in the previous sidebar, "Rights of Tenants in Foreclosed Homes." By federal law, the new owner must give you a 90-day notice to end your tenancy. In addition, if you have more than 90 days left on your lease, the new owner cannot evict you until the end of the lease unless he or she is going to use the house as his or her own primary residence.

QUESTION: I moved out a month ago and my landlord still hasn't returned my deposit. I think I should get all of it back, too.

State law proscribes how long a landlord has after move-out to provide a tenant with an accounting of the security deposit and its return in whole or in part. If damages exceed the deposit, the accounting may show an amount due from the tenant. State law may also require a walk-through near the time of move-out to determine any damages that are beyond normal wear and tear. Research your state statutes to determine what is required when it comes to rental deposits.

QUESTION: I've heard about federally funded rental housing. How do I find out more and apply for it?

The U.S. Department of Housing and Urban Development (HUD) provides answers to this and many questions related to public housing at "What is Public Housing?" webpage (www.hud.gov/offices/pih/programs/ph/).

From Landlords

QUESTION: As a landlord, what am I responsible for? And are there restrictions on what I can do?

State law governs the rights and responsibilities of both tenants and landlords. In addition, there are federal laws against discrimination in housing and regulating safety that are reflected in state and local laws. Some common restrictions on what a landlord can do include protection of tenancy privacy and access to the premises—this may mean requiring advance notice for entry except in cases of emergency maintenance, for example. Check the state statutes to find out the specific restrictions and requirements. The terms of the lease can encompass additional provisions; refer to sample lease agreements available for free from forms books in law libraries and the do-it-yourself publications described earlier and listed in the Resources Recap at the end of the chapter.

QUESTION: How do I handle the security deposit from my tenant? And is it any different from the last month's rent?

State laws are specific as to the handling of rental security deposits, and local laws may have further provisions. There are typically requirements as to whether interest must be paid on the deposit and to whom, how soon an accounting of the deposit (and/or its return, in part or whole) must be provided to the tenant after move-out, whether the tenant must be told where the deposit is being held (at what bank, for example), etc. A security deposit is different from last month's rent. Refer to state statutes for answers to these issues. There are also do-it-yourself materials available for landlords:

▶ American Bar Association, "Renting a Home," for general information for landlords and tenants (free): www.abanet.org/publiced/practical/rentinghome.html

▶ Nolo Press, "Ten Tips for Landlords" (free): www.nolo.com/legal-encyclopedia/checklist-29482.html

▶ Stewart, Marcia. 2009. *Leases and Rental Agreements*. 8th ed. Berkeley, CA: Nolo.

▶ Stewart, Marcia. 2010. *Every Landlord's Legal Guide*. 10th ed. Berkeley, CA: Nolo.

QUESTION: What are the legal reasons to evict a tenant? And how do I do an eviction?

The answers to both of these questions are determined by state statutes, so consult the state resource directories in this chapter. In general, common good cause reasons to evict a tenant are nonpayment of rent, lapse of the rental agreement (expiration of the lease), nuisance behavior, and violating terms of the rental agreement. Many local courts provide information and even forms for proceeding with an eviction (also called an unlawful detainer action). If these are not available from the court, check with local law libraries and legal aid groups or one of the do-it-yourself publications listed under the previous question and also in the Resources Recap at the end of the chapter. Especially for particularly contentious evictions and difficult tenants, it is sometimes a good idea to consult with an attorney on the matter.

> QUESTION: I rent out the house I used to live in and have had some bad experiences with renters. How can I do background screening on people and can I charge the applicant for it?

Many screening services are available directly on the Internet; however, it can be difficult to determine the reputable ones. One example of a nationwide service is www.intelius.com/tenant-screening.html. A local process server company can be another good resource for running background checks on potential tenants. Some state statutes allow landlords to charge a fee to prospective tenants for running a background check; consult your state statutes to determine what is allowed.

> QUESTION: I rent out an apartment in my house to students and the last one left behind damages that cost a lot more to repair than the security deposit covered. I gave him the move-out statement showing he owes $350 but he hasn't paid. What should I do?

Check that notices given and the move-out statement were in accordance with state law. At this point the matter may be evolving into a debt collection matter and it may be that going to small claims court or mediation or consulting an attorney is the next best step.

For resource updates, visit this book's companion website at

▶ **www.GetLaw.net**

RESOURCES RECAP		
Landlord–Tenant		
	Resource	**Notes**
Primary Sources: Federal	▶ Environmental Protection Agency, "Residential Lead-Based Paint Hazard Reduction Act of 1992" (P.L. 102-550): www.epa.gov/oppt/lead/pubs/titleten.html	
	▶ GPO Access, *Code of Federal Regulations* (*CFR*), "Housing and Urban Development" (Title 24, Section 1): www.access.gpo.gov/nara/cfr/waisidx_00/24cfrv1_00.html	
	▶ GPO Access, *Code of Federal Regulations* (*CFR*), "Housing and Urban Development" (Title 24, Section 2): www.access.gpo .gov/nara/cfr/waisidx_00/24cfrv2_00.html	

(Cont'd.)

RESOURCES RECAP *(Continued)*		
Landlord–Tenant		
	Resource	**Notes**
Primary Sources: State	▶ HUD.GOV, U.S. Department of Housing and Urban Development, "Local Renting Information": www.hud.gov/renting/local.cfm	This site provides a directory of state statutes and resources and is the best starting point for resources because state law governs landlord–tenant matters. Each state's page on the HUD website includes not only links to the state statutes but also to state-specific resources such as free tenant handbooks, sample forms, and legal aid groups.
	▶ LandlordAssociation.org, "Landlord Tenant Laws and Statutes, Executive Orders, Hazard Control Resources": www.landlordassociation.org/statelaws.html	This directory of state statutes also includes links to free tenant rights publications for some states.
	▶ WashLaw, "State Legal Resources for the United States": www.washlaw.edu/uslaw/	Click "States" in top navigation bar and then the state name in the list on the left. Look under the heading "Legislative Branch" for "Statutes" or "Code." Most states provide the ability to browse the statutes and/or to search by keyword.
Uniform and Model Acts	▶ Cornell's Legal Information Institute, "Model Residential Landlord–Tenant Code" (42 U.S.C. § 3604): www.law.cornell.edu/uscode/pdf/uscode42/lii_usc_TI_42_CH_45_SC_I_SE_3604.pdf ▶ National Conference of Commissioners on Uniform State Laws, "Uniform Residential Landlord and Tenant Act": www.law.upenn.edu/bll/archives/ulc/fnact99/1970s/urlta72.htm	
Free Online Resources: General Information	▶ American Bar Association, "Renting a Home": www.abanet.org/publiced/practical/rentinghome.html ▶ Nolo, "Ten Tips for Landlords": www.nolo.com/legal-encyclopedia/checklist-29482.html ▶ Nolo, "Ten Tips for Tenants": www.nolo.com/legal-encyclopedia/checklist-29446.html	ABA's website includes an extensive list of frequently asked questions.
Free Online Resources: State-Specific Information	▶ HUD.GOV, U.S. Department of Housing and Urban Development, "Local Renting Information": www.hud.gov/renting/local.cfm	The HUD website listing of state resources is the best launchpad for issues related to landlord–tenant law. It includes information on relevant federal law as well as a page of resources for each state.
	▶ State Attorneys General Directory (from National Association of Attorneys General): www.naag.org/attorneys_general.php	Use this listing to locate your state's attorney general website, which typically includes a directory of legal aid resources.

(Cont'd.)

RESOURCES RECAP *(Continued)*		
Landlord–Tenant		
	Resource	**Notes**
Free Online Resources: Federal Assistance and Guidelines	▶ Environmental Protection Agency, "Asbestos: Basic Information": www.epa.gov/asbestos/pubs/help.html ▶ Environmental Protection Agency, "Indoor Air Quality": www.epa.gov/iaq/ ▶ U.S. Department of Housing and Urban Development, "Housing Discrimination" (for access to a Housing Discrimination Complaint Form): portal.hud.gov/portal/ page/portal/HUD/topics/housing_ discrimination ▶ U.S. Department of Housing and Urban Development, "Welcome to the Office of Healthy Homes and Lead Hazard Control": www.hud.gov/offices/lead/ ▶ U.S. Department of Housing and Urban Development, Public and Indian Housing, "PHA Contact Information": www.hud.gov/offices/pih/pha/contacts/index.cfm	
Do-It-Yourself Publications: Books for Tenants	▶ Portman, Janet. 2009. *Renters' Rights: The Basics*. 6th ed. Berkeley, CA: Nolo. ▶ Stewart, Marcia. 2010. *Every Tenant's Legal Guide*. 10th ed. Berkeley, CA: Nolo.	
Do-It-Yourself Publications: Books for Landlords	▶ Leshnower, Ron. 2008. *Every Landlord's Property Protection Guide*. Berkeley, CA: Nolo. ▶ Portman, Janet. 2009. *Every Landlord's Guide to Finding Great Tenants*. 2nd ed. Berkeley, CA: Nolo. ▶ Stewart, Marcia. 2009. *Leases and Rental Agreements*. 8th ed. Berkeley, CA: Nolo. ▶ Stewart, Marcia. 2010. *Every Landlord's Legal Guide*. 10th ed. Berkeley, CA: Nolo.	
Treatises and Authoritative Sources	▶ *Restatement of the Law Second, Property—Landlord and Tenant*. 1977– . St. Paul, MN: West Group.	This source is not state specific; however, many states have authoritative secondary source publications such as practice materials specific to the state. As with many secondary sources, these are likely to be expensive and available only from law school libraries and larger public law libraries.

Epilogue

Questions related to landlord–tenant matters are seemingly endless; those included in this chapter represent common questions and hopefully can serve as pointers to similar questions and their answers.

Wills, Estate Planning, and Probate

QUESTION: Can I do my own will or do I need an attorney? Or maybe I need a trust. Or both? I really need to find out more.

QUESTION: I've heard it's important to have a 'living will' but don't really know what that is. I just want to be sure my wishes are made clear if I get seriously ill or injured. Is that what I need?

QUESTION: My uncle died and I'm handling his probate myself. He didn't have a lot, but it still looks like there are a lot of steps to go through. How do I get started?

Contemplating what are usually called "end of life" decisions brings up many legal questions, all of them overlaid with anxiety over the desire to leave clear instructions for family members and doctors. This might include preparing a simple will or writing up a health care directive, covering specific instructions about medical treatments to be allowed if a person is unable to give his or her own informed consent or refusal. Similarly, when a person faces the task of managing the estate of a loved one recently deceased, it can be overwhelming. In addition to handling the grief, memorials, and personal belongings, the estate may require opening a probate case, and even a "simple" probate can be complex to a grieving executor trying to navigate the court system and generate proper legal documents without an attorney's assistance. This chapter covers the resources available to help answer the most common questions that arise.

Framework for Questions in This Area of Law

People looking to prepare a will or a health care directive need to rely on state statutes as these govern this area of law. For example, it is state law that determines who inherits property if no instructions are left, in the form of a will, trust, or other legal document. However, federal laws apply to certain end-of-life decisions, particularly advance directives. An

IN THIS CHAPTER:
✔ Framework for Questions in This Area of Law
✔ Getting Started
  Understanding Key Terms
✔ Finding Answers to Frequent Questions

advance directive is a legal document that takes effect if a person cannot make decisions due to illness, serious injury, incapacity, or incompetency. There are different types of advance directives, discussed more fully later in this chapter.

In this realm of federal law the Patient Self-Determination Act (PSDA), passed by Congress in 1990, is significant. The PSDA requires most Medicare and Medicaid providers to give adult patients information about the rights granted to them by their state laws for advance health care directives. This information must be provided at the time of enrollment in a program or admission to the health care facility. This includes hospitals, long-term care facilities, health maintenance organizations (HMOs), and home health agencies. The PSDA also requires the institutions to provide community education about advance directives and prohibits discrimination against patients who do not have an advance directive.

Guiding the laws in the areas of trusts and probate are uniform codes that have been enacted into law by many states, often with modifications. The Uniform Probate Code was initially written in the 1960s and continues to be revised; it has been adopted by 18 states at this time. The Uniform Trust Code has been adopted by 21 states. However, what matters with both of these uniform codes is *how* they have been adopted (or not) within your own state's statutes. The following resources from the National Conference of Commissioners on Uniform State Laws (NCCUSL) summarize how these have been adopted in different states:

▶ Uniform Health Care Decisions Act: www.nccusl.org/Update/Act SearchResults.aspx?ActId=46

▶ Uniform Probate Code: www.nccusl.org/Update/ActSearchResults .aspx?ActId=67

▶ Uniform Trust Code: www.nccusl.org/Update/ActSearchResults.aspx? ActId=28

For an excellent discussion of the objectives and realities of uniform laws generally, see the Cornell LII *Law by Source* article: www.law.cornell .edu/uniform/uniform.html. The Uniform Health Care Decisions Acts (UHCDA) must also be mentioned here, although many states had already enacted laws governing advance directives by the time the UHCDA was approved in 1993.

Getting Started

Fortunately, several nonprofit and professional organizations provide reliable information in this area of law, specifically for the layperson. The American Bar Association (ABA) has brochures as well as more extensive publications at low or no cost to the public:

▶ "Consumer's Tool Kit for Health Care Advance Planning": www.abanet. org/aging/toolkit/

▶ "Estate Planning FAQs": www.abanet.org/rppt/public/

▶ *Guide to Wills and Estates*, Second Edition (free to download; also available for purchase): www.abanet.org/publiced/practical/books/wills/home.html

▶ *Health and Financial Decisions: Legal Tools for Preserving Your Personal Autonomy*: www.abanet.org/abastore/index.cfm?section=main&fm=Product.AddToCart&pid=4280030

In addition, your local state's bar association is likely to have information that reflects the state statutes. Go to the state bar's website and look for a heading like "Public Services" or "For the Public." To locate the website of your state's bar association, refer to Appendix 3.

Many states provide forms for a generic will and an advance health care directive; some states require that their statutory forms be used for advance health care directives. Your state's department of health may also list state-specific information and forms that are related to end-of-life planning.

Be forewarned that there are many Internet-based companies selling advance directive forms, many of which are the exact same statutory forms available for free from your state government. Always look for websites that end in ".gov," which identifies government agencies and institutions.

Understanding Key Terms

Estate planning is rife with terminology that is unfamiliar, antiquated, and also includes overlapping terms that can add to the confusion. This can be one of the biggest hurdles to beginning the process, so the first step in getting started is a basic understanding of a few key terms:

- **Advance directive**: A legal document prepared in advance that takes effect if a person cannot make decisions due to illness, serious injury, incapacity, or incompetency. The purpose of an advance directive is to protect a person's rights if he or she becomes unable to choose or communicate his or her wishes. There are different types of advance directives, with the two most common being a living will and a health care power of attorney. These two are sometimes combined into a single legal document. An advance directive may also be called a health care directive or advance medical directive.

- **Executor**: The person named in a will (or appointed by a court) to distribute the deceased person's property and pay any bills. If probate is necessary the executor must handle it or hire an attorney to do so. A woman may be called executrix. Either may also be called the personal representative in some states.

- **Guardian**: Person appointed by the court to act as the legal representative of a person determined to be mentally or physically incapable of managing his or her financial affairs. This person may be called a *conservator* in some courts. For a

---

GOOD TO KNOW

Transferring Ownership of Real Estate

Estate planning may include the transfer (or *conveyance*) of real estate into a trust or making other changes to the ownership. This kind of transaction usually calls for the advice of an attorney to be certain it is done correctly and with the fewest consequences in terms of taxes or other fees. In terms of law, transferring or selling real estate is governed by contract law that includes the *statute of frauds* (Uniform Commercial Code § 2-201), requiring that real estate transactions be in writing. A simple transfer may be accomplished through a Quit Claim Deed; however, the intricacies in this area of law and the particulars of a given situation go beyond the scope of this book. To learn more, look for your state's governing agency for real estate, typically called the department of real estate or the real estate commission. See the state-by-state directory available from Justia (www.justia.com/real-estate/resources.html).

Advance Directive Registry

Some states are cooperating in a nationwide registry of living wills and other advance directive documents. The goal is a repository of advance directive documents available online to health care professionals throughout the United States, 24 hours a day. One effort is the U.S. Living Will Registry, www.uslivingwill registry.com. Individuals register, submit their documents, and are notified yearly to update contact information and check that documents still reflect their wishes.

Several states are participating through their public health departments, but even if your state is not among them, it is possible to store documents with the registry as an individual for a one-time fee or through private health care providers. The registry's website also includes a comprehensive directory of downloadable advance directive forms from all 50 states. See uslwr.com/formslist.shtm.

discussion of guardianship, see Cornell Law School Wex (topics .law.cornell.edu/wex/guardian).

- **Health Care Power of Attorney**: A legal document signed by a person which designates another person (called the *agent* or *attorney-in-fact*) to make health care decisions should that person become incapacitated. This may also be called Medical Power of Attorney, Health Care Proxy, or Durable Power of Attorney for Health Care. This document is for health care decisions only; it is a type of special power of attorney and not the same as a general power of attorney.

- **Intestate**: Describes a person who dies without a will; the opposite of testate.

- **Living trust**: A trust created during a person's life into which assets such as real estate and accounts are placed. Typically a living trust is revocable. The person creating the trust is called the *grantor* or *settler*. The person responsible for managing the assets of the trust is the *trustee*. This can be the same person. May also be called "inter vivos trust." For an overview of living trusts, see "What Is a Living Trust?" from the American Bar Association (www.abanet.org/rpte/public/revocable-trusts .html#revocablelivingtrust).

- **Living will**: A type of advance directive giving instructions on which measures may or may not be used to prolong life in the event the person cannot give informed consent or refusal. A living will commonly includes specific directives on which life-sustaining measures may be used in cases of extreme disability without reasonable expectation of recovery. For example, these instructions may include a directive for "no heroic measures," a "natural death" directive, or DNR (do not resuscitate) instructions for terminally ill persons—a living will is a highly personal expression of an individual's wishes. For further information on living wills, see "Living Wills and Advance Health Care Directives" from the ABA at www.abanet.org/rpte/public/living-wills .html#livingwillsetc.

- **Payable-On-Death ("POD") Account**: Typically a bank account set up with one or more people designated to receive the funds in the account when the account holder dies, usually for the purpose of bypassing probate. This may also be called an informal bank account trust or revocable trust account.

- **Probate**: Probate means the entire process during which a deceased person's assets are gathered, inventoried, and then applied to pay debts and distributed to the beneficiaries. Probate includes proving the will is valid or, if the person died without a will, a determination by the court of the person's heirs—the state statutes for this are called "intestate succession" laws. Probate statutes vary from state to state and it can be wise to consult an attorney to determine if probate is necessary.

Finding Answers to Frequent Questions

QUESTION: Can I do my own will or do I need an attorney? Or maybe I need a trust. Or both? I really need to find out more.

The answers to these questions depend entirely on the individual's situation, his or her assets, family relationships, personal wishes, etc. The best answer is actually a series of more questions to probe for further information. Two free guides that can help are from the American Bar Association and the California Bar Association. Even though the latter is intended for Californians, much of the material is generic and can be useful to those in other states.

▶ American Bar Association, *ABA Guide to Wills and Estates*, Chapters 1 to 3: www.abanet.org/publiced/practical/books/wills/home.html

These chapters cover the key objectives of estate planning and the purpose of a will. Other chapters cover topics such as trusts, taxes, and disability issues.

▶ The State Bar of California, "Do I Need a Will?" (available in English, Spanish, and Chinese): www.calbar.ca.gov/Public/Pamphlets/Will.aspx

This covers types of wills, how to change a will, who should be told about a will, and other estate planning topics.

QUESTION: I've heard it's important to have a "living will" but don't really know what that is. I just want to be sure my wishes are made clear if I get seriously ill or injured. Is that what I need?

A person creates a living will to put in writing his or her specific instructions and wishes for which medical measures may (or may not) be used if the person is unable to give consent or refusal. A living will often includes instructions about what measures may be taken to prolong life if the person becomes severely ill or injured without reasonable expectation of recovery. Several organizations and their resources follow:

▶ American Academy of Hospice and Palliative Medicine, "Resources: Legal Documents": www.aahpm.org/patient/resources/legal.html

▶ American Bar Association, "Consumer's Tool Kit for Health Care Advance Planning": www.abanet.org/aging/toolkit/

▶ American Bar Association, *Health and Financial Decisions: Legal Tools for Preserving Your Personal Autonomy*: www.abanet.org/abastore/index.cfm?section=main&fm=Product.AddToCart&pid=4280030

▶ American Cancer Society, "Advance Directives": www.cancer.org/docroot/MIT/mit_3_1_1.asp

▶ National Hospice and Palliative Care Organization and the American Health Lawyers Association, "Advance Care Planning Brochures": www.caringinfo.org/PlanningAhead/acp_brochures.htm

▶ National Hospice and Palliative Care Organization and the American Health Lawyers Association, "Download Your State's Advance Directives": www.caringinfo.org/stateaddownload

▶ PBS (Public Broadcasting), "On Our Own Terms: Moyers on Dying—Resources": www.pbs.org/wnet/onourownterms/resources.html

QUESTION: I have my advance health care directive ready but don't understand who has to witness it or if it needs to be notarized. Also, who should I give it to?

State statutes govern the requirements for witnesses and whether or not your signature needs to be notarized. Refer to the "State Resources Summary: Advance Medical Directive Requirements" sidebar, and also check to see if the statutes in your state have changed since this summary was prepared. The American Bar Association recommends that you give copies to your doctor, the person you named as your agent, close relatives, and anyone else who may be involved in your care. You may also want to consider registering a copy; see the "Worth Watching: Advance Directive Registry" sidebar.

QUESTION: What is a "living trust"? Is it the same as a "living will"? Which one do I need?

A living trust is different from a living will. A living trust can substitute in part for a will (not a living will) because your assets—such as real estate and bank accounts—are placed in the living trust for your use during your lifetime and then pass to your beneficiaries at the time of your death. A living will is a type of advance directive that gives instructions on which measures can be used to prolong life in the event you are unable to give informed consent or refusal. Both documents are often part of the process of estate planning, but they serve different purposes. More information about living trusts is available from:

▶ American Bar Association, *ABA Guide to Wills and Estates*, Chapter 5: www.abanet.org/publiced/practical/books/wills/home.html

▶ The State Bar of California, "Do I Need a Living Trust?" (available in English and Spanish): www.calbar.ca.gov/state/calbar/calbar_generic .jsp?cid=10581&id=2212

QUESTION: My uncle died and I'm handling his probate myself. He didn't have a lot but it still looks like there are a lot of steps to go through. How do I get started?

The first step is often to determine if probate is necessary. Either way, the state statutes govern this area of law. Many state courts provide the necessary documents for handling probate without an attorney, but it may be wise to consider if an attorney's assistance is needed or to advise you on whether or not probate is required. Several do-it-yourself publications are available for free from the American Bar Association, as are low-cost books:

▶ *Guide to Wills and Estates* (free to download; also available for purchase): www.abanet.org/publiced/practical/books/wills/home.html

▶ "Estate Planning FAQs," including an introduction to wills, revocable trusts, advance directives, probate, and retirement planning: www .abanet.org/rppt/public/

▶ Randolph, Mary. 2010. *Eight Ways to Avoid Probate*. 8th ed. Berkeley, CA: Nolo

▶ Randolph, Mary. 2010. *Executor's Guide*. 4th ed. Berkeley, CA: Nolo.

STATE RESOURCES SUMMARY	
Advance Medical Directive Requirements	
Laws and forms vary from state to state. A few states require that their statutory forms be used and make these available at no charge. Refer also to Appendix 3 for websites with the latest versions of state statutes.	
Alabama	Alabama Bar Association, Advance Directive for Health Care: www.alabar.org/members/advdirective.pdf
Alaska	Alaska Division of Public Health, Advance Health Care Directive (Living Will): www.hss.state.ak.us/dph/director/living_will/default.htm
Arizona	Arizona Attorney General, Life Care Planning Documents: www.azag.gov/life_care/index.html
Arkansas	Arkansas Pro Bono Partnership, Advanced Directives: www.arlegalservices.org/files/FSLivingWill.pdf
California	California Medical Association, New Advance Healthcare Directive Kit: www.cmanet.org/publicdoc.cfm/7
Colorado	Colorado Bar Association, Senior Law Handbook: www.cobar.org/index.cfm/ID/726/dpwfp/Senior-Law-Handbook/
Connecticut	Connecticut Attorney General, Living Will Laws: www.ct.gov/ag/cwp/browse.asp?A=2130&BMDRN=2000&BCOB=0&C=19278
Delaware	Delaware Heath & Social Services, Advance Health Care Directive: www.dhss.delaware.gov/dsaapd/advance1.html
District of Columbia	Georgetown University Hospital, Advance Directives Online Resource: www.georgetownuniversityhospital.org/body.cfm?id=555640
Florida	Florida Bar Association, Living Wills and Advanced Directives: www.floridabar.org/
Georgia	State Bar of Georgia, Advance Directive for Health Care: www.gabar.org/communications/consumer_pamphlet_series/
Hawaii	Hawaii Department of Health, Advance Health Care Directive Handbook: hawaii.gov/health/disability-services/neurotrauma/key-services-health.html
Idaho	Idaho Secretary of State, Health Care Directive Registry and Forms: sos.idaho.gov/general/hcdr.htm
Illinois	Illinois Department of Public Health, Advance Directives: www.idph.state.il.us/public/books/advdir4.htm
Indiana	Indiana State Department of Health, Advance Directives: www.in.gov/isdh/files/advanceddirectives.pdf
Iowa	Iowa Department of Public Health, Step-by-Step Guide to Preparing Advance Directive Documents: www.aging.iowa.gov/Documents/Publications/GiftofPeaceofMind.pdf
Kansas	Kansas Bar Association, Living Wills: www.ksbar.org/public/public_resources/pamphlets/living_wills.shtml
Kentucky	Kentucky Office of the Attorney General, Living Will Packet: www.florence-ky.gov/docs/fire/ky_living_will.pdf
Louisiana	Louisiana Department of Health & Hospitals, Planning Guide for Advance Directives: www.dhh.louisiana.gov/offices/publications/pubs-62/advance_con.pdf

(Cont'd.)

STATE RESOURCES SUMMARY *(Continued)*	
Maine	Maine Department of Health and Human Services, Advance Directives Forms: www.maine.gov/dhhs/oes/resource/rit2chew.htm
Maryland	Maryland Attorney General, Advance Directives: www.oag.state.md.us/Healthpol/AdvanceDirectives.htm
Massachusetts	Massachusetts Trial Court Law Libraries, Health Care Proxy & Living Will Forms: www.lawlib.state.ma.us/subject/forms/formsf-l.html#proxy
Michigan	Michigan Department of Community Health, Advance Directives: www.michigan.gov/mdch/0,1607,7-132-2941_4868_41752---,00.html
Minnesota	Minnesota Department of Health, About Health Care Directives: www.health.state.mn.us/divs/fpc/profinfo/advdirlg.htm
Mississippi	Mississippi State Department of Health, Patient Self-Determination Act: unite.msdh.state.ms.us/msdhsite/_static/resources/75.pdf
Missouri	Missouri Bar Association, Living Wills and Other Advance Directives: www.mobar.org/99b8baa9-d44d-4756-9b40-fcdf1dd91ceb.aspx
Montana	Montana Department of Justice, Advance Health Care Directives: www.doj.mt.gov/consumer/consumer/advancedirectives.asp
Nebraska	Nebraska Department of Health & Human Services, Advance Directives in Nebraska: www.hhs.state.ne.us/ags/agselderrghts.htm
Nevada	Nevada Center for Ethics & Health Policy, Advance Directives: www.unr.edu/ncehp/ADs.html
New Hampshire	New Hampshire Bar Association, Making Medical Decisions for Someone Else: www.nhbar.org/for-the-public/publicinformationlibrary.asp
New Jersey	New Jersey Department of Health & Senior Services, Advance Directives for Health Care: www.state.nj.us/health/healthfacilities/documents/ltc/advance_directives.pdf
New Mexico	New Mexico Aging & Long-Term Services Department, Advance Health Care Directives: www.nmaging.state.nm.us/AHCD.html
New York	New York State Department of Health, Health Care Proxy Form & Instructions: www.health.ny.gov/forms/doh-1430.pdf
North Carolina	North Carolina Secretary of State, Advance Health Care Directive Registry & Forms: www.secretary.state.nc.us/ahcdr/
North Dakota	North Dakota Department of Human Services, Making Health Care Decisions: www.nd.gov/dhs/info/pubs/docs/aging/aging-healthcare-directives-guide.pdf
Ohio	Ohio Legal Rights Service, Advance Directives Publications: www.olrs.ohio.gov/topic-advance-directives
Oklahoma	Oklahoma Bar Association, Advance Directive for Health Care FAQs & Form: www.okbar.org/public/brochures/advancedQA.htm
Oregon	Oregon Senior Health Insurance Benefits Assistance Program, Advance Directives: egov.oregon.gov/DCBS/SHIBA/advanced_directives.shtml

(Cont'd.)

STATE RESOURCES SUMMARY *(Continued)*

Pennsylvania	Pennsylvania Department of Aging, Understanding Advance Directives for Health Care: www.portal.state.pa.us/portal/server.pt/document/780893/advancedirectives_pdf
Rhode Island	Rhode Island Attorney General, Health Care Power of Attorney: www.riag.ri.gov/documents/reports/healthcare/power_of_attorney.pdf
South Carolina	South Carolina Lieutenant Governor's Office on Aging, Advance Directives Brochure: www.aging.sc.gov/seniors/AdvanceDirectives/
South Dakota	Regional Health, South Dakota, Living Will Form & Instructions: www.regionalhealth.com/documents/LivingWill.PDF
Tennessee	Tennessee Department of Health, Advance Directive Forms: health.state.tn.us/AdvanceDirectives/index.htm
Texas	Texas Department of Aging and Disability Services, Advance Directives Forms/Handbooks: www.dads.state.tx.us/news_info/publications/handbooks/index.html
Utah	Utah Department of Human Services, Advance Directives Toolkit: www.hsdaas.utah.gov/advance_directives.htm
Vermont	Vermont Department of Health, Advance Directives Registry: healthvermont.gov/vadr/index.aspx
Virginia	Virginia Department for the Aging, Advance Medical Directive: www.vda.virginia.gov/advmedir.asp
Washington	Washington State Department of Health, Living Will Registry & Forms: www.doh.wa.gov/livingwill/
West Virginia	West Virginia Center for Health Ethics & Law, Advance Directives Forms & Law: www.hsc.wvu.edu/chel/center/directives.htm
Wisconsin	Wisconsin Department of Health Services, Advance Directives: www.dhs.wisconsin.gov/forms/AdvDirectives/
Wyoming	Wyoming State Bar, Durable Power of Attorney for Health Care: https://www.wyomingbar.org/pdf/forms/Info_Durable_Power_of_Attorney.pdf

For resource updates, visit this book's companion website at

▶ *www.GetLaw.net*

RESOURCES RECAP

Wills, Estate Planning, and Probate

	Resource	Notes
Primary Sources: Federal	▶ Patient Self-Determination Act (PSDA): www.ssa.gov/OP_Home/comp2/F101-508.html	The PSDA was a part of the Omnibus Budget Reconciliation Act of 1990, P.L. 101-508 (104 Stat. 143).

(Cont'd.)

RESOURCES RECAP *(Continued)*		
Wills, Estate Planning, and Probate		
	Resource	**Notes**
Primary Sources: State	▶ American Bar Association, "Health Care Power of Attorney and Combined Advance Directive Legislation": tinyurl.com/healthcarePOA (MS Word document) ▶ Cornell's Legal Information Institute, "Probate: State Statutes": topics.law.cornell.edu/wex/table_probate ▶ Washburn University School of Law, "Of Interest to All States": www.washlaw.edu/uslaw/	State statutes for advance directives State statutes for probate State statutes directory
Uniform Acts	▶ Cornell's Legal Information Institute, "Law by Source: Uniform Laws": www.law.cornell.edu/uniform/uniform.html ▶ National Conference of Commissioners on Uniform State Laws, "Uniform Health-Care Decisions Act": www.law.upenn.edu/bll/archives/ulc/fnact99/1990s/uhcda93.htm ▶ National Conference of Commissioners on Uniform State Laws, "Uniform Probate Code": www.law.upenn.edu/bll/archives/ulc/upc/2008final.htm ▶ National Conference of Commissioners on Uniform State Laws, "Uniform Trust Code": www.law.upenn.edu/bll/archives/ulc/uta/2005final.htm	
Free Online Resources	▶ American Academy of Hospice and Palliative Medicine, "Resources: Legal Documents": www.aahpm.org/patient/resources/legal.html ▶ American Bar Association, "Appendix A: Estate Planning Checklist," in *Guide to Wills and Estates*: www.abanet.org/publiced/practical/books/wills/home.html ▶ American Bar Association, "Consumer's Tool Kit for Health Care Advance Planning": www.abanet.org/aging/toolkit/ ▶ American Bar Association, "Estate Planning FAQs": www.abanet.org/rppt/public/ ▶ American Bar Association, *Guide to Wills and Estates*: www.abanet.org/publiced/practical/books/wills/home.html ▶ American Bar Association, *Health and Financial Decisions: Legal Tools for Preserving Your Personal Autonomy*: www.abanet.org/abastore/index.cfm?section=main&fm=Product.AddToCart&pid=4280030 ▶ American Cancer Society, "Advance Directives": www.cancer.org/docroot/MIT/mit_3_1_1.asp ▶ International Association for Hospice and Palliative Care, "IAHPC Directory" (by state): www.hospicecare.com/yp/index.php?cat=10&subcat=111 ▶ National Hospice and Palliative Care Organization and the American Health Lawyers Association, "Advance Care Planning Brochures": www.caringinfo.org/PlanningAhead/acp_brochures.htm	Free to download; also available for purchase

(Cont'd.)

RESOURCES RECAP *(Continued)*		
Wills, Estate Planning, and Probate		
	Resource	**Notes**
Free Online Resources *(Cont'd.)*	▶ National Hospice and Palliative Care Organization and the American Health Lawyers Association, "Download Your State's Advance Directives": www.caringinfo.org/stateaddownload ▶ PBS (Public Broadcasting), "On Our Own Terms: Moyers on Dying—Resources": www.pbs.org/wnet/onourownterms/resources.html	
Do-It-Yourself Publications: Books	▶ American Bar Association Division for Public Education. 2006. *Legal Guide for Americans Over 50*. Chicago: American Bar Association. ▶ American Bar Association Division for Public Education. 2009. *American Bar Association Guide to Wills and Estates*. Chicago: American Bar Association. ▶ American Bar Association Division for Public Education. 2009. *Guide to Legal, Financial, and Health Care Issues: You and Your Aging Parents*. Chicago: American Bar Association. ▶ Clifford, Denis. 2007. *Simple Will Book*. 7th ed. Berkeley, CA: Nolo. ▶ Clifford, Denis. 2008. *Quick and Legal Will Book*. 5th ed. Berkeley, CA: Nolo. ▶ Clifford, Denis. 2009. *Make Your Own Living Trust*. 9th ed. Berkeley, CA: Nolo. ▶ Clifford, Denis. 2010. *Plan Your Estate*. 9th ed. Berkeley, CA: Nolo. ▶ Randolph, Mary. 2010. *Eight Ways to Avoid Probate*. 8th ed. Berkeley, CA: Nolo. ▶ Randolph, Mary. 2010. *Executor's Guide*. 4th ed. Berkeley, CA: Nolo.	
Do-It-Yourself Publications: Software	▶ Quicken Willmaker Plus. Updated annually. Berkeley, CA: Nolo.	
Treatises and Authoritative Sources*	Anderson, R. W. 2003. *Understanding Trusts and Estates*. 3rd ed. New York: Mathew Bender. Bogert, G. G. 1977– . *The Law of Trusts and Trustees*. Rev. 2nd ed. St. Paul: West Group. *Restatement of the Law Third, Trusts*. 2003– . St. Paul: West Group.	
*These sources are likely to be available only from law school libraries and larger public law libraries.		

Debts, Collections, and Credit

QUESTION: I won in small claims court a couple of months ago and got a judgment against the guy who still owed me money for the car he bought from me. But he still hasn't paid it. What can I do? How do I collect what he owes me?

QUESTION: A collection agency is trying to take money out of my paycheck and I don't even know what it's for. How do I find out? Can they really do this? And it doesn't leave enough for me to pay rent.

These two narratives tell flipsides of the same story. The first is the voice of a creditor who has a court order or judgment stating that a person owes him a certain amount of money. His concern is how to proceed with enforcing the unpaid judgment and collecting what is due. The second is the voice of the debtor who owes money to a creditor and, in this case, that creditor has evidently engaged a collection agency to handle the collection process. This chapter addresses the questions that typically arise for people on both sides of a creditor–debtor dispute; it also covers common questions when a person has concerns related to credit problems.

Framework for Questions in This Area of Law

As in the preceding chapters, the first consideration is determining if the applicable law is federal, state, or local—or a combination. Money judgments in creditor–debtor actions are typically the outcome of state court actions, and the actions related to collections will likewise be driven by state statutes and court rules. However, certain aspects of creditor–debtor actions, particularly those in place to protect the consumer or debtor, are guided by federal law or by uniform or model acts at the national level that have been adopted in varying forms at the state level within state statutes. Examples of these include the Consumer Protection

IN THIS CHAPTER:

- ✔ Framework for Questions in This Area of Law
  - Multistate Matters
  - Matters Involving Contracts
- ✔ Getting Started
  - Debtor: Basic Starting Information
  - Creditor: Basic Starting Information
  - Facing Foreclosure
- ✔ Finding Answers to Frequent Questions
- ✔ References

Act, Federal Wage Garnishment Law, Fair Debt Collection Practices Act, Consumer Credit Protection Act, and the Uniform Commercial Code. As an example, both the Federal Wage Garnishment Law and state laws establish exemptions to types of income that can be garnished by a creditor. Similarly, in terms of enforcement, the Federal Trade Commission enforces the Fair Debt Collection Practices Act (FDCPA), but many states have their own debt collection laws and regulations.

Multistate Matters

Another jurisdictional consideration in collection matters is that a creditor might need to collect from a debtor who no longer resides in the state where the judgment was entered. In this instance, a creditor may be able to refile the judgment as a "foreign judgment" in the other state in order to begin a collection action there. State laws where the foreign judgment is being filed will apply to this type of action. Some states have adopted the Uniform Enforcement of Foreign Judgments Act, another example of a uniform or model act.

Notice that in this context "foreign judgment" does not refer to judgments from outside of the United States but from another state. Refer to the U.S. Department of State publication *Enforcement of Non-U.S. Judgments* as a starting point for information on enforcing a non-U.S. judgment in a U.S. federal court. This can be found at: travel.state.gov/law/judicial/judicial_691.html.

Matters Involving Contracts

Often a creditor–debtor matter will involve a contract; for example, an agreement with a construction contractor to perform work on a person's home or an agreement to purchase a vehicle. Contract law is intricate, and many factors come into play: whether the agreement was in writing or oral, whether the service or product was provided in whole or in part, whether modifications were agreed to, whether a licensed or unlicensed contractor was involved, and what specific area of law is involved in the contract: employment, real estate, intellectual property, to name just a few. The various considerations go beyond the scope of this book. To gain a general understanding of contracts, see topics.law.cornell.edu/wex/contract.

Getting Started

First, some basic information is necessary as a foundation before beginning to find answers to questions in the creditor–debtor arena.

Debtor: Basic Starting Information

A debtor may begin with a question about garnishment, having been alerted to a collection action by an employer or a notice about deductions from a paycheck or bank account. Knowing what is behind the garnishment is one of the first steps for a debtor: it may be that earlier notices were received and not heeded or understood but, whatever the reason, the debtor will be helped by learning what is in the court file to find out the nature of the judgment, the amount (which might include interest and fees), and if the judgment has been assigned to a collection agency for action. This often means going to the clerk of the court to get a copy of the documents in the case file from which the judgment arose.

Creditor: Basic Starting Information

Much like the debtor, the creditor needs basic information to get started with a collection action. This might include doing the following:

- Determining how long the debtor has to pay: this may be driven by state statute, the terms of the judgment itself, the original contract, or a combination of factors. For "old" debts there might also be considerations related to a **statute of limitations**.

- Determining if there is interest and/or fees accruing and at what rate. The interest, if any, may be written into the judgment or contract or it may be statutory.

If a creditor wants to proceed with a garnishment action, a few terms and players need to be understood. The creditor who begins a garnishment action is the *garnishor*, and the holder of the debtor's assets is the *garnishee* (or *garnishee-defendant*), whereas the debtor is the *defendant*. Examples of a garnishee-defendant include a bank that holds the debtor's savings or checking account or the debtor's employer.

Facing Foreclosure

The devastating impact of home foreclosure has been headline news the last few years, with good reason. The delinquency rate for residential properties, measuring mortgages at least 90 days delinquent, was at its highest ever recorded level in the third quarter of 2009. One in 14 mortgages in the United States now meets this standard, up from one in 22 just a year ago. In some locales, the rate is much higher: in Las Vegas 21.7 percent of home mortgages are more than 90 days delinquent, and in Miami the rate is 28.8 percent (Fitch, 2010).

A foreclosure affects not only the individual homeowner but the entire community in the form of depressed home values and often increased crime rates as homes are left unoccupied. Most of this chapter focuses on debts that are not related to home mortgage debt; however, homeowners who are facing foreclosure are often facing the biggest debt crisis of their lives. This section covers legal resources specifically helpful to those who are homeowners needing information about foreclosure.

UNDERSTANDING REDEMPTION:
If your home has been sold at a foreclosure sale (also called a trustee sale), many states allow for a "redemption period" during which you can

---

WORTH WATCHING

Consumer Financial Protection Bureau (CFPB)

The Consumer Financial Protection Bureau was established as part of the Consumer Protection Act of 2010 (P.L. 111-203, H.R. 4173), signed into law on July 21, 2010. In describing the CFPB, President Barack Obama stated, "Never again will folks be confused or misled by the pages of barely understandable fine print that you find in agreements for credit cards, mortgages, and student loans. The Consumer Financial Protection Bureau will be a watchdog for the American consumer, charged with enforcing the toughest financial protections in history" (White House, 2010). There is little argument that consumers have been damaged by the practices of the mortgage and credit card industries and considerable debate continues over the best solutions. This new federal agency is one to watch.

reclaim your home. The requirements and timelines are determined by state statutes. The U.S. Department of Housing and Urban Development (HUD) provides several resources for homeowners:

▶ HUD.GOV, "Avoiding Foreclosure": portal.hud.gov/portal/page/portal/HUD/topics/avoiding_foreclosure

FORECLOSURE RESCUE SCAMS:
The U.S. Treasury Department posts advisories about predatory practices of companies and individuals looking to take advantage of those in foreclosure or mortgage default:

▶ Comptroller of Currency, Administrator of National Banks, "OCC Consumer Tips for Avoiding Mortgage Modification Scams and Foreclosure Rescue Scams": www.occ.treas.gov/ftp/ADVISORY/2009-1.html

FORECLOSURE LAWS, STATE BY STATE:

▶ "United States Foreclosure Laws": www.foreclosurelaw.org.
This website is recommended by HUD as a resource for looking up the statutes in your state related to foreclosure.

REFINANCING AND MODIFICATION OF HOME MORTGAGES:

▶ MakingHomeAffordable.gov: www.makinghomeaffordable.gov
This website is a joint effort of the White House, Treasury Department, and HUD.

Finding Answers to Frequent Questions

QUESTION: My employer told me that she has to start garnishing my wages. I won't have enough left over to pay rent. How do I keep that from happening?

Garnishment is the result of a court-issued writ of garnishment, but there are limits to how much of a person's income can be garnished to pay off a debt. These limits are determined by both state and federal law. For example, a percentage of a person's income as well as some or all of income from sources such as public assistance, Social Security, unemployment compensation, or child support may be claimed as exempt from garnishment. Most state courts provide state-specific forms for filing a [petition for] claim of exemption. See also the Federal Wage Garnishment Law (15 U.S.C. § 1671), available from: www.dol.gov/esa/whd/garnishment.

QUESTION: I'm confused about where the judgment came from and how the collection action started in the first place. Maybe I just didn't keep good records. How do I find out more?

The court file will include information on the creditor and the judgment amount and what interest and fees might be included, whether determined by statute or original contract or agreement. The judgment will indicate a court and case number; you can go to the courthouse and look up the

GOOD TO KNOW

Debt Collector Dos and Don'ts

The federal Fair Debt Collections Practice Act (FDCPA) is the authority for what a debt collector can and cannot do according to law, and the Federal Trade Commission (FTC) is responsible for enforcement of the act. Under the FDCPA, third-party debt collectors are prohibited from using deceptive or abusive conduct in the collection of consumer debts. Debt collectors may not, for example, subject debtors to repeated telephone calls, threaten legal action that is not actually contemplated, or reveal to other persons the existence of the debts. The FTC website includes an extensive frequently asked questions publication. Here are a few highlights:

- How to stop a debt collector from contacting you
- Times of day a debt collector may phone you and when it may not
- What a debt collector *must* tell you about the debt
- What's not allowed: what a debt collector may not say or do

Refer to www.ftc.gov/bcp/edu/pubs/consumer/credit/cre18.pdf.

case file to see all documents related to the judgment and garnishment action. The file will also show if the judgment was assigned to a collection agency.

QUESTION: How can I complain about the practices of a collection agency or a dispute about a debt?

For resource updates, visit this book's companion website at

▶ *www.GetLaw.net*

RESOURCES RECAP		
Debts, Collections, and Credit		
	Resource	**Notes**
Primary Sources: Federal	▶ Cornell's Legal Information Institute, "Consumer Credit: An Overview": topics.law.cornell.edu/wex/Consumer_credit; www.dol.gov/compliance/laws/comp-ccpa.htm	Provides access to the Consumer Credit Protection Act, CCPA
	▶ Cornell's Legal Information Institute, "Law by Source: Uniform Laws—Uniform Commercial Code Locator": www.law.cornell.edu/uniform/ucc.html	
	▶ GPO Access, "Fair and Accurate Credit Transactions Act of 2003" (FACTA) (P.L. 108-159): www.gpo.gov/fdsys/pkg/PLAW-108publ159/content-detail.html	
	▶ Federal Trade Commission, "Fair Credit Reporting Act" (15 U.S.C. § 1681): www.ftc.gov/os/statutes/fcrajump.shtm	
	▶ Federal Trade Commission, "Fair Debt Collection Practices Act" (15 U.S.C. § 1692): www.ftc.gov/bcp/edu/pubs/consumer/credit/cre27.pdf	
	▶ Federal Trade Commission, "Legal Resources—Statutes Relating to Consumer Protection Mission": www.ftc.gov/ogc/stat3.shtm	
	▶ Travel.State.Gov, "Enforcement of Judgments": travel.state.gov/law/judicial/judicial_691.html	
	▶ United States Department of Labor, Wage and Hour Division (WHD), "Federal Wage Garnishments": www.dol.gov/whd/garnishment/index.htm	Provides access to the Federal Wage Garnishment Law (15 U.S.C. § 1671)
Primary Sources: State	▶ United States Foreclosure Laws: www.foreclosurelaw.org	Provides access to foreclosure laws by state Refer also to Chapters 4 and 5 and Appendix 3.
Free Online Resources: Credit and Collection Information	▶ Federal Trade Commission, "Credit and Your Consumer Rights": www.ftc.gov/bcp/edu/pubs/consumer/credit/cre01.shtm	
	▶ Federal Trade Commission, "Debt Collection FAQs: A Guide for Consumers": www.ftc.gov/bcp/edu/pubs/consumer/credit/cre18.pdf	
	▶ Federal Trade Commission, "Free Annual Credit Reports": www.ftc.gov/freereports	
	▶ National Association of Attorneys General, "Current Attorneys General": www.naag.org/attorneys_general.php	Includes a state directory
		(Cont'd.)

RESOURCES RECAP (Continued)		
Debts, Collections, and Credit		
	Resource	**Notes**
Free Online Resources: Foreclosure Information	▶ Comptroller of Currency, Administrator of National Banks, "OCC Consumer Tips for Avoiding Mortgage Modification Scams and Foreclosure Rescue Scams": www.occ.treas.gov/ftp/ADVISORY/2009-1.html ▶ HUD.GOV, "Avoiding Foreclosure": portal.hud.gov/portal/page/portal/HUD/topics/avoiding_foreclosure ▶ MakingHomeAffordable.gov: www.makinghomeaffordable.gov	
Do-It-Yourself Publications: State-Specific Materials	▶ California Courts Self-Help Center: www.courtinfo.ca.gov/selfhelp/smallclaims/collect.htm	This is just one example. Many states have court-provided packets of forms for this purpose. As with other common legal matters, state courts, public law libraries, and local legal aid organizations often provide online forms for this purpose. Refer to the resources in Chapter 6 and Appendix 3.
Do-It-Yourself Publications: Books	▶ Elias, Stephen. 2009. *Foreclosure Survival Guide*. 2nd ed. Berkeley, CA: Nolo. ▶ Leonard, Robin, and John Lamb. 2009. *Credit Repair*. 9th ed. Berkeley, CA: Nolo. ▶ Leonard, Robin, and Margaret Reiter. 2009. *Solve Your Money Troubles: Debt, Credit, & Bankruptcy*. 12th ed. Berkeley, CA: Nolo.	

The federal Fair Debt Collections Practice Act is enforced by the Federal Trade Commission (FTC), and you can file a complaint with them. In addition, the state's attorney general or district attorney website may also have consumer information that will be helpful. See the directory of state attorneys general at www.naag.org/attorneys_general.php.

QUESTION: I got served with a summons and complaint from a collection agency. I don't think I owe anything, so do I have to respond or can I just ignore it?

Yes, you do need to respond. The summons and complaint mean that a lawsuit has been filed against you. Very likely there is language in the summons saying that you have a certain number of days to file an answer or the collection agency can go to court to get a default judgment against you. If you do not respond, you will not even receive notice of the judgment. Once there is a judgment, the next step can be garnishment of wages or bank accounts. Refer to the resources in Chapter 7.

QUESTION: I got a judgment in small claims court but it still hasn't been paid. I want to start an enforcement action to try to collect. Where do I start?

There are many kinds of collection actions. Garnishment is one common way to collect on a debt, and some states have court-provided packets of forms and instructions for this purpose. (An example from California is provided in the Resources Recap at the end of the chapter.) Public law libraries are another resource. In addition to garnishment—and depending on the jurisdiction—a creditor might be able to secure a writ to force the sale of certain of a debtor's assets, start the process for a judicial lien on real property, or other collection actions. These go beyond the scope of this book, and the advice of an attorney may be appropriate.

QUESTION: I've paid off all my debts, but now my credit report still shows some of them as unpaid. How can I get that fixed?

The FTC website (www.ftc.gov/freereports) provides helpful how-tos, FTC Facts for Consumers, with tips for clearing up problems on a credit report. This publication also links to the FTC's service for requesting a free copy of your credit report and warnings about impostor "free report" services. It also covers the Fair and Accurate Credit Transaction Act (FACTA). See www.ftc.gov/bcp/edu/pubs/consumer/credit/cre34.pdf.

References

Fitch, Stephane. 2010. "Soaring Mortgage Defaults May Kill The Housing Recovery." *Forbes Magazine* (February 26). Available: www.forbes.com/2010/02/26/real-estate-advisor-personal-finance-housing-defaults.html (accessed August 10, 2010).

White House, Office of the Press Secretary. 2010. "Statement by the President to the Press, September 17, 2010." Available: www.whitehouse.gov/the-press-office/2010/09/17/statement-president-press (accessed September 18, 2010).

Bankruptcy

QUESTION: "I have so many debts that I'm thinking I should find out about bankruptcy. Where do I start to learn about it and what it would mean for me?"

The previous chapter addressed the realm of debtor–creditor questions. Perhaps the ultimate question a debtor can ask is about bankruptcy. Quite often a person has heard about bankruptcy as a means to get out from under an unmanageable level of debt but is likely to know very little about how to proceed.

It should be noted, however, that it is not unusual for the initial question to be focused on bankruptcy—the Big B—when in fact other information needs are at the core of a person's query. Further exploration during a reference interview may reveal, for example, that the person has received a summons and complaint from a collection agency and leaped to the conclusion that bankruptcy is the next logical step. It also may be that a library patron wants to avoid discussing the "real question" due to embarrassment or lack of understanding or basic fear of the unknown— common obstacles when facing an intimidating situation and certainly exacerbated when correspondence from debt collectors is involved. So the person poses the question, "I need to know about bankruptcy," with the hope that the overly simplified question will be taken at face value and further probing won't occur, even if the ultimate answer would not address the true information need. This chapter assumes that the information need truly is about bankruptcy, but reviewing the preceding chapter as well as the sidebar "When One Question Masquerades as Another" (p. 156) is recommended.

Framework for Questions in This Area of Law

Some fundamental distinctions will be helpful when seeking information about bankruptcy: first, bankruptcy law is entirely the province of the federal legal system; second, there are different types of bankruptcies,

When One Question Masquerades as Another

In the arena of questions related to personal finance the anxiety level is particularly high and may be further fueled by a sense of urgency to respond to a debt collector's letter or phone call. Ross and colleagues (2009) have written about how one question can masquerade as another, and this phenomenon is especially prevalent in the circumstances described in this and the preceding chapter:

> When a patient comes into the doctor's office and says, "I need a prescription for prednisone," the doctor doesn't reach immediately for the prescription pad. He or she first asks some question in order to understand the nature of the original problem and its symptoms. Similarly the purpose of the reference interview is to get back, as far as possible, to the original informational need. Until you do this, you don't really know what kind of question you are dealing with. One experienced librarian [in the study] reported, "The woman came in and said she wanted books about the Titanic. It turned out she had a great-aunt who had survived the Titanic sinking and she wanted the passenger list to find this lady's name. So it was a genealogy question masquerading as information about the Titanic." The job of the savvy librarian is to strip off the masquerade. (Ross et al., 2009: 29)

and a layperson is likely to be concerned with only one or two of these types since those contemplating business or corporate bankruptcies are likely to already have attorneys to handle it; and third, resource currency (making sure one has the most up-to-date information) is critical in this fast-changing area of the law.

Federal Law Governs

As discussed in Part I of this book, some areas of the law involve both federal and state law, some areas involve only state law, and some areas are entirely governed by federal law. Bankruptcy is governed by Federal Law, specifically Title 11 of the U.S. Code. There are three main types of bankruptcy filings, each referring to a chapter in the Title 11 code. For example, "11 U.S.C. § 707" refers to a section in the Chapter 7 bankruptcy code, and "11 U.S.C. § 1322" refers to a section within the Chapter 13 code. The title comes first, and the § symbol refers to a section. So "11 U.S.C. § 707" indicates Title 11, section 707, in the U.S. Code. Sometimes "U.S.C.A." will appear in a citation; the "A" indicates the annotated version published by West. U.S.C.S., for United States Code Service, is another annotated version of the U.S. Code, published by LexisNexis. Refer to the chapters in Part I for further discussion of the kinds of information typically found in statute and code annotations. The following are types of bankruptcy:

- Chapter 7, "Liquidation," or sometimes called "straight bankruptcy": The most common type for individuals, a Chapter 7 bankruptcy provides for the sale of a debtor's nonexempt property and the distribution of the proceeds to creditors.

- Chapter 11, "Reorganization": Chapter 11 is generally used by corporations or partnerships but may also be used by individuals to seek relief. In this type of bankruptcy a debtor typically proposes a plan of reorganization to keep its business alive and pay creditors over time.

- Chapter 13, "Debt Adjustment": Chapter 13 provides a way for an individual with a regular income to adjust debts over time. It allows a debtor to keep property and pay debts over a set period of time, usually three to five years.

There are a few less common types of bankruptcies (such as Chapter 12 for family farmers or fisherman), but these are not discussed here.

Choosing from among the different types of bankruptcy involves multiple considerations—such as the specific nature of assets and debts and how the debt was incurred—and this is an area of law where an attorney's advice can be essential to traversing the legal processes and making fully informed decisions. In fact, most attorneys who work in bankruptcy law confine their practices to only bankruptcy law (or to bankruptcy and a few related areas like collections) because it is such a specialized area. Fortunately some do offer free consultations—check the Yellow Pages or a lawyer referral service (see Chapter 6) to find out what is available locally.

The federal district courts for bankruptcy have excellent websites that include downloadable templates for the basic documents needed to file for bankruptcy, such as the bankruptcy petition. There may be local rules specific to a regional court so be sure to utilize the website for the appropriate district. For example, Chicago is in the Illinois Northern Bankruptcy District Court and Carbondale is in the Illinois Southern District. A court directory that can help you find your regional court is located at www.uscourts.gov/courtlinks/.

The federal courts now use electronic filing ("e-filing"), meaning that all court documents are submitted in PDF format through the courts' websites and also made available online. The federal courts' system is referred to as CM/ECF, for case management and electronic case files. The date each court began using e-filing varies; refer to the U.S. courts webpage for "Courts Accepting Electronic Filings," which includes a section on bankruptcy courts (www.uscourts.gov/FederalCourts/CMECF/Courts.aspx).

Currency: Be Sure You Have the Most Recent Information

In October 2005, the federal bankruptcy code underwent a massive revision and the law continues to be updated. Be sure that any materials consulted reflect the latest code. For example, since the 2005 revision, personal bankruptcies require a "means test" (based on income over the last several years and other factors) and include a requirement for credit counseling. Even in a Chapter 7 "liquidation" bankruptcy, some kinds of debts can be discharged while others cannot. If one of the do-it-yourself publications in the Resources Recap at the end of the chapter is consulted, be sure to check for the latest forms online on the court websites and do not rely on the samples provided in the books.

Getting Started

An authoritative and reliable starting point is "Bankruptcy Basics" from the U.S. Courts website: www.uscourts.gov/bankruptcycourts/bankruptcybasics.html. This resource even includes a collection of short videos explaining different aspects of bankruptcy, such as the filing itself, the creditors' meeting, etc. There is also a guide specifically for those who are self-represented, called "Filing for Bankruptcy without an Attorney." It is important to note that this guide advises:

> While individuals can file a bankruptcy case without an attorney, or pro se, it is extremely difficult to do it successfully. It is very important that a bankruptcy case be filed and handled correctly. The rules are very technical, and a misstep may affect a debtor's rights. For example, a debtor whose case is dismissed for failure to file a required document, such as a credit counseling certificate, may lose the right to file another case or lose protections in a later case, including the benefit of the automatic stay. Bankruptcy has long-term financial and legal consequences—hiring a competent attorney is strongly recommended. ("Filing for Bankruptcy without an Attorney," 2009)

Another helpful and free guide is available from the American Bar Association (ABA), "Bankruptcy Pros and Cons." It covers the two major forms of personal bankruptcy, Chapter 7 and Chapter 13, and also discusses other options a person may want to consider.

If a person would benefit from seeing "how it is done" or wants to track a particular bankruptcy case, the online records are available at low cost. Documents filed in bankruptcy cases are public record and in electronic format going back several years. The PACER (Public Access to Court Electronic Records) Service is available to individuals at a low cost (currently $0.08 per page); registration is online by credit card at pacer.psc.uscourts.gov. PACER provides access to bankruptcies and all federal court cases, with a few exceptions. Refer to the court lists on the PACER website (www.pacer.gov/psco/cgi-bin/links.pl).

Finding Answers to Frequent Questions

As described at the start of this chapter, bankruptcy is a complex area of law where an attorney's advice can be critical to making fully informed decisions. In addition, a person is typically best served by an attorney who specializes in bankruptcy law. That said, common questions involve the need to understand the choices, consequences, and considerations, even if few people will file their own bankruptcies without the assistance of an attorney.

QUESTION: I need to know what the basic options are when it comes to bankruptcy. Is there more than one kind of bankruptcy for personal debts? What about for a small business?

Refer to the section at the beginning of this chapter, Federal Law Governs, that describes the different types of bankruptcies. For further information, consult the following:

▶ "Bankruptcy Basics" (free): www.uscourts.gov/bankruptcycourts/ bankruptcybasics.html

▶ Elias, Stephen, Albin Renauer, and Robin Leonard. 2009. *How to File for Chapter 7 Bankruptcy.* 16th ed. Berkeley, CA: Nolo.

▶ "Filing for Bankruptcy without an Attorney" (free): www.uscourts .gov/bankruptcycourts/prose.html

▶ Leonard, Robin, and Stephen Elias. 2010. *Chapter 13 Bankruptcy: Keep Your Property & Repay Debts Over Time.* 10th ed. Berkeley, CA: Nolo.

QUESTION: How do I choose between a Chapter 7 and Chapter 13 bankruptcy?

Guidance for making this decision goes beyond the scope of this book. One initial consideration to know, however, will be that a person planning to file for bankruptcy is required to get credit counseling from a government-approved organization within 180 days before filing. Refer to the self-help publications listed in the previous answer for basic information. Many bankruptcy attorneys offer a brief, free consultation. It can be worthwhile to investigate this possibility in your community.

QUESTION: Are there some debts that cannot be discharged in bankruptcy?

Yes. Student loans, child support, fines for criminal violations, and certain other debts, including recent income taxes, cannot be discharged in bankruptcy. Refer to the Free Online Resources sections in the Resources Recap at the end of this chapter; all of these discuss the laws governing dischargeable debts. Specific information about what may be discharged may call for professional legal advice.

QUESTION: What about debt consolidation—is that the same as bankruptcy or something different?

Debt consolidation is typically done to lower the total cost of credit. Refer to the Federal Trade Commission's publication "Facts for Consumers: Knee Deep in Debt" (www.ftc.gov/bcp/edu/pubs/consumer/credit/cre19.shtm).

QUESTION: How can I look up someone's bankruptcy petition? Can I follow the progress of an active bankruptcy?

Refer to the PACER online service or, for older cases, to the clerk of the court:

WORTH WATCHING

RECAP the Law

RECAP the Law is an online public archive of court documents from U.S. federal district and bankruptcy courts that launched as a beta version in August 2009. RECAP is an independent project of the Center for Information Technology Policy at Princeton University and is hosted by the Internet Archive.

RECAP is an add-on to the Firefox web browser. If a person enables the RECAP add-on, any documents purchased are automatically added to the RECAP public archive where they will then be available for free to others. In addition, there is an "R" indicator on the PACER court docket next to any documents available from RECAP; this means you do not need to pay for the full document through PACER and can instead click the "R" link and download it for free from RECAP. RECAP is a key player in the movement toward making court records freely available to the general public via the Internet. RECAP describes three ways it is working to achieve this goal:

> Most obviously, we are directly increasing public access to legal documents by creating a free repository that anyone can access. Second, by donating bandwidth and CPU cycles to the cause of public access, we are reducing the load on the PACER servers and making it feasible for the courts to make more documents freely available with the computing resources they already have. Finally, we think that building and running RECAP will give us the opportunity to study the practical challenges involved in large-scale open access to public documents. We hope to learn lessons that will help the judiciary improve its own systems. (www.recapthelaw.org/why-it-matters/)

Not surprisingly, RECAP has been the subject of some controversy because it allows users to bypass the per-page fee levied by PACER. It has also been heralded as a bold and much-needed move toward greater accessibility.

> Citizens deserve open and easy access to all public court documents. Until public access becomes a matter of policy rather than blocked by PACER's artificial pay wall, independent efforts like RECAP continue to fill a critical gap in our ability to foster a more participatory and engaged democracy. (Ari Schwartz, Center for Democracy and Technology. Available: https://www.recapthelaw.org/about/what-people-are-saying/ [accessed November 22, 2009])

RECAP also has spin-off projects to promote further accessibility of legal information. One venture is FedThread that allows for anyone using the *Federal Register* to make annotations and create collaborative "conversations" online, perform advanced searches, and automatically receive new hits on a search topic.

▶ PACER (Public Access to Court Electronic Records): pacer.psc.uscourts .gov/

▶ United States Courts, "Court Locator": www.uscourts.gov/courtlinks/

QUESTION: My creditors are trying to collect on some really old debts. Maybe I don't really need bankruptcy? Isn't there a limit to how long they have before they can sue me over the debt?

Yes, there are "time barred debts," and the **statute of limitations** varies according to the nature of the original debt and state law. Refer to the Federal Trade Commission's publication "Facts for Consumers: Time-Barred Debts" (www.ftc.gov/bcp/edu/pubs/consumer/alerts/alt144 .shtm). In addition, each state's attorney general typically has information about time limits on debt collection. For a directory of state offices, see the National Association of Attorneys General website (www.naag .org/attorneys_general.php).

For resource updates, visit this book's companion website at

▶ **www.GetLaw.net**

RESOURCES RECAP		
Bankruptcy		
	Resource	**Notes**
Primary Sources: Federal	▶ Cornell's Legal Information Institute, "Federal Rules of Bankruptcy Procedure" (2009): www.law.cornell.edu/rules/frbp/ ▶ Cornell's Legal Information Institute, "Title 11—Bankruptcy": www.law.cornell.edu/uscode/html/uscode11/usc_sup_01_11 .html	
Free Online Resources	▶ American Bar Association, "Bankruptcy Pros and Cons": www.abanet.org/publiced/practical/bankruptcy.html ▶ Consumer Bankruptcy Center (American Bankruptcy Institute): consumer.abiworld.org ▶ Cornell's Legal Information Institute, "Bankruptcy: An Overview": topics.law.cornell.edu/wex/Bankruptcy ▶ Federal Trade Commission, "Before You File for Personal Bankruptcy: Information about Credit Counseling and Debtor Education": www.ftc.gov/bcp/edu/pubs/consumer/credit/ cre41.shtm ▶ Federal Trade Commission, "Facts for Consumers: Knee Deep in Debt": www.ftc.gov/bcp/edu/pubs/consumer/credit/cre19 .shtm ▶ GPO Access, "Bankruptcy Abuse Prevention and Consumer Protection Act of 2005" (P.L. 109-8): frwebgate.access.gpo.gov/ cgi-bin/getdoc.cgi?dbname=109_cong_public_laws&docid= f:publ008.109.pdf ▶ Nolo, "Bankruptcy, Chapter 7, Chapter 13: Free Law Resources": www.nolo.com/resource.cfm/catID/462A9501-9B21-4E09- A08C5A7B8AF51A79/213/161/	

(Cont'd.)

RESOURCES RECAP *(Continued)*	

Bankruptcy		
	Resource	**Notes**
Free Online Resources *(Cont'd.)*	▶ United States Courts, "Bankruptcy Basics": www.uscourts.gov/ bankruptcycourts/bankruptcybasics .html ▶ United States Courts, "Bankruptcy Resources": www .uscourts.gov/bankruptcycourts/resources.html ▶ United States Courts, "Filing for Bankruptcy without an Attorney": www.uscourts.gov/bankruptcycourts/prose.html ▶ United States Courts, "Glossary": www.uscourts.gov/library/ glossary.html	Defines bankruptcy-related terms
Courts and Case Tracking	▶ PACER, Public Access to Court Electronic Records: www.pacer.gov ▶ PACER, Public Access to Court Electronic Records, "Case Management/Electronic Case Files (CM/ECF)": www.pacer.gov/documents/press.pdf ▶ PACER, Public Access to Court Electronic Records, "PACER Case Locator": www.pacer.gov/pcl.html ▶ United States Courts, "Court Locator": www.uscourts.gov/ courtlinks/ ▶ United States Courts, "Courts Accepting Electronic Filings": www.uscourts.gov/FederalCourts/CMECF/Courts.aspx ▶ U.S. Courts, "Judiciary Privacy Policy" (including for electronic case files): www.privacy.uscourts.gov	General information about the CM/ECF system
Do-It-Yourself Publications	▶ Bergman, Paul, and Sara Berman. 2008. *Represent Yourself in Court*. 6th ed. Berkeley, CA: Nolo. ▶ Elias, Stephen, Albin Renauer, and Robin Leonard. 2009. *How to File for Chapter 7 Bankruptcy*. 16th ed. Berkeley, CA: Nolo. ▶ Leonard, Robin, and Stephen Elias. 2010. *Chapter 13 Bankruptcy: Keep Your Property & Repay Debts Over Time*. 10th ed. Berkeley, CA: Nolo.	
Treatises and Authoritative Sources*	▶ *Collier Bankruptcy Practice Guide*, 15th ed. 2007– . New York: Mathew Bender. Six volumes with updates. ▶ *Collier Consumer Bankruptcy Practice Guide*, 1997– . New York: Mathew Bender. ▶ *Collier on Bankruptcy*, 16th ed. 2009– . New York: Mathew Bender. 26 volumes with updates. ▶ *Norton Bankruptcy Law and Practice*, 3rd ed. 2008/2009– . St. Paul, MN: Thomson West. 13 volumes with updates.	Procedural guide written for bankruptcy attorneys Transaction-based practice manual intended primarily for attorneys who are solo practitioners or in small firms Most comprehensive treatise on bankruptcy A combination of treatise and practice materials

*These sources are likely to be available only from law school libraries and larger public law libraries.

References

"Filing for Bankruptcy without an Attorney." 2009. Available: www.uscourts .gov/bankruptcycourts/prose.html (accessed August 10, 2010).

Ross, Catherine Sheldrick, Kirsti Nilsen, and Marie L. Radford. 2009. *Conducting the Reference Interview: A How-To-Do-It Manual for Librarians.* 2nd ed. New York: Neal-Schuman.

Employment and Unemployment

Introduction

Employment law can cover many aspects of our working life. This chapter will cover three major areas of employment law: employment discrimination, unemployment benefits, and workers' compensation. A fourth section will cover smaller miscellaneous areas in which people are likely to want legal information: wages and hours, wrongful termination, and privacy. This chapter will not tell you how to litigate cases of employment discrimination or how to file unemployment or workers' compensation claims; it will lead you to sources that will tell you how to do those things.

The chapter does not cover a large area known as "labor law" because traditionally this is the area of federal law that concerns the relations between unions and management. Because unions and management typically have their own attorneys, it is less likely that public librarian patrons will be in need of this type of law.

Getting Started

The following list of sources will provide you with a broad overview right from the beginning about employment law, including aspects not covered in this chapter:

▶ American Bar Association (ABA): www.abanet.org/publiced/practical/books/family_legal_guide/home.html

The prestigious ABA publishes a very wide-ranging and authoritative book titled the *ABA Family Legal Guide* that is available for download, or you can buy it in hard copy online.

▶ Cornell's Legal Information Institute: topics.law.cornell.edu/wex/table_labor

These webpages on labor and employment law provide a list of links to statutes for each state.

▶ Nolo: www.nolo.com/legal-encyclopedia/employee-rights/index.html
"Lighter," but still helpful, this portion of the Nolo website provides information about employee rights.

Alternatively, a good public library may have the following two books, or you can buy them online if you can afford to do so:

▶ Reps, Barbara K. 2007. *Your Rights in the Workplace*. 8th ed. Berkeley, CA: Nolo.

▶ Steingold, Fred S. 2009. *The Employer's Legal Handbook*. 9th ed. Berkeley, CA: Nolo.

For resource updates, visit this book's companion website at

▶ *www.GetLaw.net*

RESOURCES RECAP		
Getting Started		
	Resource	**Notes**
Free Online Resources	▶ Cornell's Legal Information Institute, "Labor and Employment Laws of the Fifty States, District of Columbia, and Puerto Rico": topics.law.cornell.edu/wex/table_labor ▶ Nolo, "Employee Rights in the Workplace: Free Law Resources": www.nolo.com/legal-encyclopedia/employee-rights/index.html	
Do-It-Yourself Publications	▶ American Bar Association. *ABA Family Legal Guide*. Available: www.abanet.org/publiced/practical/books/family_legal_guide/home.html. ▶ Reps, Barbara K. 2007. *Your Rights in the Workplace*. 8th ed. Berkeley, CA: Nolo. ▶ Steingold, Fred S. 2009. *The Employer's Legal Handbook*. 9th ed. Berkeley, CA: Nolo.	

Framework for Questions in Employment Discrimination

Like many areas of the law, employment discrimination is a vast area. It can cover the failure to hire, the failure to promote, and selective firing or layoffs, and it can cover quitting one's work due to discriminatory working conditions. It can involve federal law or state law or both. Federal, state, and local statutes or ordinances may prohibit discrimination based on race, gender, age, nationality, disability, sexual orientation, or pregnancy. Furthering an employment discrimination claim often involves administrative agencies such as the Equal Employment Opportunity Commission or counterparts on the state level and sometimes even the county or city level. Such claims may also often involve informal settlements, mediation, arbitration, or litigation.

While the workers' compensation and unemployment insurance systems discussed elsewhere in this chapter are specifically designed for citizens to navigate on their own, and while there are similar governmental agencies involved with discrimination claims, if you are pursuing a discrimination claim consider retaining counsel. Prior to this step you can find out a good deal about the law on your own.

Sketched in the following sections are sufficient resources for determining if under specific circumstances you have a discrimination claim. From those sources you should also be able to identify the governmental agencies that might be involved in furthering that claim or at least in preserving that claim prior to the running out of any time limits.

Finding Answers to Frequent Questions about Employment Discrimination

QUESTION: I feel I was not hired/not promoted/fired/forced to quit because of discrimination by my boss/supervisor/coworker based on my race/national origin/color/gender/age/disability/religion.

Unless there is good reason to do otherwise, start with federal law, then state law, then investigate your county and city for possible agencies focused on discrimination. If starting with federal law, start with the Equal Employment Opportunity Commission (EEOC), particularly its website (www.eeoc.gov/). More details about EEOC are given in this section's Resources Recap. Next, the Cornell Legal Information Institute, discussed previously and throughout this book, has several sections devoted to employment law and employment discrimination. Finally, listed in this chapter are a host of print resources that one may find in public libraries or, if need be, in a nearby law library.

After this overview, the researcher may already be deeply embroiled in federal primary sources, but if not, those main primary sources—specifically, federal statutes—are listed in the federal primary law section below. However, the researcher should not forget state law. State law may often provide alternative or additional recourse for those discriminated against in employment. Some state law sources, or places to go to find links to state law sources, are listed in the state primary law section in this chapter. One may have to be especially tenacious in searching out these sources. If there is not a state agency that is easily identified, start by looking at the state's attorney general or executive website or the state bar association. Finally, investigate the county or city in which the claim arises. Many counties and cities have "human rights commissions" or some similarly named agencies that may focus on discrimination in housing or employment or both.

Resources in Employment Discrimination

Most workplace discrimination cases involving federal law will involve the Equal Employment Opportunity Commission. The basic EEOC starting point is www.eeoc.gov/. The place to begin to see what sorts of practices are prohibited under federal law and to find links to the pertinent statutes and regulations is www.eeoc.gov/laws/practices/index.cfm.

The laws enforced by EEOC prohibit an employer from discriminating against an applicant or a current employee based on a person's color, race, national origin, sex (including pregnancy), age (40 or older), religion, disability, or genetic information. Retaliating against a person because he or she complained about discrimination, filed a charge of discrimination, or participated in an employment discrimination investigation or lawsuit is also illegal. For an online overview of discrimination law that includes at least a mention of state antidiscrimination law, you can go to Cornell's Legal Information Institute website (topics.law.cornell.edu/wex/Employment_discrimination).

Many secondary sources can be consulted on employment discrimination. Most of them are multivolume, scholarly sets usually available only in law libraries. Some one-volume books that might be useful are the following:

▶ Lewis, Harold S., Jr., and Elizabeth J. Norman. 2004. *Employment Discrimination Law and Practice*. 2nd ed. St. Paul, MN: Thomson West.

▶ Player, Mack A. 2004. *Federal Law of Employment Discrimination in a Nutshell*. 5th ed. St. Paul, MN: Thomson West.

The larger, multivolume sets include the following:

▶ Larson, Lek K. 1994– . *Employment Discrimination*. 2nd ed. New York: Mathew Bender.

▶ Lindemann, Barbara, and Paul Grossman. 1996. *Employment Discrimination Law*. 3rd ed. St. Paul, MN: Thomson West.

Some additional print guides regarding specific discriminatory practices include the following:

▶ Coleman, John J. 1991– . *Disability Discrimination in Employment: Law and Litigation*. St. Paul, MN: West (Clark Boardman Callaghan).

▶ Eglit, Howard C. 1993– . *Age Discrimination*. 2nd ed. St. Paul, MN: West (Clark Boardman Callaghan).

Primary Sources: Federal Law of Employment Discrimination

Title VII of the Civil Rights Act of 1964, 42 U.S.C. § 2000e et seq., is the primary federal statute that prohibits discrimination on the basis of race, color, religion, sex, national origin, age, or disability. The Equal Employment Opportunity Commission EEOC is the federal agency that enforces Title VII. The EEOC website (www.eeoc.gov/) is a good starting point for an explanation of the law as well as for links to the law itself. For a starting point for the statutes and regulations, go to this portion of the EEOC website: www.eeoc.gov/laws/index.cfm.

Another site about discrimination is provided by Cornell's Legal Information Institute (topics.law.cornell.edu/wex/Employment_ discrimination). This site provides a good jumping off point for both an explanation of the law and the actual text of the federal statutes concerning discrimination. You will see two tabs, "Overview" and "Resources." For the links to the statutes, click on the "Resources" tab.

Primary Sources: State Statutes in Employment Discrimination

The best access on the Internet to a comprehensive list of state statutes, regulations, and agencies is the Washburn University School of Law's site (www.washlaw.edu/). While it may not get you directly to state statutes on discrimination, it remains the best place to begin your search if you are not already familiar with your state's websites for statutes and regulations. Once you are at the homepage, look on the right-hand navigation column and you will see "States." Look for your state under that heading. Another resource for linking to state law is Justia: www.justia .com/index.html. Again, scroll down the page a little and you will find "US States." A third site that lists links to all the statutory and administrative codes for all of the states is www.re-quest.net/g2g/codes/state/ index.htm#OK. Like many sites, some of the links are outdated, but with some persistence these links will get you to the codes you need for your state. Then it will be a matter of subject searching for discrimination and its specific subtypes—racial, age, gender, etc.

Do-It-Yourself Publications in Employment Discrimination

Nolo is the champion of "self-help" legal publications. Here are four that have something to say about employment discrimination:

▶ England, Deborah C. 2009. *The Essential Guide to Handling Workplace Harassment and Discrimination*. Berkeley, CA: Nolo.

▶ Guerin, Lisa, and Amy DelPo. 2009. *The Essential Guide to Federal Employment Laws*. 2nd ed. Berkeley, CA: Nolo.

▶ Reps, Barbara K. 2007. *Your Rights in the Workplace*. 8th ed. Berkeley, CA: Nolo.

▶ Steingold, Fred S. 2009. *The Employer's Legal Handbook*. 9th ed. Berkeley, CA: Nolo.

Some additional emerging issues may arise in the library as legal questions concerning workplace discrimination. For instance, increasingly there are fears that employers may discriminate in hiring, firing, or promotion decisions based on genetic information. On this issue, start with the National Workrights Institute's page on genetic discrimination (www.workrights.org/issue_genetic.html).

Discriminating against someone based on their off-site lifestyle also arises from time to time as a legal question. On this issue, start with

Finding the Answers to Legal Questions

For resource updates, visit this book's companion website at

▶ **www.GetLaw.net**

the National Workrights Institute's page on lifestyle discrimination (www.workrights.org/issue_lifestyle.html). For a thorough paper on the many aspects of potential "lifestyle" discrimination, begin at www.workrights.org/issue_lifestyle/ldbrief2.pdf.

RESOURCES RECAP		
Employment Discrimination		
	Resource	**Notes**
Primary Sources: Federal	▶ Title VII of the Civil Rights Act of 1964, 2 U.S.C. § 1331 et seq.	
Primary Sources: State	▶ Washburn University School of Law: www.washlaw.edu/	For locating individual states' statutes See Appendix 3 in this book to locate an individual state's statutory code online.
Free Online Resources	▶ Cornell's Legal Information Institute, "Employment Discrimination: An Overview": topics.law.cornell.edu/wex/Employment_discrimination ▶ Equal Employment Opportunity Commission: www.eeoc.gov/ ▶ National Workrights Institute, "Learn More about Genetic Discrimination": www.workrights.org/issue_genetic.html ▶ National Workrights Institute, "Learn More about Lifestyle Discrimination": www.workrights.org/issue_lifestyle.html ▶ National Workrights Institute, "Lifestyle Discrimination: Employer Control of Legal Off Duty Employee Activities": www.workrights.org/issue_lifestyle/ldbrief2.pdf	
Do-It-Yourself Publications	▶ England, Deborah C. 2009. *The Essential Guide to Handling Workplace Harassment and Discrimination.* Berkeley, CA: Nolo. ▶ Guerin, Lisa, and Amy DelPo. 2009. *The Essential Guide to Federal Employment Laws.* 2nd ed. Berkeley, CA: Nolo. ▶ Reps, Barbara K. 2007. *Your Rights in the Workplace.* 8th ed. Berkeley, CA: Nolo. ▶ Steingold, Fred S. 2009. *The Employer's Legal Handbook.* 9th ed. Berkeley, CA: Nolo.	
Treatises and Authoritative Sources	▶ Coleman, John J. 1991– . *Disability Discrimination in Employment: Law and Litigation.* St. Paul, MN: West (Clark Boardman Callaghan). ▶ Eglit, Howard C. 1993– . *Age Discrimination.* 2nd ed. St. Paul, MN: West (Clark Boardman Callaghan). ▶ Larson, Lek K. 1994– . *Employment Discrimination.* 2nd ed. New York: Mathew Bender. ▶ Lewis, Harold S., Jr., and Elizabeth J. Norman. 2004. *Employment Discrimination Law and Practice.* 2nd ed. St. Paul, MN: Thomson West.	

(Cont'd.)

EMPLOYMENT DISCRIMINATION *(Continued)*		
Bankruptcy		
	Resource	**Notes**
Treatises and Authoritative Sources *(Cont'd.)*	▶ Lindemann, Barbara, and Paul Grossman. 1996. *Employment Discrimination Law.* 3rd ed. St. Paul, MN: Thomson West. ▶ Player, Mack A. 2004. *Federal Law of Employment Discrimination in a Nutshell.* 5th ed. St. Paul, MN: Thomson West.	

Framework for Questions in Unemployment Compensation

Unemployment compensation, also known as unemployment insurance (UI) and as "unemployment benefits," concerns payments made by the government to people who are unemployed. While eligibility for benefits is largely determined by each state, unemployment compensation is actually a joint enterprise of the federal government and the individual states. For the basic framework of who gets benefits and who does not, you will look to state law, specifically state statutes, regulations, and decisions concerning the unemployment system for an individual state. But to get an overview of this area of law in general and to get an easy entry to the departments in each state that administer these benefits, it is best to start at the federal level.

One caution is particularly important: most states will not allow someone to draw *both* unemployment benefits *and* workers' compensation. Often when you are hurt on the job you become unemployed for a period of time, and too often people think that it is okay to draw both types of benefits. This is usually not allowed, and trying to do so will mean having to pay back some or all of the benefits and possibly facing charges of fraud.

Finding Answers to Frequent Questions about Unemployment Compensation

QUESTION: I quit my job and everyone tells me that because of that I cannot get unemployment benefits. Is this true?

Each state will have a slightly different answer to this question, but it bears investigating because in many states you can qualify for unemployment benefits even if you quit your job, depending on the reason. The statutes and regulations in the state in which you were employed will tell you whether you might qualify. Start by locating the department or commission that is in charge of granting or denying unemployment benefits for your state. In some "gray areas" you may also be guided by court and administrative decisions concerning unemployment benefits for your state.

> QUESTION: I got fired when a new manager came on and didn't like me and everyone tells me that because I got fired I cannot get unemployment benefits. Is this true?

Again, each state will have a slightly different answer to this question, but it bears investigating because in many states you can qualify for unemployment benefits even if you get fired, depending on the reason. The statutes and regulations in the state in which you were employed will tell you whether you might qualify. Start by locating the department or commission that is in charge of granting or denying unemployment benefits for your state. In some "gray areas" you may also be guided by court and administrative decisions concerning unemployment benefits for your state.

Resources in Unemployment Compensation

For a general online overview from the federal vantage point, start at www.dol.gov/dol/topic/unemployment-insurance/index.htm. For an overview of the general process in the states to granting or denying unemployment benefits, start at workforcesecurity.doleta.gov/unemploy/uifactsheet.asp. For a clickable map that will help you locate the agency or department or commission in charge of unemployment benefits for individual states, start at workforcesecurity.doleta.gov/unemploy/. Or a bigger, more easily used map to get you to your state's agency for unemployment is at www.servicelocator.org/OWSLinks.asp. For advocacy and up-to-date news about developments in unemployment insurance law, start at www.nelp.org/site/issues/category/unemployment_insurance/.

Beware: the recent recession created high unemployment and spawned a large number of shyster sites on the web, sites that say they will help people apply for unemployment benefits but are really just selling the unemployed products of various sorts. While there are millions of reputable ".com" sites on the web, we recommend you prefer ".gov" and ".org" sites when looking for information and help with unemployment (or for that matter, help in many areas of the law).

For the most comprehensive and "free" source, the in-print *CCH Unemployment Insurance Reporter* is the place to start. It will be found only in big law libraries. You can access it through subscription online databases at some libraries, but these will be few and far between. We recommend instead the "free" web sources listed here or accessible through these sources.

Primary Sources: Federal Statutes about Unemployment Compensation

While unemployment compensation is a joint federal–state program, the federal statutes and regulations are not much assistance to the individual who is seeking unemployment benefits. However, if one's interests are less practical, the place to find entry into the federal statutes and regulations is the U.S. Department of Labor's page (workforcesecurity.doleta .gov/unemploy/laws.asp#FederalLegislation).

Primary Sources: State Statutes about Unemployment Compensation

A simple "X unemployment insurance compensation" query in Google, with your state's name in place of the "X," will probably get you to the website for the agency that administers unemployment in your state and links to the statutes. For example, we entered "Minnesota unemployment insurance compensation" in Google and the first result was this one: www.uimn.org/. This is the government site for unemployment insurance in Minnesota; it contains information for employers as well as applicants for unemployment. A link, "UI Law," gets you to links for all the statutes and regulations pertaining to UI in Minnesota.

A similar search for North Carolina yielded as the first result a link to the Employment Security Commission of North Carolina: www.ncesc .com/default.aspx. This is the agency in the state that determines UI benefits. While it did not have easy links to the law itself, it did have ample information for employers and for applicants, including information about how to file a claim. Try it for your state; it should work to get you to the site you need.

Do-It-Yourself Publications in Unemployment Compensation

Nolo is the biggest name and publisher in self-help legal publications. It has a book published in 2007 that covers many "employee rights" issues, including unemployment compensation:

▶ Guerin, Lisa, and Amy DelPo. 2009. *The Essential Guide to Federal Employment Laws.* 2nd ed. Berkeley, CA: Nolo.

▶ Reps, Barbara K. 2007. *Your Rights in the Workplace.* 8th ed. Berkeley, CA: Nolo.

For resource updates, visit this book's companion website at

▶ *www.GetLaw.net*

RESOURCES RECAP		
Unemployment Compensation		
	Resource	**Notes**
Primary Sources: Federal	▶ U.S. Department of Labor, "Federal Legislation": workforce security.doleta.gov/unemploy/laws.asp#FederalLegislation	
Primary Sources: State	▶ Washburn University School of Law: www.washlaw.edu	For locating individual states' statutes See Appendix 3 in this book to locate an individual state's statutory code online.

(Cont'd.)

RESOURCES RECAP (Continued)		
Unemployment Compensation		
	Resource	**Notes**
Free Online Resources	▶ National Employment Law Project, "Unemployment Insurance": www.nelp.org/site/issues/category/unemployment_insurance/ ▶ Nolo, "Employee Rights in the Workplace: Free Law Resources: www.nolo.com/legal-encyclopedia/employee-rights/index.html ▶ Nolo, "When You Are Entitled to Employment Compensation: Free Legal Information": www.nolo.com/legal-encyclopedia/article-29898.html ▶ U.S. Department of Labor, "Unemployment Insurance (UI)": www.dol.gov/dol/topic/unemployment-insurance/index.htm ▶ U.S. Department of Labor, Employment and Training Administration, "State Unemployment Insurance Benefits": workforcesecurity.doleta.gov/unemploy/uifactsheet.asp ▶ U.S. Department of Labor, Employment and Training Administration, "Unemployment Insurance": workforcesecurity.doleta.gov/unemploy/	
Do-It-Yourself Publications	▶ Guerin, Lisa and Amy DelPo. 2009. *The Essential Guide to Federal Employment Laws*. 2nd ed. Berkeley, CA: Nolo. ▶ Reps, Barbara K. 2007. *Your Rights in the Workplace*. 8th ed. Berkeley, CA: Nolo.	
Treatises and Authoritative Sources	▶ *CCH Unemployment Insurance Reporter*	Limited availability through large law libraries or online subscription databases

Nolo also has an excellent "free" website (www.nolo.com/legal-encyclopedia/employee-rights/index.html) that provides information about employee rights. A specific page within that source has information about unemployment compensation: www.nolo.com/legal-encyclopedia/article-29898.html.

Framework for Questions in Workers' Compensation

Workers' compensation arose in part as an effort to preclude workers from suing their employers for injuries or illnesses arising from one's job. Thus, if one is injured on the job, most of the time the only recourse is through the workers' compensation system. This means that a "tort" suit, or a personal injury suit, is usually not available to those who are injured on the job. Exceptions to this rule exist, but they are rare. Therefore, much like unemployment compensation, although there is a federal component of workers' compensation, most of what is of interest to most injured workers and employers will be on the state level: state statutes, regulations, and decisions.

The process of getting workers' compensation benefits will therefore vary in all the states. It is essential that someone seeking those benefits track down the agency, the statutes, and the regulations in one's state. Usually, getting those benefits does not involve long and drawn out litigation, but often there will be administrative hearings and appeals.

Even with the variety between the states, usually if you are accidentally injured or develop an occupational disease, workers' compensation will be available. The injury must arise out of and be "in the course of" your employment. For instance, one gray area is if you slip and fall in the icy parking lot of your employer on the way to or from work. Some will argue that is "in the course" of employment; others will say it is not. The "course of employment" requirement will also likely exclude coverage of injuries received from crimes, commuting, or roughhousing at work. Independent contractors will also likely be excluded from coverage as will some employees of very small businesses.

The "benefits" one may receive usually include reasonable medical expenses and death benefits as well as "lost-time benefits" due to temporary or permanent disability and partial or total disability. Again, the only way to find out short of hiring an attorney is to find the agencies and laws in your state pertaining to these benefits.

One caution is particularly important and bears repeating: most states will not allow someone to draw *both* workers' compensation benefits *and* unemployment benefits. Often when you are hurt on the job you become unemployed for a period of time, and too often people think that it is okay to draw both types of benefits. This is usually not allowed, and trying to do so will mean having to pay back some or all of the benefits and possibly facing charges of fraud.

Finding Answers to Frequent Questions about Workers' Compensation

QUESTION: I fell off scaffolding at my job and twisted my ankle; the next day I couldn't get to work. What can I do now?

This "classic" injury on the job is most likely covered by workers' compensation, though exceptions always exist. The first thing to do is to notify the employer of your injury and most likely to seek immediate medical care.

QUESTION: I've been typing for my job for the past 20 years and now I've developed problems in my hands and wrists. What can I do?

These types of "repetitive motion injuries" are increasingly recognized as compensable under most workers' compensation systems. You can apply and find out, or you can get some sense of your chances by doing some of the research mentioned later in this chapter.

QUESTION: I've been under so much stress at work that I developed digestive problems. Can I get workers' comp for that?

The reach of compensable injuries or illnesses has generally expanded over recent years, so the answer is, "It depends." You will have to do some research to find out what is likely to happen in the state in which you apply for workers' compensation.

Resources in Workers' Compensation

It is most likely that workers' compensation will be handled by an agency of state government, unless you are a federal employee. Fortunately, a comprehensive website (www.comp.state.nc.us/ncic/pages/all50.htm) lists the workers' compensation agency websites for all 50 states. This is probably the best place to begin if you are seeking workers' compensation.

Alternatively, a simple "X workers' compensation statutes" query in Google, with your state's name in place of the "X," *may* get you to the website for the agency that administers unemployment in your state. Profit-making companies and firms again have entered the picture, so be careful what links you decide to depend on. As noted regarding unemployment compensation, many ".com" sites say the site will help you get benefits but are essentially an advertisement for services or products. While this is not a bad thing in itself, beware of what you are getting into if you explore these sites and enter your name and social security number and other personal information. Again, we recommend you stick to ".gov" and ".org" sites.

Primary Sources: Federal Statutes in Workers' Compensation

If you are a federal employee, you may qualify for workers' compensation through a federal program. For that, check here: www.dol.gov/dol/topic/workcomp/index.htm. Otherwise, most workers' compensation questions are going to be resolved in each state.

Primary Sources: State Statutes in Workers' Compensation

The website with a comprehensive list of links to each state's workers' compensation agency is www.comp.state.nc.us/ncic/pages/all50.htm, and it is the place to begin to track down the appropriate statutes and regulations.

Do-It-Yourself Publications about Workers' Compensation

If you are lucky, an enterprising lawyer or writer may have published a separate book on how to qualify for workers' compensation in your state. Most likely, however, no one has published such a book. You may find useful the following three more "scholarly" books that a large public library, a law library, or an academic library in your area may have. While these sources are not exactly short, self-help books for laypeople, they will help get you started:

- ▶ Hood, Jack. B., Benjamin A. Hardy, and Harold S. Lewis. 2005. *Workers' Compensation and Employee Protection Laws in a Nutshell*. 4th ed. St. Paul, MN: West Group.

- ▶ Jasper, Margaret C. 2008. *Workers' Compensation Law*. 2nd ed. New York: Oceana.

- ▶ Larson, Arthur, and Lex K. Larson. 1952– . *The Law of Workmen's Compensation*. New York: Mathew Bender.

For resource updates, visit this book's companion website at

▶ *www.GetLaw.net*

RESOURCES RECAP		
Workers' Compensation		
	Resource	Notes
Primary Sources: Federal	▶ U.S. Department of Labor, "Workers' Compensation": www.dol.gov/dol/topic/workcomp/index.htm	
Primary Sources: State	▶ State workers' compensation statutes: www.comp.state.nc.us/ncic/pages/all50.htm ▶ Washburn University School of Law: www.washlaw .edu	For locating individual states' statutes See Appendix 3 in this book to locate an individual state's statutory code online.
Free Online Resources	▶ Links to workers' compensation agency websites for all 50 states: www.comp.state.nc.us/ncic/pages/all50.htm	
Treatises and Authoritative Sources	▶ Hood, Jack. B., Benjamin A. Hardy, and Harold S. Lewis. 2005. *Workers' Compensation and Employee Protection Laws in a Nutshell*. 4th ed. St. Paul, MN: West Group. ▶ Jasper, Margaret C. 2008. *Workers' Compensation Law*. 2nd ed. New York: Oceana. ▶ Larson, Arthur, and Lex K. Larson. 1952– . *The Law of Workmen's Compensation*. New York: Mathew Bender.	

Framework for Other Employment Law Questions

At least three other areas of concern frequently raise legal questions that can be researched in a public library: (1) wages and hours, (2) wrongful discharge, and (3) privacy. Very broadly speaking, there is a good deal of legal protection for workers regarding wages and hours; there is far less legal recourse for workers regarding discharge and invasions of one's "privacy" at the workplace. The following books provide general information about these areas and others, but begin from two different vantage points—the employee's and the employer's:

▶ Reps, Barbara K. 2007. *Your Rights in the Workplace*. 8th ed. Berkeley, CA: Nolo.

▶ Steingold, Fred S. 2009. *The Employer's Legal Handbook*. 9th ed. Berkeley, CA: Nolo.

For quick, thumbnail summaries of some of the areas of workplace "rights," begin with the Nolo legal encyclopedia on that topic (www.nolo.com/legal-encyclopedia/employee-rights/index.html).

Wages and Hours

Analogous to the EEOC's role in enforcing antidiscrimination statutes, the U.S. Department of Labor has a role in enforcing many of the laws concerning wages and hours. Starting at the U.S. Department of Labor's Wage and Hour Division's website (www.dol.gov/whd/index .htm) is a good idea. You can also be helped by DOL's "advisor" site on wages and hours (www.dol.gov/elaws/flsa.htm).

A good collection point is Cornell Legal Information Institute's pages on labor and employment law (topics.law.cornell.edu/wex/table_labor). This site will also provide you a list of links to statutes and relevant agencies for each state concerning wages and hours. Briefly, issues that arise regarding wages and hours can include minimum wage, overtime pay, break time, meal break time, and travel time. Begin with the federal statute titled the Fair Labor Standards Act, FLSA, 29 U.S.C. § 201 et seq., which is available from the government site frwebgate.access.gpo .gov/cgi-bin/usc.cgi?ACTION=BROWSE&TITLE=29USCC8& PDFS=YES and from the Cornell site www.law.cornell.edu/uscode/ 29/ch8.html. Keep in mind, however, that one's state likely has its own statutes pertaining to some or all of these issues. Many states set the minimum wage level higher than the federal level. Search your state statutes beginning at the Washburn site www.washlaw.edu/uslaw/ index.html. Two print sources may be worth tracking down:

▶ Kearns, Ellen C. ed. 1999– . *The Fair Labor Standards Act*. Washington, DC: Bureau of National Affairs.

▶ Ossip, Michael J., and Robert M. Hale. Eds. 2006. *The Family and Medical Leave Act*. Washington DC: Bureau of National Affairs.

Wrongful Discharge

As for "wrongful discharge," the legal phrase concerning a claim that a person was fired for the wrong reasons, you must first determine what that wrong reason might have been. Generally speaking, workers working without a contract or a union-negotiated collective bargaining agreement are considered "employees at will" and they can be fired for any reason or for no reason at all. This is a harsh rule but it is a long-standing one in our society. Due to this rule, proving a "wrongful discharge" is an uphill battle. If discrimination was the cause of the job separation, then rather than a "wrongful discharge" case one is more likely to have a discrimination claim, as discussed previously.

One place to begin to find out about the possibilities of a "wrongful discharge" claim is this website from the Worker Rights Institute (www.workrights.org/issue_discharge.html). Two print sources that you may find in a public library or a law library are these:

▶ Holloway, William J., and Michael J. Leech. 1993. *Employment Termination: Rights and Remedies.* 2nd ed. Washington, DC: Bureau of National Affairs.

▶ Westman, Daniel P., and Nancy M. Modesitt. 2004– . *Whistleblowing: The Law of Retaliatory Discharge.* 2nd ed. Washington, DC: BNA Books.

Workplace Privacy

Your right to "privacy" at your workplace is even more problematic. In general, the workplace is the "property" of the employer, but governmental employees may have some protection for privacy afforded by Constitutional law. The majority of people who work for a private employer will not have this protection and therefore will have little "expectation of privacy" sufficient to protect a person's privacy at the workplace. This is generally true regarding an employee's work computer and bodily fluids for drug testing. Furthermore, employee monitoring, what others might call privacy invasion, can take many forms: camera surveillance, microphones in the workplace, and more commonly monitoring of phone calls, e-mail, and computer use.

While the news is generally not good for an employee seeking to have "privacy" at work, some organizations are working on the issue and may lead you to legal resources. Here are five organizations and some of the specific websites they provide. They are listed in the order of those providing the most focused and complete information on privacy in the workplace:

- National Workrights Institute: www.workrights.org/. For drug testing, start here: www.workrights.org/issue_drugtest.html. For employee monitoring, start at www.workrights.org/issue_ electronic.html. To get right to some of the law in the area, start at www.workrights.org/issue_electronic/em_common_law.html.

- Workplace Fairness: www.workplacefairness.org/. For privacy, start here: www.workplacefairness.org/sc/privacy.php.

- Privacy Rights Clearinghouse: www.privacyrights.org/about _us.htm#contact. For privacy, start here: www.privacyrights .org/fs/fs7-work.htm.

- The American Civil Liberties Union (www.aclu.org/) covers many areas of the law, but employment law is not directly one of them. Many of the topics with which the organization is concerned, however, do have ties to issues in the workplace, so it is a place to investigate.

Do not forget that the ACLU has individual state organizations in many states and those state organizations, specifically starting with the websites, may provide some leads to legal assistance.

For resource updates, visit this book's companion website at

▶ *www.GetLaw.net*

Another organization, 9 to 5, the National Association of Working Women, potentially can provide information on privacy in the workplace, though the current website (www.9to5.org/) is still a little light on the issue. These areas, particularly wrongful discharge and workplace privacy, are in flux. Different states may provide more or less protection to workers in one or some of these areas of the law. Additionally, a creative,

RESOURCES RECAP		
Other Employment Law Questions		
Wages and Hours	**Resource**	**Notes**
Primary Sources: Federal	▶ Fair Labor Standards Act, FLSA, 29 U.S.C. § 201 et seq.	
Primary Sources: State	▶ Washburn University School of Law: www.washlaw.edu	For locating individual states' statutes See Appendix 3 in this book to locate an individual state's statutory code online.
Free Online Resources	▶ Cornell's Legal Information Institute, "Labor and Employment Laws of the Fifty States, District of Columbia, and Puerto Rico": topics.law.cornell.edu/wex/table_labor ▶ Cornell's Legal Information Institute, "U.S. Code: Chapter 8—Fair Labor Standards": www.law.cornell.edu/uscode/29/ch8.html ▶ GPO Access, "United States Code: Chapter 8—Fair Labor Standards" (Fair Labor Standards Act, FLSA, 29 U.S.C. § 201 et seq.): frwebgate.access.gpo.gov/cgi-bin/usc.cgi?ACTION=BROWSE&TITLE=29USCC8&PDFS=YES ▶ U.S. Department of Labor, "Fair Labor Standards Act Advisor": www.dol.gov/elaws/flsa.htm ▶ U.S. Department of Labor, Wage and Hour Division: www.dol.gov/whd/index.htm	
Treatises and Authoritative Sources	▶ Kearns, Ellen C. ed. 1999– . *The Fair Labor Standards Act.* Washington, DC: Bureau of National Affairs. ▶ Ossip, Michael J., and Robert M. Hale, eds. 2006. *The Family and Medical Leave Act.* Washington, DC: Bureau of National Affairs.	
Wrongful Discharge	**Resource**	**Notes**
Treatises and Authoritative Sources	▶ Holloway, William J., and Michael J. Leech. 1993. *Employment Termination: Rights and Remedies.* 2nd ed. Washington, DC: Bureau of National Affairs. ▶ Westman, Daniel P., and Nancy M. Modesitt. 2004– . *Whistleblowing: The Law of Retaliatory Discharge.* 2nd ed. Washington, DC: BNA Books.	

(Cont'd.)

RESOURCES RECAP *(Continued)*		
Other Employment Law Questions		
Workplace Privacy	**Resource**	**Notes**
Free Online Resources	▶ American Civil Liberties Union: www.aclu.org ▶ National Workrights Institute: www.workrights.org ▶ National Workrights Institute, "Electronic Monitoring in the Workplace: Common Law and Federal Statutory Protection": www.workrights.org/issue_electronic/em_common_law.html ▶ National Workrights Institute, "Learn More about Drug Testing": www.workrights.org/issue_drugtest.html ▶ National Workrights Institute, "Learn More about Electronic Monitoring": www.workrights.org/issue_electronic.html ▶ Privacy Rights Clearinghouse: www.privacyrights.org/about_us.htm#contact ▶ Privacy Rights Clearinghouse, "Fact Sheet 7: Workplace Privacy and Employee Monitoring": www.privacyrights.org/fs/fs7-work.htm ▶ Workplace Fairness: www.workplacefairness.org/ ▶ Workplace Fairness, "Privacy": www.workplacefairness.org/sc/privacy.php	

bright, enthusiastic attorney or freelance researcher may be able to make a difference too.

Conclusion

This chapter has concerned three specific areas of employment law: employment discrimination, unemployment compensation, and workers' compensation. It has also covered three smaller or developing areas: wages and hours, wrongful discharge, and workplace privacy. These areas encompass only a portion of employment law, but if your research concerns one of these areas, the resources provided here should help you find if not the final answer to your questions at least a good start to finding it.

Criminal Law

Framework for Questions in This Area of Law

This chapter focuses on four subtopics in criminal law: the rights of the accused, crimes and criminal codes, criminal procedure, and criminal defenses. In seeking information about criminal law, it is easy to become overwhelmed. Many disciplines besides the law are concerned with crimes—criminals, criminal psychology, criminology, the sociology of crime, the history of the criminal law, and more. Though this literature is of interest, and sometimes of particular application to criminal law, questions about it are beyond both the scope of this chapter and of "legal research" generally. The researcher looking for this material will therefore need to consult other sources.

But even the researcher who focuses on the narrower topic of "criminal law" per se is still faced with a big area. It involves constitutional law, statutory law, court rules, and case law interpreting constitutions, statutes, and court rules. Criminal law research can also involve administrative law, such as how the department of corrections in a particular jurisdiction is to be run. Questions in criminal law also can involve federal, state, local, and tribal law.

The basic framework for questions in criminal law therefore, except on the most general level, first involves the question of jurisdiction. The researcher must decide whether the area of interest involves federal or state law. At times the researcher will need both federal and state law, but an organized search will focus first on one jurisdiction and then the other. The materials in this chapter are therefore always organized with this in mind, separating out in most instances federal and state materials.

However, the person seeking information about criminal law must also be aware of the limitations of the research. If you are charged with a crime, you should first get a lawyer if at all possible. Usually, if you are charged with a felony, an attorney will be appointed if you cannot afford to pay one. In any event, getting representation should be the first priority, not legal research.

This chapter assumes you are interested in criminal law for less immediate reasons: either you want information about criminal law for academic, journalistic, or other broad purposes or you or someone you know has been charged with a crime and you want to know more about the criminal justice process or about the charges, their consequences, or defenses to those charges. Nothing in this chapter should be interpreted to be providing legal advice to anyone, especially those charged with a crime.

Getting Started

Criminal law is a major division in the law, the other side of which is civil law. Most of this book concerns aspects of civil law, and this chapter is the only one focused solely on criminal law. In some ways, these two huge areas are very separate provinces. If you have some familiarity with civil law, do not assume everything is the same in criminal law. Often there are separate rules of procedure for criminal cases and for civil cases; some jurisdictions even have separate trial courts and appellate courts for civil cases and criminal cases. If you are unfamiliar with these different provinces, you will need to immerse yourself for awhile in learning some general concepts in criminal law.

Where you start depends on your situation and your experience. Usually it is best to start in secondary sources. An entire chapter is devoted to this topic in this book, but here are some specific suggestions.

If you have access to a large public law library, start with one of the two national legal encyclopedias, *Corpus Juris Secundum* (*CJS*) or *American Jurisprudence 2d* (*AmJur2d*), specifically the volumes in those sets on criminal law and then possibly the volumes on constitutional law. Then you might track down some of the treatises that are listed in the Resources Recap at the end of this chapter. In general, the secondary sources in print on criminal law will be more reliable than the free online sources.

Using secondary sources helps you develop a sense of whether your topic involves federal or state law, what other finer grained concepts you need to research, and what more specialized vocabulary you can use for further searching in indexes or search engines. You can then begin to find online the primary sources—statutes, court opinions, regulations—that most concern you. Look for the criminal code, the criminal rules of procedure, evidence rules, and other such material for the jurisdiction involved.

To help you with this process, the "Finding Answers" section is organized around four major subtopics in criminal law: rights of the accused, particular crimes or offenses, procedural law, and defenses. In each area ask yourself whether you need state or federal law; if you need both state and federal law, decide which type to seek first.

Finding Answers to Frequent Questions

Rights of the Accused

QUESTION: My 17-year-old son was stopped for speeding and the police searched the car's glove compartment and found a bottle of beer. Can they do that?

QUESTION: I was watching *Cops* the other night and when they arrested a guy they did not read him his Miranda rights like they do on *Law & Order*. Where do those rights to an attorney and to remain silent come from?

These questions all raise issues of the rights that people have in relation to the government, either federal or state, and the government can act through only its agents or employees—the police officer, the prosecutor, the administrative rule maker. To investigate what rights people have in relation to the government, you will usually begin with constitutional law. It may be federal constitutional law or state constitutional law, or both. Often in researching the questions of rights, it is best to explore both jurisdictions.

If you are new to this area of the law, start with secondary sources, such as encyclopedias and treatises. You will learn that most of these rights on the federal level begin with the original Bill of Rights to the U.S. Constitution, the first ten amendments. If you identify a specific amendment that pertains to your question, such as the Fourth Amendment's protections against unlawful search and seizure, then you can focus your search in the secondary and primary sources that concern that amendment. You will also find that just reading the fourth amendment will not be terribly helpful without reading some current court cases, particularly from the U.S. Supreme Court, concerning the breadth of protection provided by that amendment.

Most of the time you will also want to explore the constitutional protections given by the constitution in the state in which your question arises. Often state constitutions can provide additional rights to those granted under the federal constitution or can provide more far-reaching protection of the rights originally granted under the federal constitution. In either instance, you will want to explore your state's constitution.

After consulting some secondary sources, usually the most efficient way to find what rights exist and the breadth of those rights is to search the annotated United States Code for federal constitutional rights and the annotated statutory code for your state. These annotated codes will not only provide the text of the constitution in which you are interested but also provide citations to court cases that have interpreted the provisions of that constitution. You can also search in the case digests (further explained in the legal research chapter) for the jurisdiction in which you are interested to find citations to opinions that have delineated the rights of the accused.

Remember, neither annotated codes nor digests are available on the "free" web, though they are available through Westlaw or Lexis. If you begin or turn to the web for help in finding legal information about the rights of the accused, consult the Cornell Legal Information Institute's pages on criminal law and procedure (topics.law.cornell.edu/wex/category/criminal_law_and_procedure). Finally, if you have access to a law library you may find the following treatises helpful, among others you are likely to find there:

▶ Cook, Joseph G. 1996. *Constitutional Rights of the Accused.* 3rd ed. St. Paul, MN: West (Clark Boardman Callaghan).

▶ LaFave, Wayne R. 2004. *Search and Seizure: A Treatise on the Fourth Amendment.* 4th ed. St. Paul, MN: West Group.

▶ Rudenstein, David S., Peter C. Erlinder, and David C. Thomas. 1990. *Criminal Constitutional Law.* New York: Mathew Bender.

Crimes and Criminal Codes

QUESTION: My father has been charged with assault. Is that a felony or a misdemeanor?

QUESTION: I read that kidnapping is a federal crime. Why isn't it a state crime?

Crimes, or specific offenses, are creations of statutory law. Legislatures decide what acts "against the people" will be considered crimes. Statutes therefore define what crimes are punishable in a particular jurisdiction, what the degrees of those crimes will be, what elements must be proved to convict someone of a particular crime, whether the crime is a misdemeanor or a felony, and often what punishments may be given for convictions of specific crimes. In other words, if you are researching about specific crimes or offenses you will have to research in the statutory codes. You can do this, as you know, in print in annotated codes or on the free web, usually on each state's legislature's website.

If you are researching federal crimes, begin with Title 18 of the United States Code. If all you want are the statutes themselves, you can find them easily online either at the GPO Access website, specifically www.gpoaccess.gov/uscode/browse.html, or at the Cornell site (www.law.cornell.edu/uscode/718/usc_sup_01_18.html). But if you want citations to cases that have interpreted these statutes, start in Title 18 in the United States Code Annotated or the United States Code Service, the two annotated codes discussed often in this book, particularly in Chapter 3. These codes are available in print and through Westlaw or Lexis.

If you are researching about a particular crime or offense in your state, you will need to research the criminal code for your state, which is usually a part of the overall statutory code for your state. If you do not know the volume or title number for your state's criminal code, start with the Cornell Legal Information Institute's list of links to each state's criminal code (topics.law.cornell.edu/wex/table_criminal_code). Finally, if you have access to a law library you may find these treatises helpful, among others you are likely to find there:

▶ LaFave, Wayne R., and Austin W. Scott, Jr. 1986. *Substantive Criminal Law*. 2nd ed. St. Paul, MN: West Group.

▶ Torcia, Charles E. 1993. *Wharton's Criminal Law*. 15th ed. St. Paul, MN: West (Clark Boardman Callaghan).

Criminal Procedure

QUESTION: My daughter was charged with vehicular homicide three months ago, but she has not been tried yet. When do they have to try her?

QUESTION: What happens at an arraignment?

QUESTION: If the Constitution says there can be no cruel or unusual punishment, how come they can execute people?

QUESTION: If I testify at my trial, can the prosecution talk about my juvenile conviction?

Researching criminal procedure—the procedure that governments must follow in trying, convicting, and imprisoning people charged with crimes—is a little trickier, in some ways a little more complex, than researching crimes and offenses as discussed previously. As noted in the prior subsection, crimes and offenses are largely creatures of statutory law, but criminal procedure can involve many different types of law: constitutions, statutes, cases, and court rules. Consequently, some of what was said about researching the rights of the accused and about researching crimes and offenses applies in researching criminal procedure.

Again, the first question always is whether you need federal or state law. As far as the constitutional aspects of criminal procedure—issues such as speedy trial, the right to confront witnesses, the right to be free from self-incrimination—you would begin with federal constitutional law research. You would also want to check your state's constitution, which might provide greater protections than the federal constitution.

Then, if the jurisdiction of interest is federal, you would move from constitutional law to statutory law. Look in the United States Code, Title 18, for statutes concerning criminal procedure as more fully discussed in the prior section. Also, look for a copy of the Federal Rules of Criminal Procedure and the Federal Rules of Evidence. Here are some PDF versions: www.uscourts.gov/RulesAndPolicies/FederalRulemaking/RulesAndForms.aspx. Refer to Chapter 3 for further information about finding federal court rules.

If the jurisdiction of interest is a specific state, you would repeat the process in the prior paragraph, but in your state's statutory code. If you do not know what title or volume of your state's statutory code concerns criminal procedure, return to the Cornell site, but to a different page: topics.law.cornell.edu/wex/table_criminal_procedure.

You will also need to find your state's court rules for criminal procedure and for evidence. Often you can find these online, which can be helpful for questions such as deadlines or page limits and that sort of thing. Court rules can often be critical in criminal law situations and are not always easy to interpret. Therefore, find an annotated version. Annotated versions of the court rules will provide you with not only the exact language of the rules but also citations to court cases that have interpreted those rules.

When you are looking for court rules keep in mind that there will be rules of general application to the entire jurisdiction, such as all the federal district courts or all the trial courts in your state, but that there will be local court rules too. That is, the federal district court in the southern district of New York will follow the federal rules of criminal procedure but may also have rules for proceedings in the Southern District of New York. These local rules may often add additional or more specific requirements to those rules for the jurisdiction generally. Chapter 3 tells you how to find these local rules. Finally, the following treatise is very well-respected and is likely at your local law library:

▶ LaFave, Wayne R., Jerold H. Israel, and Nancy J. King. 2004. *Criminal Procedure*. 4th ed. St. Paul, MN: Thomson West.

Criminal Defenses

QUESTION: He hit me first. So, when I hit him back, isn't that self-defense?

QUESTION: He forced her to go into the bank with the gun. Isn't that duress sufficient to relieve her of guilt?

QUESTION: What does "not guilty by reason of insanity" mean?

QUESTION: They offered me drugs first. Isn't that entrapment?

Defenses to criminal charges can range from "They got the wrong guy" to "I wasn't even in the country at the time" to insanity and duress. Defenses to crimes can be creations of case law, but most often you begin your research about criminal defenses in the statutory code. Find the online statutory code for your state, find the titles or volumes concerning crimes and offenses or punishments or other such related terms, and you will like find sections on criminal defenses.

You can also find reliable information about criminal defenses, specifically links to state criminal codes but also specific links to information about defenses at the Cornell Legal Information Institute's website on criminal law and procedure: topics.law.cornell.edu/wex/category/criminal_law_and_procedure. Additionally, if you have access to a law library you may find the following treatise helpful, among others you are likely to find there:

▶ Robinson, Paul H. 1984. *Criminal Law Defenses*. St. Paul, MN: West Group.

Finally, although this book has frequently advised a person charged with any type of crime to hire an attorney, one area in which you can get direct help in representing yourself is with traffic tickets. Nolo has both a book and a website that will help you with this:

▶ Brown, David. 2007. *Beat Your Ticket: Go to Court and Win*. 5th ed. Berkeley: Nolo.

▶ "Five Strategies for Fighting a Traffic Ticket." Available: www.nolo .com/legal-encyclopedia/article-30091.html.

For resource updates, visit this book's companion website at

▶ *www.GetLaw.net*

RESOURCES RECAP		
Criminal Law		
	Resource	**Notes**
Primary Sources: Federal	▶ U.S. Code ▶ U.S. Code Annotated ▶ U.S. Code Service	
Primary Sources: State		For a list of statutory codes for your state, see Appendix 3. See Chapter 4 on state primary sources in this book for further information on this code.
Free Online Resources	▶ Cornell's Legal Information Institute, "Criminal Law and Procedure": topics.law.cornell.edu/wex/category/criminal_law_and_procedure ▶ Nolo, "Five Strategies for Fighting a Traffic Ticket": www.nolo.com/legal-encyclopedia/article-30091.html ▶ United States Code: www.gpoaccess.gov/uscode/	
Do-It-Yourself Publications	▶ Brown, David. 2007. *Beat Your Ticket: Go to Court and Win*. 5th ed. Berkeley: Nolo. ▶ Nolo, "Five Strategies for Fighting a Traffic Ticket." Available: www.nolo.com/legal-encyclopedia/article-30091.html.	
Treatises and Authoritative Sources*	▶ *American Jurisprudence 2d* (*AmJur 2d*). 1998–2010. Eagan, MN: West. Volumes on criminal law and constitutional law.	Legal encyclopedia
	▶ Cook, Joseph G. 1996. *Constitutional Rights of the Accused*. 3rd ed. St. Paul, MN: West (Clark Boardman Callaghan).	
	▶ *Corpus Juris Secundum* (*CJS*). 1999-2010. Eagan, MN: West. Volumes on criminal law and constitutional law.	Legal encyclopedia
	▶ LaFave, Wayne R. 2004. *Search and Seizure: A Treatise on the Fourth Amendment*. 4th ed. St. Paul, MN: West Group.	
	▶ LaFave, Wayne R., Jerold H. Israel, and Nancy J. King. 2004. *Criminal Procedure*. 4th ed. St. Paul, MN: Thomson West.	
	▶ LaFave, Wayne R., and Austin W. Scott, Jr. 1986. *Substantive Criminal Law*. 2nd ed. St. Paul, MN: West Group.	
	▶ Robinson, Paul H. 1984. *Criminal Law Defenses*. St. Paul, MN: West Group.	
		(Cont'd.)

RESOURCES RECAP *(Continued)*		
Criminal Law		
	Resource	**Notes**
Treatises and Authoritative Sources* *(Cont'd.)*	▶ Rudenstein, David S., Peter C. Erlinder, and David C. Thomas. 1990. *Criminal Constitutional Law*. New York: Mathew Bender. ▶ Torcia, Charles E. 1993. *Wharton's Criminal Law*. 15th ed. St. Paul, MN: West (Clark Boardman Callaghan).	

*Hundreds of treatises and hornbooks concern the various subtopics of criminal law. The best idea is to go to a law library and find the criminal law section or the section of the library holding the classification numbers concerning criminal law and browse.

Collection: Building a Basic Collection or Website

Part IV is intended for public library staff wanting to create a basic website, or perhaps just a single webpage, with links to relevant legal information for their local community. It also provides advice on how to build a small hard-copy collection at minimal cost. The first two chapters cover print sources that are not available online or in pay-for-view databases and discuss the general nature of free legal information on the web—megaportals, law school library sites, public library sites—and how it differs from what is included in pay-for-view databases like Lexis and Westlaw. These chapters provide tips on how to sift through and evaluate self-help law books and websites, often an intimidating array and host to unique concerns such as jurisdiction, relevancy, bias, and authenticity. The final chapter provides how-to information for creating a basic website of legal links and building a small, low-cost collection of print resources.

What's Online, What's Not, and When to Use What

Introduction

Finding legal resources has always been a little complex for a variety of reasons that have been discussed often in this book. Modern advances in technology have not made the process less complex. The researcher today is faced with not only the different types of law and jurisdictions but with three major repositories: print sources in libraries, free online sources on the web, and pay-for-view online databases. This chapter will attempt to make some generalizations about how to choose which repository to use in specific situations or searches. The initial sections will discuss the question of choice from the point of view of the type of material one is seeking: primary law or secondary sources. Then some generalizations will be provided focused on search strategies in relation to the three major repositories.

Primary Law

First, as a general rule, all primary law—enacted law, case law, and administrative law—can be found in all three places: in print, on the free web, and in pay-for-view databases. If you already have a specific citation to a specific piece of law and what is needed is the text of that piece of law, then you are likely to choose the free source: the print version at the library or the version on the web. Second, however, some caution must be used if you intend to quote the cited material to a court or for some other "official" purpose. In that instance, you would want the most authoritative version and, like it or not, in most states the free online sources are not considered "authentic" or "official." You then may need to find the official version, which is usually the one in print. Third, another caution is that if the researcher wants something more than just the text represented by the citation, such as a case that interprets the cited statute, then the free online sources are not likely one's best source. The print sources or the pay-for-view sources are more likely to

IN THIS CHAPTER:
- ✔ Introduction
- ✔ Primary Law
- ✔ Secondary Sources
- ✔ When to Use Print Sources
- ✔ When to Choose Free or Pay-for-View Online Databases
- ✔ Comparing and Combining Print, Free Online, Pay-for-View Repositories
- ✔ Conclusion

help in these situations. Finally, if you do not have a specific citation to a specific piece of law but need instead to do a subject search in statutes or cases or regulations, then again the free web is likely to be more hit or miss. You might get lucky, but you might not find what you need. For subject searching—finding out what primary law exists about a particular subject in a particular jurisdiction—print or pay-for-view sources are again the most reliable.

Secondary Sources

Everyone knows that the web represents a massive network of information. You would expect, therefore, to find thousands of "secondary sources" about the law on the free web. In some respects, that is true. The trouble is that most of it is not the type of secondary source recognized in traditional legal research. The authoritativeness of secondary material, of "commentary on the law" on the web is difficult to assess, and it therefore should be accessed and relied on with great caution. It is also unlikely that you would want to quote such secondary material to a court.

Traditional, reliable, authoritative secondary sources are still largely found only in print, in large law libraries, and at the pay-for-view databases Westlaw and Lexis. However, given that secondary sources may be wide-ranging commentaries on the law, you are less likely to have a specific citation to a specific section of a secondary source. It is not unheard of, but it is less likely than with primary law. Therefore, using secondary sources in the pay-for-view databases, while handy, is likely to be costly.

Therefore, as a general rule, the most time- and cost-efficient way to find authoritative secondary sources remains print sources in large law libraries. If cost is not a consideration, however, the pay-for-view databases will save travel time and may yield quick results for a skilled online searcher, but the serendipity factor of browsing in secondary print sources should not be discounted. Flipping through print secondary sources often yields some lucky "accidental" finds, finds that are not purely luck because the materials have been organized in such a way as to keep related material close together.

When to Use Print Sources

In general, aside from the previous specific suggestions as to types of law, here are some good rules of thumb for choosing to research in print sources: First, if you need general background information about an area of law with which you are unfamiliar, using print sources may be most helpful. Second, if you are researching particularly complex concepts or legal theories, this is very time consuming. Time is money, but in pay-for-view databases it is usually lots of money. Print will save you some money, and the serendipity factor seems to happen more consistently in print. The very precision of online searching tends to rob a researcher of this serendipity factor. Third, if your research involves an area of the law using many common or not terribly unique terms or words, then researching will likely be easier and more efficient in print sources. Commonplace terms, ambiguous words, or words with many synonyms make online searching challenging and possibly costly. In these situations the easy access of flipping through tables of contents, indexes, and text sections in print may be most helpful. Fourth, historical materials, though sometimes available in all three repositories if important enough, are more likely to be found in print. Though more historical materials are appearing both in the free online and pay-for-view sources, often you will need to resort to a library with printed materials. Fifth, if your research calls for a good deal of creativity and inventiveness because the mandatory authority you do find is opposed to your position, then again print sources may be a way of spending enough time to let good luck and serendipity help you find a new way of looking at things. Finally, you should use print sources when online searching has either provided you with too much information or too little. Finding material in print may help you see the relationships between large amounts of material and may allow you thereby to order it better and focus more pointedly. Conversely, if you have found too little information online, print sources may unlock the door in a variety of ways, not the least of which is putting one in proximity to a human who can help: a librarian.

When to Choose Free or Pay-for-View Online Databases

In many ways, one chooses pay-for-view databases for just the opposite reasons one would choose print, but it may help to discuss those choices in terms specific to online searching. First, if your search involves unique search terms rather than common or ambiguous words or phrases, then online search engines are likely to get one quickly to the "right stuff." Similarly, if your research involves unique factual terms—a rhinoplasty rather than surgery (in general)—then again the online search engines may yield quicker, more accurate, more precise results. Similarly too, if the legal issue that one is researching can itself be couched in narrow terms, then again the online search engines will help.

Second, if you're doing work in a relatively new, developing area of the law, often print sources will be behind the times and online sources will be the best and maybe only source. Third, print sources are not always the best for doing cross-jurisdictional searching. It can be done, but it is more laborious than doing such work online. More and more, even on the "free" web, sites make it easy for the researcher to compare and contrast the laws of the various states on specific subjects. For instance, the Cornell Legal Information Institute's site that has been mentioned throughout this book compiles links to all the states' statutes on specific areas of the law, such as the criminal and criminal procedure codes.

A fourth situation in which you might have no choice but to use online sources is when you are seeking "unpublished" material. For instance, though the practice varies from state to state, often courts will designate many decisions as "unpublished." These decisions in fact do not get published in print but usually can be found online. Usually, though not always, and the practice is changing, you are advised not to cite this unpublished material to a court. It may nevertheless be helpful information, and most of the time you can find it only online. Fifth, when money is not the biggest concern but time may be, then the online databases may be the fastest way to find something, especially something very specific for which you already have a citation.

Finally, if you are "updating" the law in the traditional sense of "Shepardizing," then almost every researcher would agree that this is done much more easily online. Moreover, many law libraries will provide this service for free at terminals for public use.

Comparing and Combining Print, Free Online, Pay-for-View Repositories

Probably the best strategy, if you have time and money, is to do your research in all three sources. This is particularly true when you need to both browse material—often easier done in print—and to find very specific words or phrases, which is done most easily with online search engines. As for choosing between free web and pay-for-view databases, aside from all of the considerations discussed, see the Good to Know sidebar "Free versus Pay-for-View Online Sources."

GOOD TO KNOW		
Free versus Pay-for-View Online Sources		
Evaluative Criteria	**Free Online**	**Pay-for-View Online Databases**
Currency	Varies, and not always apparent	Prompt posting, predictable, and currency usually stated
Completeness	Mostly very recent material only, though this is changing for the better	Very thorough, typically, of both current and historical material
Searchability/ease of use	Varies, but often hard to tell how sophisticated the search engine is	Basic to highly sophisticated capabilities, not always easily learned, and often easily forgotten
Stability	Unpredictable; some sites keep material previously posted, some sites shift older material to different sites, some just disappears	Everything that has been posted will likely remain, though there is some variation on this, especially with case law

Many of the tips, suggestions, and strategies discussed were developed by Mary Hotchkiss, Nancy McMurrer, and Peggy Jarrett, in *Fee-Based Electronic Resources: The Future of Legal Research* (University of Washington CLE, January 17, 2000).

Conclusion

Finding legal information has become more complex with the advent of the Internet. Finding legal information in print was never easy, but now that this information can appear sometimes in print, sometimes online, sometimes in both formats, the search can be even more puzzling than in the past. This chapter has given the reader some guidelines for making choices in seeking legal information. By following these guidelines, and with persistence and patience, the legal researcher will develop a good sense of where to turn first for specific types of legal information.

Evaluating the Trustworthiness of Websites and Self-Help Law Books

Introduction

Whether to trust what you find on the Internet has been an important concern since the Internet's inception. The trustworthiness of *legal information* on the web is especially challenging because of two factors that are relatively unique to legal information: jurisdiction and obsolescence. But the trustworthiness of legal information on the web also involves many other factors. These factors have been widely discussed concerning the web in general, and many websites discuss these factors. Of these factors, the top-level domain name provides possibly one of the most central clues, after jurisdiction and timeliness, in evaluating the trustworthiness of legal information on the web.

Another consideration regarding trusting legal information is the distinction made throughout this book between primary law and secondary authority. Remember that "primary law" means enacted law, regulatory law, and case law, and that the first of these, enacted law, includes constitutions, statutes, court rules, and local ordinances. "Secondary authority" or "secondary sources" in general means not the law itself but commentary about the law, someone else telling the reader what the law is. Evaluating trustworthiness is slightly different for these two types of legal information. When you find primary law on the web, the first three factors are probably the most important: jurisdiction, obsolescence, and domain. When you find secondary authority on the web, these first three factors are important too but in some ways even more critical are the typical questions one asks of websites in general. These fall under some broad criteria that will be discussed: scope of coverage, authorship, and authority.

All of these considerations also should arise in evaluating whether to trust one of the many self-help legal books that are published throughout the United States. This chapter ends with a brief section about these books.

Jurisdiction

The "primary law" in every state will have significant similarities, but there will be very important differences as well. Therefore, when you are looking for the law on the web you must make sure that what you find pertains to the jurisdiction in which you are interested. In other words, legal information is a trustworthy guide for you only if it pertains to your jurisdiction, whether that is a particular state or federal jurisdiction. If this distinction is unclear for you, reviewing chapters one and two of this book would be helpful.

Statutes

Obviously, statutory law, the laws enacted by the legislature for your state, will be unique to your state. The workers compensation statutes, for instance, will be different for every state. The "rules of the road," or statutes, pertaining to vehicles will be different for every state. Therefore, you will likely want to find only statutes that apply in your state. However, you may be searching for federal statutory law as well, so you will want to make sure you are finding federal and not state statutes. Sometimes you need both federal and state statutes, so you can get easily confused when you are new to the process and if you are not engaged in the process of evaluating the trustworthiness of the information you are finding.

Regulations

Similar to statutes, administrative regulations promulgated by a state's administrative agencies will be unique to each state. The regulations pertaining to, for instance, the process for awarding or declining unemployment benefits will be tailored to each state. One cannot be guided in how to apply for unemployment benefits by the regulations for any state other than the one in which one is applying for those benefits. Also similar to statutes, on occasion you may be looking for federal regulations rather than or in addition to state administrative regulations. Therefore, as you are "surfing," be sure you know what the website you are looking at is providing: Is it state or federal administrative regulations?

Case Law

Case law is a little different from statutes and regulations. Court opinions will be mandatory authority only for the state governed by the court that issued the opinion. In other words, the opinions from the Wisconsin Supreme Court will be mandatory authority only in Wisconsin. However, opinions may be *persuasive authority* in jurisdictions other than the state that issued it. Thus, if you are in Alabama but find a Wisconsin Supreme Court opinion that is helpful to your legal work, you can always cite the opinion to an Alabama court, though the Alabama court does not have to rule the same way but may be *persuaded* to do so. In terms of trustworthiness, one can likely "trust" that the Wisconsin Supreme Court opinion is "good law" so long as it passes the other tests for trustworthiness, but it will not have mandatory effect outside of Wisconsin.

U.S. Supreme Court opinions, however, are a little different too. In most instances, especially when construing the meaning of the U.S. Constitution or federal statutes, these opinions will be mandatory authority in all jurisdictions. Thus, one can "trust" that an opinion from the U.S. Supreme Court states the law for the entire country so long as the opinion is from a reliable, trustworthy source and has not since been overruled by a later case, which raises the issue of obsolescence.

Obsolescence

Legal information can become obsolete, often quite quickly. The law is constantly changing, so in deciding whether to trust the legal information you find on the web you must always determine whether it is the most recent, up-to-date information or is it obsolete.

Legislatures are constantly enacting new or amended statutes. This is what legislatures do, so you can be sure that statutory compilations will be constantly changing. Administrative agencies also exist to administer government functions, and in so doing those agencies are constantly promulgating new or changed regulations. Regulations change even more often than statutes, so do not trust that you have the latest regulation until you are certain that you do. Case law too changes often. A specific opinion, once published, will not be rewritten, but a later case may well reverse or overrule an earlier opinion. Furthermore, there is an interplay here as well. Cases may invalidate statutes or regulations. Subsequently, legislatures may enact new statutes to in essence nullify prior court decisions, so obsolescence is a constant concern in trusting the legal information you find on the web.

This is especially true because the Internet is notorious for having websites still on display that have not been updated in a decade or more. You must always make sure that what you find is up to date. A good, trustworthy website will provide this information to you. If it does not, be wary of trusting the site to provide you the most recent law. Even if you are able to determine that the website you are hoping to trust has been recently updated, you should always independently "update" the law through the methods discussed elsewhere in this book, particularly in the chapter on the legal research process.

Domain

Websites are produced by all sorts of individuals and entities—companies, universities, bloggers, artists, thieves, governments, nonprofit organizations, etc. On the web, many of these different entities are differentiated by the domain designation contained in the site's URL. For-profit entities will most often have ".com" or sometimes .biz in the URL, governments will have ".gov," nonprofit organizations will have ".org," and educational institutions will usually have ".edu" in the URL. In determining the trustworthiness of the legal information you find on the web you should always determine who has produced the website where you find the information. Distinguishing between these top-level domain indicators may also help you see that some sites that pretend to be authoritative, official sites are really hoaxes. For instance, the www.whitehouse.gov is the official site for the nation's executive; any domain extensions after "whitehouse" that are not ".gov" are hoaxes.

One of the signs of trustworthiness is that who created the website should be very easy to determine from the face of the website itself. If it is not, be careful. You can also do some sleuthing on your own by running a search on the URL in the "Who Is?" database, which can be accessed at several websites, including www.whois.net (this is the simplest one), www.register.com (look for the "Who Owns It?" button), and www.net worksolutions.com (look carefully for the "WHOIS" hyperlink). In addition to the creator of the website, be guided to by the entity designation in the URL along the following lines.

.gov

For legal information, the government that creates that information is a likely place to find trustworthy information. But finding a ".gov" site should not alleviate all concern. First, it must be a site concerning your jurisdiction, and it must be updated frequently and not be merely a site containing historical information. For instance, many state governments have had a few constitutions over the years. Some of the old, no longer in effect constitutions for these states are online for historical interest. But if you want to find what is currently in effect, you could be misled if you are not careful to make sure that in addition to being a ".gov" site, it is also up to date.

Additional, more technical concerns can arise too. For instance, even though ".gov" sites will post constitutions, statutes, regulations, and cases, in most instances this information is not considered "official." Most states still hold to the print-centric view that the "official" version of a statute or case or regulation is the hard copy, printed version and not the online version. Depending on the purpose of your search, this somewhat arcane fact should not deter you from finding legal information at ".gov" sites, but it is something to consider if you are citing or quoting the information you find on the Internet to a court or in some other "official" capacity.

.edu

Educational institutions, particularly schools of law, are often great and trusted resources for legal information. Many of the sites operated by these schools have been mentioned throughout this book. With some exceptions, however, it is likely that websites operated by specific law schools will concentrate on displaying legal information for the state where the law school is located. Often, it will have federal law too, but the state law collections are very likely to be focused just on one state. If it is your state, great; if not, use caution.

.org

Numerous nonprofit organizations have websites that include legal information. Many of these websites are fabulous, and some of them have been discussed in this book. Some of these organizations, however, will be advocates for particular points of view. This is not a bad thing in itself, but you must evaluate the trustworthiness of the information provided at these sites while recognizing that it may come with a particular slant. The site may be highlighting information that furthers its point of view and downplaying or neglecting information that is opposed to it.

.com

In general, companies exist to make money through selling you something. This is not necessarily a bad thing either, but it means that at the very least the information provided on these sites may be provided with a particular point of view that *may* influence how the information is presented. Therefore, using these sites as a source for legal information calls for the same caution in using .org sites: is there a particular point of view being promoted, and is that reflected in the information provided?

Scope of Coverage

Given the amount of legal information in the world, websites with legal information will often limit the amount of information posted. Often this limitation is a chronological one; for instance, the site will post only cases decided since 1990 while there may be case law in that jurisdiction going back to the 1800s. Other sites may only publish "landmark" case opinions but not all case opinions, and the one you need may well be not considered a "landmark." Or the site will publish only currently in force statutes but no historical material, or sometimes vice versa.

A related concern is that to thoroughly answer a legal question the researcher may need not just statutory law but case law and maybe regulatory law. But a particular website may publish only one of these and may not come with the warning that you will need other law as well. So while the website itself is "trustworthy," it might, unintentionally, lead you to feel mistakenly that you have found all there is to find about a particular legal question. So in evaluating trustworthiness, be sure to find out a website's self-imposed limitations in chronology, selectivity, and completeness.

Authorship

While "authorship" on .gov sites of primary law is typically not a problem, when one is relying on secondary authority, a primary concern is who the author is. You should be able to determine this easily. If you cannot, your trust meter should be alerted. Once you have determined who the author is, you should also be able to assess on some level the author's credentials. The website should provide this information for you. Does the writer have the usual indicia of expertise? What educational background does the writer have? What is the writer's past or current employment? Does the writer have a record of writing in the area?

Furthermore, does the writer have a particular point of view? The law is a contentious arena and often people have strongly held opinions on an issue. Again, this is not a bad thing in itself, but in evaluating trustworthiness you should be aware of the particular point of view being promoted. At the very least you should probably look for others writing from a different or opposing point of view, at least to satisfy yourself that an author on which you want to rely has presented a fair and full statement of the issue.

Authority

Again, particularly when evaluating the trustworthiness of secondary sources on the web, a series of questions pertains to the authority relied on by the author. What authority is the author relying on? Primary law? Only other secondary authority? Does the author provide full and accurate cites to this authority? The thorough researcher would have to also evaluate the trustworthiness of the authority relied on by the author. Is the authority relied on from the relevant jurisdiction? Is it up to date? What was its source?

Additional Resources

Evaluating the trustworthiness of legal information on the web is an ongoing concern among legal professionals. The brief guide provided in this chapter should serve you well in many situations, but additional resources on this question are readily available. The Access to Electronic Legal Information Committee of the American Association of Law Libraries has produced a number of resources for evaluating government-related websites. Though often the criteria in the guides appear more prescriptive than purely evaluative, the considerations may be particularly helpful for librarians deciding whether a certain site is sufficiently trustworthy and valuable to be included in the library's list of hyperlinks for legal information. Here are those sites:

- ▶ "Executive Branch Website Evaluation Criteria": www.aallnet.org/committee/aelic/execcrit.html
- ▶ "General Website Evaluation Criteria": www.aallnet.org/committee/aelic/criteria.html
- ▶ "Judicial Branch Website Evaluation Criteria": www.aallnet.org/committee/aelic/judcrit.html

▶ "Legislative Website Evaluation Criteria": www.aallnet.org/committee/aelic/legcrit.html

▶ "Local Government Website Evaluation Criteria": www.aallnet.org/committee/aelic/localcrit.html

Self-Help Law Books

A number of publishers publish books intended to help nonlawyers negotiate different aspects of their lives that involve the law. Books about do-it-yourself divorces, do-it-yourself wills, do-it-yourself traffic ticket defenses, and so forth, proliferate. Nolo is probably the biggest national publisher of these books, and you will notice that this company's books are often in their fifteenth or sixteenth editions. This is a good sign: the books are frequently updated.

Timeliness, or what was discussed as "obsolescence," is therefore one of the major considerations in whether to trust self-help legal books. While websites can be updated instantly, the book publishing process is much longer, so you can predict, given what was said about the constant change characteristic in the law, that any self-help legal book is likely to become outdated fairly quickly. Always check the copyright date at the beginning of the book and remember that this gives you only a general and vague idea of how recent the information in the book might be. Of course, the book publishing world is coming up with ways to "update" books quickly too, so look in the book or at the publisher's website to see if there are updates for the book.

Jurisdiction is again a major concern for the trustworthiness of self-help books. Most of them are written for a specific state and will provide only general and perhaps completely misleading guidance for any other state. Particularly in areas in which these self-help books tend to be written—divorces, wills, real estate—the law is very state specific, so make sure the book you wish to trust is up to date and pertains to your state.

The publisher is also a clue to trustworthiness just as the domain designation is for websites. Some publishers—West, Lexis, Bancroft Whitney, and Nolo—are well-known, long-established, and in general can be trusted to publish reliable law books so long as the other criteria are satisfied. This is not to say you should not trust a book on doing your own divorce that is published by a company no one has ever heard of, but some caution is probably merited. In these instances, particularly, the considerations regarding author and authority will be important.

The book should provide you some sense of the authority to be accorded the author of the book. Is the author an attorney? A judge? Does the author work in the area that is the topic of the book? Does the author have a particular prejudice or point of view? What is it? What can you find out about the author by going on the web? If you cannot answer most of these questions, then fully trusting the book may be a mistake. Finally, what authority does the author rely on? Is it up to date? Is it from your jurisdiction? Does the author provide you accurate citations so that you can find for yourself the authority that the author relies on? Is the authority primary law or other authors?

If you are able to answer most of these questions about a specific self-help book you are considering, then you should be able to come to a well-informed decision about whether to trust the resolution of your likely significant legal problem to the advice provided in the book.

Conclusion

Whether you are doing your own research for legal information or you are helping others to do that research, either directly or through providing them a list of resources, you will want to keep trustworthiness as a constant concern. This chapter has attempted to provide a useful list of criteria by confining the list to six considerations: jurisdiction, obsolescence, domain, scope, author, and authority. However, as you have read, there are related subissues that sometimes come into play in each of these six criteria depending in part on whether you are evaluating primary law sources or secondary authority sources. But with these six considerations in mind you should be able to make a quick assessment of whether a website bears further exploration and reliance.

Creating a Library Webpage and Basic Legal Collection

The rising cost of information—with legal information costs rising even faster than other types—is a grave concern to librarians charged with making information available to the public. Demand in public libraries for legal information is up at the same time budgets and staffing levels are down. This chapter, as the culmination of the book, summarizes the resource suggestions provided throughout the book, framed in the context of the public library and the role of the public librarian. It outlines which of the many sources discussed are essential to a collection that aims to inform its public about legal information and also must function within the constraints of a limited budget—or no budget at all.

The two previous chapters in this book, covering "when to use what" and tips for evaluating the trustworthiness of free legal information, should be used as background, as these address what to keep in mind when making selections about the resources to include, whether for your library's hard copy legal collection or as legal resource links on the library's webpage.

The chapter focuses first on how to make free sources of online legal information easily accessible through a basic webpage of links and, second, on ways to build a low-cost print collection of key hardcopy legal reference resources. A preliminary step for either of these efforts is determining the legal information needs of your particular public library and community.

Deciding What Your Library Needs

Assessing the specific needs of the constituents of your public library and community is the objective of entire books, workshops, and professional conferences, so this chapter will not attempt to provide the breadth or depth of these other sources. The purpose here is to consider your library patrons' most urgent and frequent legal information needs and then to keep these in mind when creating a legal information webpage or a basic collection of hardcopy materials. For example, libraries near a

U.S. border may want to include a cluster of web links for information about types of identification needed for border crossings; libraries in states hard hit by foreclosures may want multiple links as well as hard copy self-help resources about homeowner's and tenant's rights in these situations. Local librarians will know best the particular and most pressing needs of the local community for legal information.

In addition to addressing community-driven information needs, there are certain basic legal resources that should be considered as part of the core of any public library legal reference collection. One helpful resource to use as a checklist is from the American Association of Law Libraries (AALL). AALL publishes an online "Public Libraries Toolkit—Collections" designed to guide public librarians with collection development for legal research materials. The toolkit (www.aallnet.org/sis/lisp/collect.htm) has bibliographies for federal and secondary materials as well as state-specific guides for 30 states.

The next two sections in this chapter contain suggestions and practical tips for (1) building a simple webpage of links to the most commonly requested websites for legal information and (2) creating a small and low-cost hard copy collection of core legal reference sources appropriate for a small public library.

> Knowledge is of two kinds: we know a subject ourselves, or we know where we can find information upon it.
> —Samuel Johnson (1709–1784)

Building a Basic Website of Local Legal Links

As with any website, "content is king," so it is important to focus first on what it is your local community needs to know. Later on you can add in "nice-to-know" information that is less frequently requested. The structure of the webpages can reflect this bifurcation, with a main page for Legal Resource Links and a secondary page of More Legal Links. This can keep the main page from becoming both overwhelming and difficult to navigate, a good usability practice in website design. One simple way to incorporate legal research links into your library's website is to present the links in a Legal Questions or FAQ section within an existing Reference or Resources page (see, e.g., Figure 17.1).

Organizing the legal information links can present a challenge. Use the topical clusters in the next section to help make sure all important categories of local legal information are considered for inclusion.

Topical "Clusters" for Your Site

Here is a structure of topical clusters or categories that can work well for a typical legal resource links webpage:

- **Statutes, laws, and regulations**. Linking to a nearby law library or legal megaportal can make covering this big area easy; see the following section, Shortcuts: Megaportals and Piggybacking.
- **Local code and ordinances**. Include links for nearby municipalities and counties.

Creating a Library Webpage and Basic Legal Collection

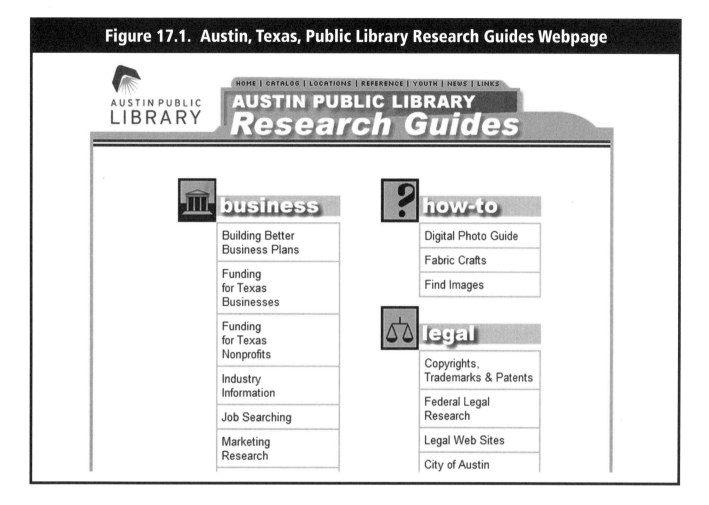

Figure 17.1. Austin, Texas, Public Library Research Guides Webpage

- **Case law.** Provide links to free sources; check Appendixes 2 and 3 for ideas.

- **Local courts.** A directory of contact information and websites for local trial courts, bankruptcy court, and federal courts. (The Federal Court Finder and Map from the U.S. Courts website, www.uscourts.gov/courtlinks/, can be used as a shortcut.)

- **Local court rules.** An easy way to find court rules by state is on the Public Library of Law website (www.plol.org/Pages/Search.aspx).

- **"Hot" topics.** This can include the most frequently requested information, such as small claim court forms, divorce information, probate, unemployment benefits, and landlord–tenant resources.

- **Attorney directory,** such as the one provided by the state bar association. There are also national directories like Martindale-Hubbell, Avvo.com, and Lawyers.com, but these depend on attorney participation so are not comprehensive.

- **Legal dictionary.** See Appendix 1 for online dictionaries that might be included.

- **Legal megaportals.** Examples are Cornell's LII and WashLaw.

If a secondary More Legal Links page is appropriate, a second tier of topical clusters can be created:

- **Other states' information**. This might include nearby states or simply linking to a megaportal page for all states, such as www.washlaw.edu/uslaw.

- **People finders**. An attorney directory is a must-have, but legal matters frequently require looking up other people, such as professional licensees, contractors, and business owners, as well as company records. See the Quick Tip sidebar "Finding Information about People" (p. 214) for ideas on what to include.

- **Research guides and tutorials**. Most law school libraries provide research guides that explain the basics of legal research in specific areas of the law. Another example is the collection of short tutorials available from the Public Library of Law (www.plol.org/Pages/Resources.aspx).

There is no single right way to construct a webpage of legal information links, and these topical clusters are intended to suggest ways to group resources appropriate for your community. Many public libraries have exemplary websites incorporating legal information links, local courts and code, and community legal aid resources. Figures 17.2 through 17.6

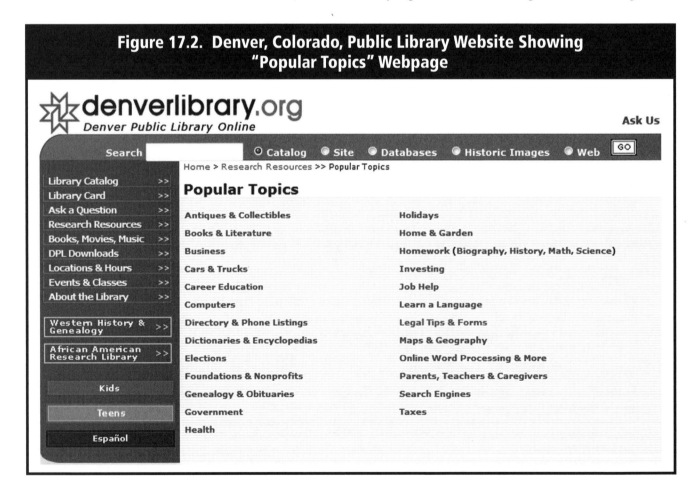

Figure 17.2. Denver, Colorado, Public Library Website Showing "Popular Topics" Webpage

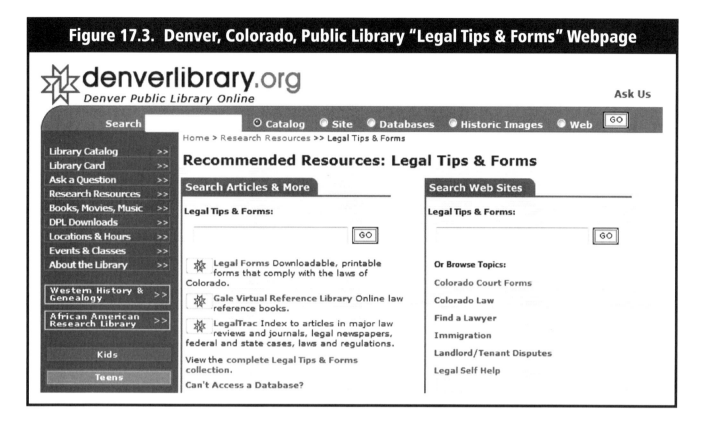

Figure 17.3. Denver, Colorado, Public Library "Legal Tips & Forms" Webpage

demonstrate a variety of implementations, including two from fairly large public library systems—Denver, Colorado, and Ann Arbor, Michigan—and one from the New Jersey State Library:

- The "Legal Tips & Forms" link on the webpage in Figure 17.2 opens the webpage shown in Figure 17.3.

- The "Laws & Legislation" link on the webpage in Figure 17.4 opens the webpage shown in Figure 17.5.

- The New Jersey State Library website (Figure 17.6) is a good example of combining links for state, federal, and general legal information web resources on a single page.

Shortcuts: Megaportals and Piggybacking

When it comes to legal research guides and directories there is no need to create materials from scratch, although it may well be that your library will develop (or already has) its own quick reference guides customized for the local community. These might include information on the local courts—including links to local court rules, forms, and clerk contact information—or codes for nearby cities and counties. However, for most purposes, it is possible to take advantage of existing websites from law school libraries and larger public law libraries. Shortcuts to megaportals like WashLaw.edu and "piggybacking" links to law library websites add breadth to your own webpage and also mean that much less updating and maintenance is necessary on your own.

Figure 17.4. Ann Arbor, Michigan, Public Library Website Showing "Research, Select Sites"

Figure 17.5. Ann Arbor, Michigan, Public Library "Laws and Legislation" Webpage

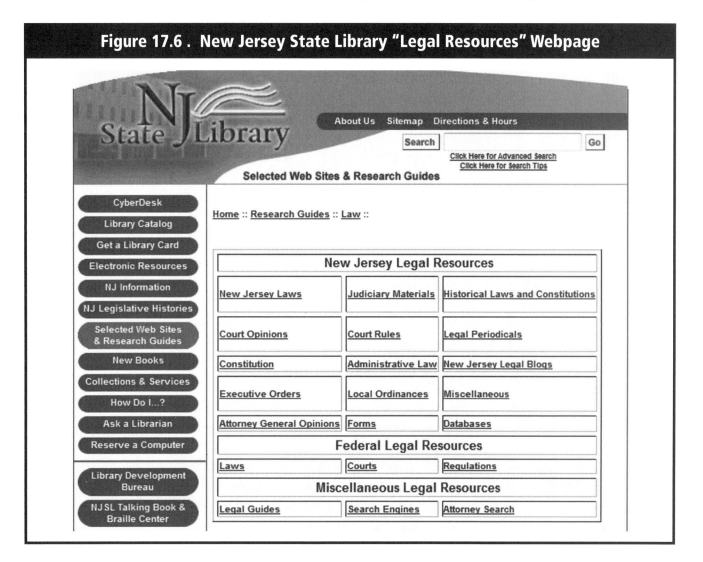

Figure 17.6 . New Jersey State Library "Legal Resources" Webpage

Figures 17.7 and 17.8 show a law school library site that works well as a piggyback target. It has resources for the local state jurisdiction (Illinois), links to local court forms, and research guides.

Another potentially great piggyback target is your state's bar association website. Many of these have a section created specifically for public use. Figure 17.9 is an example from the Michigan State Bar Association.

State courts very often provide forms for legal matters in which people are most likely to represent themselves. Figure 17.10 shows the court forms website for Colorado.

In addition to state court-provided forms, there are megaportals for other legal forms. As mentioned in earlier chapters, the Internet abounds with websites advertising free legal forms—some of which are not actually free—and caution is advised. A few reliable sources for free or low-cost legal forms are listed here. Refer also to Appendixes 2 and 3.

▶ Internet Legal Research Group, "ILRG Legal Forms Archive": www .ilrg.com/forms/

CLOSER LOOK

Access to Court Records

It would be an odd result indeed were we to declare that our courtrooms must be open, but that transcripts of the proceedings occurring there may be closed, for what exists of the right of access if it extends only to those who can squeeze through the door?

—*United States v. Antar*, 38 F.3d 1348 (1995)

Figure 17.7. Southern Illinois University Law Library Legal Topics Page

Figure 17.8. Southern Illinois University Law Library Legal and Litigation Forms Webpage

Figure 17.9 . Michigan State Bar Association's Online Legal Help Center

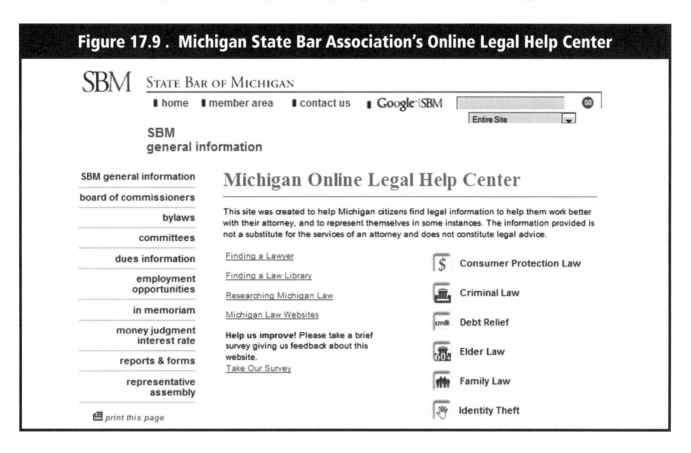

Figure 17.10. Colorado State Court Forms Website

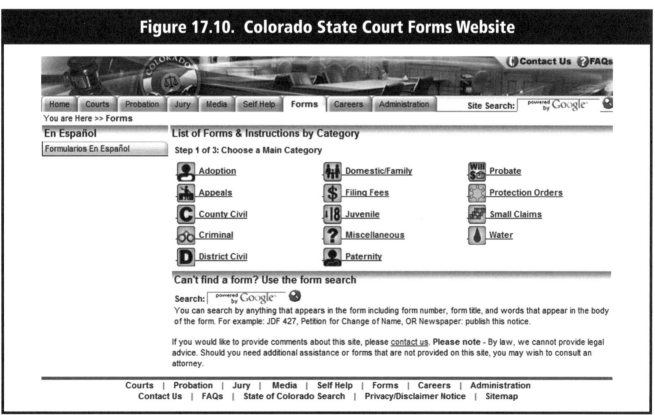

▶ Nolo, "eForms, eFormKits, and eGuides": www.nolo.com/products/all-downloadable-forms/

▶ Public Library of Law, "Legal Forms and Documents": partners.uslegal forms.com/partners/plol/

Linking to (and from) Your OPAC

Anyone working in a public library is well aware of the difficulties encountered by patrons trying to look up any topic at all using controlled vocabulary terms in an online catalog, or OPAC. Including a short list of controlled vocabulary terms on the library webpage, such as Library of Congress subject headings, that are recommended for searches on common legal topics can be effective, particularly those that are nonintuitive:

- Civil procedure
- Domestic relations
- Employees—Dismissal of
- Forms (Law)
- Pro se representation—United States
- Probate law and practice
- Rental housing—Management

The list of suggested terms can be incorporated into the legal information webpage directly—organized by topic cluster—or described in a research guide about how to get the best results from the OPAC.

Easy Tools for Website Creation

Perhaps the best advice for those wanting to build a simple website is that, no, you do not have to learn HTML and, no, you do not need to use an HTML editor or WYSIWYG (what you see is what you get) code generating tool. You can create an attractive and fully functional website using blogging or wiki tools that are available for free.

- **Wiki tools**. A *wiki* is built using collaborative web-based software that allows multiple users to create and modify a website's content. The content can include webpages, including images, and a repository for documents. You can restrict access for modifying the content to specific users or "editors." The wiki software provides templates and color palettes that are "ready to wear"—a website can be quickly up and running and the creator can focus on its content and organization. The leading wiki software is PBworks, which has a free version as well as subscription versions with more features and storage. Other providers are Socialtext and Microsoft Sharepoint.

- **Blogging tools**. A *blog* (from the term "web log") can provide some of the same capabilities as a wiki, but blogs are most often known for serving as a kind of online journal or collection of news postings and, second, for allowing others to comment on the blog's content. There has been an explosion in blogs in the past few years and they have gained in legitimacy as well. There are even search engines dedicated to retrieving from blog content, such as Technorati and Google Blog Search. A few leading tools for creating blogs are Wordpress.com, Tumblr.com, and Blogger. Entire websites are actually blogs with extensive content and hyperlinks.

Figures 17.11 and 17.12 offer two examples that illustrate creative implementation of wiki and blogging software to create a website of resource links. Figure 17.11 shows a public library website built as a wiki using PBworks that also links directly to its OPAC. Figure 17.12 shows a public library blog created using Wordpress blogging software.

In addition to wikis and blogs, at least one other tool that can be used for creating webpages with resource links is worth mentioning. These are the many social (or shared) bookmarking websites that make it possible not only to save your own bookmarked websites online but also to share them, with everyone or only those you choose. You can also see what others are bookmarking, the general idea being that this is an indication of both the current popularity and value of a website; that is, the more

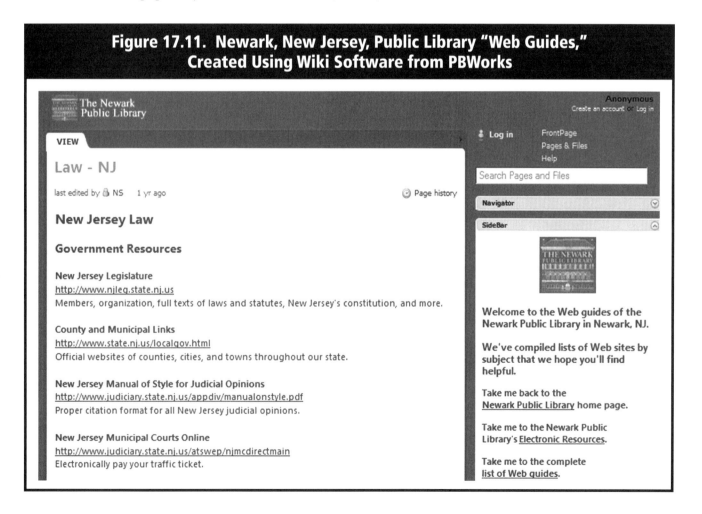

Figure 17.11. Newark, New Jersey, Public Library "Web Guides," Created Using Wiki Software from PBWorks

Figure 17.12. Shelf Talk, a Blog Created by the Staff of the Seattle Public Library Using Wordpress

times the site is getting bookmarked, the more likely it is to be a useful and reliable site. Libraries have found it effective to post their collection of favorite bookmarks on websites like Delicious (delicious.com) (Rethlefsen, 2007). Libraries can create a bookmark collection for a

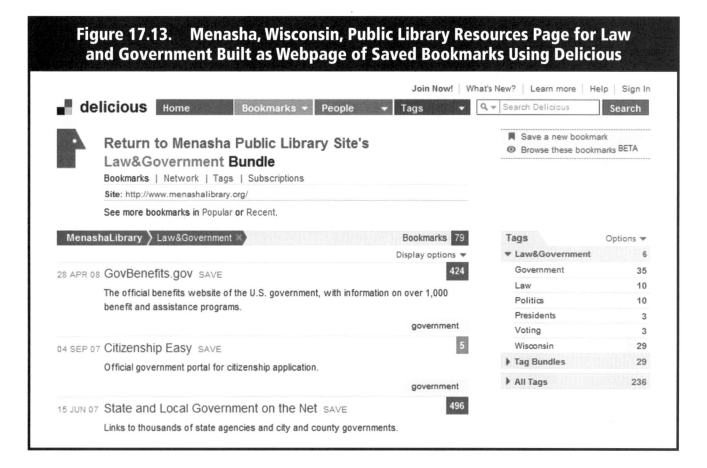

Figure 17.13. Menasha, Wisconsin, Public Library Resources Page for Law and Government Built as Webpage of Saved Bookmarks Using Delicious

specific purpose or audience, and some have replaced traditional pathfinders with "link rolls" using a bookmarking website. (There are many other social bookmarking websites in addition to Delicious, including StumbleUpon and Digg.) See Figure 17.13 for an example of a resource page created as a collection of bookmarks using Delicious.

If you do want to learn about HTML and have more control over the look and organization of your website, excellent tutorials and resources are available. Both the American Library Association and American Association of Law Librarians have materials available for getting started (Christensen, 2007).

Finally, in addition to online sources, it is enormously useful to have at least a small selection of hardcopy materials for legal information. The next section covers practical advice on how to build a basic print collection of legal reference publications.

Building a Basic Print Collection—On a Shoestring, or No String, Budget

The cost of law books can put them out of reach of many public libraries. The good news is that law books depreciate even faster than new cars. The average new car loses 21 percent of its value in the first year, and another 17 percent in the second year. By comparison, the value of new law books falls by more than 80 percent after purchase (Svengalis, 2008: 45).

A basic print collection of legal reference materials for a public library will include unannotated state statutes, a legal dictionary, and do-it-yourself books. The cost of annotated state statutes will make this out of reach for most public libraries, but it is often possible to acquire a used or hand-me-down set. Likewise there are resources for secondhand secondary sources, like state-specific practice materials, described next.

Secondhand Book Sources

Providing access to the most current statutes and regulations is critical, and this can be done through free online sources. Secondary sources, such as legal encyclopedias and some treatises, are still useful for legal research even when not the most recent edition. The cost difference between a new edition and a used edition is huge. Major online vendors like Amazon, AbeBooks, Alibris, and Powells are good sources of used law books, and the following book dealers specialize in secondhand legal materials.

▶ Law Book Exchange: www.lawbookexchange.com

▶ Legal Books Distributing: www.legalbooksdistributing.com

▶ William S. Hein: www.wshein.com

Hand-Me-Down Book Sources

Another resource for used law books is other libraries. Law libraries at large law firms often discard old editions and are happy to donate these to public libraries. Take advantage of professional organizations and librarian-oriented electronic discussion lists to communicate that your library is looking for donations of recent editions of legal volumes. This can be an excellent way to procure secondary sources like treatises and practice materials that would otherwise be prohibitively expensive to add to your collection. County law libraries and other publicly funded law libraries also can be a source of discarded volumes that are still recent enough to be usable.

Do-It-Yourself Book Publishers

Finally, there are several well-respected publishers of do-it-yourself legal books written for nonlawyers. In fact, there are so many books of this sort it is hard to keep up with them. The authors of this book have taken the position of being selective about the resources recommended and have emphasized low-cost materials that are both readily available and from reliable, authoritative sources.

When shopping for do-it-yourself legal books it is important to pay attention to both jurisdiction and currency. Fortunately, a few of these do-it-yourself publishers also distribute some of their legal information online at no or low cost and may provide online previews of the book content as well. The following publishers lead the pack for do-it-yourself legal books:

► Nolo: www.nolo.com

Undoubtedly the foremost publisher of self-help books, Nolo has extensive offerings in all areas of law that are most likely to touch the lives of people doing their own legal work or who are simply curious about the law and legal research. Nolo also provides free online resources such as legal forms and a layperson's legal dictionary. Nolo is not strictly for the end user and actively promotes its books to libraries. For example, with certain restrictions, Nolo will replace their books that are stolen from libraries. See www.nolo.com/library/replacement-policy.html.

► Oxford University Press Legal Almanac Series: www.oup.com/us/catalog/general/series/LegalAlmanacSeries/

A sampling of recent titles in this series from Oxford University Press includes employment discrimination, consumer rights, and AIDS law. The books in the Legal Almanac series are somewhat higher priced than those from Nolo or Sphinx, but they are also typically hardcover, and used copies are readily available.

► Sphinx Publishing: www.sphinxlegal.com/

Sphinx is another highly regarded publisher of do-it-yourself books; it has fewer titles than Nolo, but it is worthwhile to review its offerings and low-cost downloadable forms as well. Sphinx also includes more than 20 books in Spanish for nonattorneys.

Final Words

At a time when public libraries are faced with smaller budgets, fewer staff, and reduced hours, the demand for legal information has never been greater. More and more people are faced with questions that bring them into contact with the court system or with challenges related to consumer or financial woes. Their first line of defense is finding information, getting started with basic knowledge of legal systems, and building

For resource updates, visit this book's companion website at

► **www.GetLaw.net**

RESOURCES RECAP		
Creating a Basic Legal Collection		
	Resource	**Notes**
Collection Development Resources	► American Association of Law Libraries, "Public Library Collection Guidelines for a Legal Research Collection": www.aallnet.org/sis/lisp/collect.htm ► American Association of Law Libraries, "Public Library Toolkit": www.aallnet.org/sis/lisp/toolkit.htm	
		(Cont'd.)

RESOURCES RECAP *(Continued)*		
Creating a Basic Legal Collection		
	Resource	**Notes**
Topical Cluster Resources	▶ Public Library of Law (state court rules directory): www.plol.org/Pages/Search.aspx ▶ Public Library of Law, "Resources" (including tutorials on legal research): www.plol.org/Pages/Resources.aspx ▶ United States Courts, "Court Locator": www.uscourts.gov/courtlinks/ ▶ WashLaw, "Of Interest to All States": www.washlaw.edu/uslaw	
Legal Forms	▶ Internet Legal Research Group, "ILRG Legal Forms Archive": www.ilrg.com/forms/ ▶ Nolo, "eForms, eFormKits, and eGuides": www.nolo.com/products/all-downloadable-forms/ ▶ Public Library of Law, "Legal Forms and Documents": partners.uslegalforms.com/partners/plol/	
Do-It-Yourself Book Publishers	▶ Nolo: www.nolo.com ▶ Oxford University Press, "Legal Almanac Series": www.oup.com/us/catalog/general/series/LegalAlmanacSeries/ ▶ Sphinx Publishing: www.sphinxlegal.com	
Secondhand Book Dealers	▶ Law Book Exchange: www.lawbookexchange.com ▶ Legal Books Distributing: www.legalbooksdistributing.com ▶ William S. Hein: www.wshein.com	

understanding of how to represent themselves or to locate the legal resources in their communities. The ideas and suggestions presented here are intended to support public libraries, particularly smaller libraries, in addressing those needs effectively and economically.

References

Christensen, B. N. 2007. "Create Your Own Online Site: A Step-by-Step Guide for the Amateur Web Designer." *AALL Spectrum* 11, no. 8: 6–7, 32–33. Available: www.aallnet.org/products/pub_sp0706/pub_sp0706_ProDev.pdf (accessed August 11, 2010).

Rethlefsen, M. L. 2007. "Tags Help Make Libraries Del.icio.us." *Library Journal* 132, no. 15 (September 15): 26–28.

Svengalis, K. F. 2008. *Legal Information Buyer's Guide and Reference Manual.* North Stonington, CT: Rhode Island Lawpress.

Glossary

The Glossary defines terms **highlighted** throughout the book. To look up other legal terms in all-purpose legal dictionaries that are available for free online, refer to one of the sources described in the sidebar.

administrative law: A type of primary law consisting of rules and regulations and sometimes decisions in specific cases made by administrative agencies, known as *regulatory law*.

ADR: Alternative dispute resolution.

advance directive: A legal document that takes effect if a person cannot make decisions due to illness, serious injury, incapacity, or incompetency.

annul: To annul a marriage means it is as if the marriage never happened.

arbitration: A type of ADR, in arbitration (unlike mediation) the arbitrator is the decision maker and not the parties. After hearing from both sides, the arbitrator renders a decision that is binding and is enforceable as a court judgment.

case law: That type of primary law made by the courts; also known as judge-made law or decisions or opinions, all terms used interchangeably.

CFR: *Code of Federal Regulations.*

child custody: There are two types of child custody: physical custody, involving who is responsible for caring for the child, and legal custody, involving who is responsible for making decisions such as those affecting the child's education, religion, and medical treatment.

citatory: A case citator is used to find later cases that cite a given case.

codification: The process through which session laws are assigned numbers according to their subject matter and then published in statutory codes arranged by those numbers.

GOOD TO KNOW

Legal Glossaries Online

- ABANET Glossary from the American Bar Association
www.abanet.org/publiced/ glossary.html
An extensive glossary of legal terms intended for laypersons is available from the American Bar Association Division for Public Education.

- *Plain English Law Dictionary* from Nolo
www.nolo.com/dictionary/
Browsable for free online and also available in print and iPhone format for purchase, the *Plain English Law Dictionary* is intended for those who have no legal background and want to understand legal terms in simple language.

- U.S. Courts Commonly Used Terms
www.uscourts.gov/library/glossary.html
A quick lookup tool provided by the U.S. Courts website, this list of common legal terms is especially helpful for matters governed by federal law, such as bankruptcy.

- WEX from Cornell Legal Information Institute
topics.law.cornell.edu/wex/all
Another glossary that serves as a kind of combination legal dictionary and encyclopedia is WEX from the Cornell Legal Information Institute. WEX has been created through the collaborative efforts of attorneys across the country and is intended for both legal professionals and laypersons. WEX also provides a collection of in-depth articles on legal topics (topics.law.cornell.edu/ wex/category/wex_articles).

collaborative law: A type of ADR. In collaborative law the parties agree that they will not go to court to resolve differences, and their respective attorneys agree to withdraw if their clients change their minds and decide to litigate the matter.

commingling: Commingling happens when separate property of one person is mixed or combined with the separate property of the other.

common law: Though this phrase is often used as synonymous with case law, it is more technically the type of case law that makes law when there is no enacted law or regulatory law being interpreted in the case.

common law marriage: Common law marriage means that state law recognizes the relationship between a couple as to certain legal rights, duties, and responsibilities or community property.

constitutions: Considered a type of enacted law, though usually made by constitutional conventions rather than legislatures, constitutions are the "highest law of the land," meaning that all other laws must comply with the constitution.

depository library: In the context of legal information, a library that automatically receives materials such as state case reporters and must make them available to the public.

digest: A case digest contains short summaries of points of law from court decisions, arranged by topic.

dissolution: Legal term for divorce.

headnote: A short paragraph added to the case report by the publisher that summarizes a point of law in the case.

indigent: Having few financial resources.

jurisdiction: As the term is used most often in this book, *jurisdiction* refers either to whether a federal or state court has the power to adjudicate the dispute or, second, to the geographic area over which the power of a court is exercised. More technically, *subject matter jurisdiction* means that a particular court will have jurisdiction to rule only on certain subjects, and *personal jurisdiction* means that courts will have power over people only within a certain geographic area. This "area" can encompass the entire country if it is the United States Supreme Court or a small portion of a state if it is a county superior court.

legal separation: An alternative to dissolution (divorce) typically chosen by couples due to reasons of religious beliefs or needing to retain spousal benefits.

litigant: A person, company, or other entity who is a party in a lawsuit.

mediation: The most common type of alternative dispute resolution, mediation comes in various forms, but all involve specific stages facilitated by a professional mediator. Typically these include ensuring that both sides fully express their concerns, confirming that each side has been heard by the other, brainstorming on possible solutions, and agreement on the settlement terms.

no fault divorce: Neither spouse needs to prove wrongdoing or fault on the part of the other.

ordinance: A type of enacted law that is made by county or city councils.

parallel citations: Sets of citations to the same court decision published in different reporters. For example, there are three parallel citations in the following: *Lemon v. Kurtzman*, 403 U.S. 602; 91 S. Ct. 2105; 29 L.Ed.2d 745 (1971).

P.L.: Public Law, referring to the United States.

pocket part: A paper pamphlet inserted in the back of hardbound volumes of legal books. Pocket parts typically contain changes in the law and other updates.

postnuptial: Occurring after marriage.

practice materials: These materials are a type of secondary source that provide specific information about how to "practice" or carry out specific tasks in the legal system.

precedent: The narrow definition of this term in the law is a prior court decision that must be followed in future cases; it is not an absolute, however, because prior court decisions can be reversed or overruled by later court decisions.

prenuptial: Occurring before marriage. Also called premarital.

primary law: Primary law is "the law," as opposed to commentary about the law, and it is the phrase given to enacted law, case law, and regulatory law. It is usually what the legal researcher needs to find.

pro bono: When a lawyer represents a client for free.

pro se: Describing a person who is representing himself or herself in a legal matter. "Pro se" is Latin for "for oneself." Sometimes the term *pro per* is used.

public defender: A free, court-appointed attorney, usually in felony cases.

putative father: The man presumed to be the father of a child.

regulatory law: A type of primary law consisting of rules and regulations made by administrative agencies. It is also known as *administrative law*.

reporter: A series of books containing the full text of court opinions. Also called *case reporter*.

reporters: This is the general term given to the sets of books that publish the full text of court opinions in chronological order.

secondary sources: Secondary sources constitute commentary on the law, but these sources are not "the law" itself, as contrasted with primary law.

session laws: Prior to statutes being arranged and published by topic in statutory codes, they are first published usually with a PL number or other similar designation indicating the session of the legislature that enacted them.

slip opinions: The initial print publication of a court opinion.

spousal support: Also called alimony or spousal maintenance.

statute of limitations: A law that sets a time limit for filing an action in a civil case or for prosecuting a criminal case.

statutory law: A type of law that is enacted by federal or state legislatures.

temporary orders: In a divorce or separation, temporary orders can cover concerns such as residential schedules for the children, child support, and payment of bills.

USC: Abbreviation for United States Code, the federal statutes, used in legal citations. USCA and USCS are annotated versions of the U.S. Code and may also appear in legal citations.

Recommended Legal Resources Online

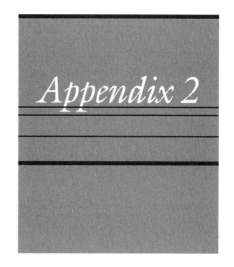

Appendix 2

Appendix 2 summarizes the key resources mentioned throughout the chapters of the book. Available online and for free, they provide broad coverage of the law and general legal topics. Sources specific to one area of law—for example, family law or criminal law—are covered only within the appropriate chapter. Think of these resources as go-to-every-time, bookmark-for-sure websites for legal information.

Legal Megaportals

General Legal Information

- Cornell Legal Information Institute (LII)
  www.law.cornell.edu/
- LawGuru—The Internet Law Library
  www.lawguru.com/ilawlib/
  Formerly the U.S. House of Representatives Internet Law Library.
- WashLaw—A Free Service of Washburn University School of Law
  www.washlaw.edu/

General Self-Help Resources

- American Bar Association (ABA) Family Legal Guide
  www.abanet.org/publiced/practical/books/family_legal_guide/
- Nolo Legal Encyclopedia
  www.nolo.com/legal-encyclopedia/
- Nolo Plain-English Law Dictionary
  www.nolo.com/dictionary/

Legal Aid Directories

- www.LawHelp.org/
  A gateway to nonprofit legal aid providers in the United States, with

IN THIS APPENDIX:

✔ Legal Megaportals
  General Legal Information
  General Self-Help Resources
  Legal Aid Directories
  Legal Topic Directories

✔ Federal Sources
  Statutes
  Regulations
  Court Rules
  Case Law
  Courts and Agencies
  Forms

✔ State Sources
  Directories
  Statutes

✔ Other Law
  Tribal Law
  Uniform Laws and Acts

✔ Understanding Legal Citations

For updates to links in this appendix, check the authors' website at

▶ *www.GetLaw.net*

the mission of helping low and moderate income people find free legal aid programs in their communities.

- www.FindLegalHelp.org/
  A service of the ABA, with links to legal aid resources in all 50 states and Canada.

Legal Topic Directories

- Cornell LII Wex
  topics.law.cornell.edu/wex
- Cornell University Law Library Legal Research Engine
  library.lawschool.cornell.edu/WhatWeDo/ResearchGuides/Legal-Research-Engine.cfm
- HGExperts Areas of Practice
  www.hg.org/practiceareas.html
- Justia Legal Practice Areas
  www.justia.com/sitemaps.html
- Nolo Legal Topics
  www.nolo.com/legal-research/
- WashLaw Legal Resources by Subject
  www.washlaw.edu/subject/

Federal Sources

Statutes

- Constitution—National Archives
  www.archives.gov/exhibits/charters/constitution.html
  Includes text-only version and high-resolution images of the original document.
- Federal Law Collection—Cornell LII
  www.law.cornell.edu/federal/
- Pending Legislation in Current Congress—Library of Congress THOMAS
  thomas.loc.gov/
- Statutes and Regulations—USA.gov (gateway to statutes, regulations, and more)
  www.usa.gov/Topics/Reference_Shelf/Laws.shtml

Regulations

- Code of Federal Regulations (CFR)—Cornell LII
  www.law.cornell.edu/cfr/
- Code of Federal Regulations (CFR)—Government Printing Office (GPO)
  www.gpoaccess.gov/cfr/retrieve.html
- Federal Register—Government Printing Office (GPO)
  www.gpoaccess.gov/fr/index.html

- Research Guide to the Federal Register and Code of Federal Regulations
  Law Librarians' Society of the District of Columbia
  www.llsdc.org/fed-reg-cfr/

Court Rules

- Federal Rules of Civil Procedure, Criminal Procedure, Evidence, and
  Appellate Procedure
  www.law.cornell.edu/rules/

Case Law

- U.S. Supreme Court—Official Site
  www.supremecourtus.gov/
- U.S. Supreme Court—Cornell LII
  www.law.cornell.edu/supct/
- U.S. Supreme Court—Oyez
  www.oyez.org/
  Selected case law, videos, and other U.S. Supreme Court media.
- U.S. Circuit Courts of Appeal and District Courts—Official Sites
  Check the individual court's own website for official opinions. Refer
  to the Court Directory at www.uscourts.gov/courtlinks/.
- U.S. Circuit Courts of Appeal—Cornell LII
  www.law.cornell.edu/federal/opinions.html
- U.S. District Courts—Cornell LII
  www.law.cornell.edu/federal/districts.html

Courts and Agencies

- Federal Court Directory—U.S. Courts Official Website
  www.uscourts.gov/courtlinks/
- Federal Court Locator—Villanova University School of Law Library
  www.law.villanova.edu/Library/Research%20Guides/Federal%20Co
  urt%20Locator.aspx
- Federal Agency Directory
  www.lib.lsu.edu/gov/

Forms

- U.S. Government Official Website for Federal Forms
  www.forms.gov/

State Sources

Directories

- American Bar Association (ABA) State Directory
  www.findlegalhelp.org/state.html

- Cornell Topical Index to State Statutes
  topics.law.cornell.edu/wex/state_statutes
- State Governments Directory—Library of Congress
  www.loc.gov/rr/news/stategov/stategov.html

Statutes

- For detailed information on individual states, see Appendix 3.
- State Statutes Megaportal
  www.washlaw.edu/uslaw/
  Click "States" in top navigation bar, then the state name in the left-hand list. Look under the heading "Legislative Branch" for "Statutes" or "Code." Most states provide the ability to browse the statutes or to search by keyword.

Other Law

Tribal Law

- National Indian Law Library
  narf.org/nill/triballaw/onlinedocs.htm
- Ross-Blakley Law Library Indian Law Portal
  www.law.asu.edu/library/RossBlakleyLawLibrary/ResearchNow/IndianLawPortal.aspx

Uniform Laws and Acts

- Cornell LII—Uniform Laws
  www.law.cornell.edu/uniform/
- National Conference of Commissioners on Uniform State Laws
  www.nccusl.org/Update/DesktopDefault.aspx?tabindex=2&tabid=60
- University of Pennsylvania Law School
  www.law.upenn.edu/bll/archives/ulc/ulc.htm

Understanding Legal Citations

- Chapter 5, "Legal Research Basics," in this book
  Pay particular attention to the section "Citations: Known Item Searching."
- *The Bluebook: A Uniform System of Citation*, 19th Edition
  www.legalbluebook.com
  The authoritative source for legal citation standards is *The Bluebook*, published by the Harvard Law Review Association. It's available by subscription; however, the next source listed reflects the latest basic information in *The Bluebook* and is available for free.

Appendix 2: Recommended Legal Resources Online

- *Introduction to Basic Legal Citation* (online ed. 2010) by Peter W. Martin
  www.law.cornell.edu/citation/
- *Citation Manual* of the Association of Legal Writing Directors (ALWD)
  www.alwd.org/publications/citation_manual.html
  Some sections of the manual are available for free online.

State Law Resources Online

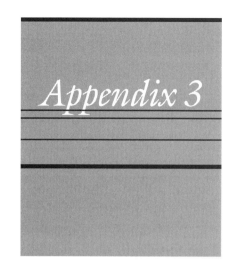

Appendix 3

The authors thank the following students at San Jose State University School of Library and Information Science's spring 2010 course on legal resources for helping to compile this table: Chezire Aclimandos, Lauren Anderson, Steven Ayala, Rachelle Bedia-Nitrini, Felishia Boggs, Jessica Brasch, Michael Carrillo, Marcy Chernowski, Cecillia Chu, Malinda Crom, C. Deane, Contrano Evans, Stacie Galli, Leah Granger, Mark Hancock, Kate Hanley, Bill Hardy, Tricia Lee, Maria Mascolo, Gina McCoy, Renee Ruzicka, Keith Sepke, Melissa Sobel, Samantha Stevens, Sharon Tani, Steve Tomalin, Edward Williams, and Katrina Yarrington.

For updates to links in this appendix, check the authors' website at

▶ *www.GetLaw.net*

*For appellate court opinions (i.e., case law), more than one website may be available.

ALABAMA	
Resource	**URL**
State's Homepage	www.alabama.gov/portal/index.jsp
Executive Branch (Governor)	www.alabama.gov/sliverheader/Welcome.do?url=governor.alabama.gov/
Legislative Branch	www.legislature.state.al.us/
Constitution	www.legislature.state.al.us/misc/history/constitutions/constitutions.html alisondb.legislature.state.al.us/acas/ACASLoginFire.asp
Statutory Code	www.legislature.state.al.us/CodeofAlabama/1975/coatoc.htm alisondb.legislature.state.al.us/acas/ACASLoginFire.asp
Judicial Branch (the courts)	judicial.alabama.gov/ judicial.alabama.gov/appellate.cfm judicial.alabama.gov/supreme.cfm judicial.alabama.gov/civil.cfm judicial.alabama.gov/criminal.cfm www.alacourt.gov/JudicialCircuits.aspx
	(Cont'd.)

Finding the Answers to Legal Questions

ALABAMA (Continued)	
Resource	**URL**
Appellate Court Opinions/Case Law*	judicial.alabama.gov/appl_faqs.cfm www.findlaw.com/11stategov/al/alca.html
Administrative Code (regulations)	www.alabamaadministrativecode.state.al.us/
State Bar Association	www.alabar.org/

ALASKA	
Resource	**URL**
State's Homepage	www.alaska.gov/
Executive Branch (Governor)	gov.state.ak.us/
Legislative Branch	w3.legis.state.ak.us/index.php
Constitution	ltgov.alaska.gov/services/constitution.php
Statutory Code	www.legis.state.ak.us/basis/folio.asp
Judicial Branch (the courts)	www.courts.alaska.gov/
Appellate Court Opinions/Case Law*	government.westlaw.com/akcases/ www.findlaw.com/11stategov/ak/akca.html
Administrative Code (regulations)	www.legis.state.ak.us/basis/folioproxy.asp?url=wwwjnu01.legis.state.ak.us/ cgi-bin/folioisa.dll/aac
State Bar Association	https://www.alaskabar.org/index.jsp

ARIZONA	
Resource	**URL**
State's Homepage	az.gov/
Executive Branch (Governor)	www.governor.state.az.us/
Legislative Branch	www.azleg.gov/
Constitution	www.azleg.state.az.us/constitution.asp
Statutory Code	www.azleg.state.az.us/arizonarevisedstatutes.asp
Judicial Branch (the courts)	www.supreme.state.az.us/welcome.htm
Appellate Court opinions/Case Law*	www.cofad1.state.az.us/ www.apltwo.ct.state.az.us/
Administrative Code (regulations)	www.azsos.gov/public_services/table_of_contents.htm
State Bar Association	www.azbar.org/

(Cont'd.)

ARKANSAS

Resource	URL
State's Homepage	portal.arkansas.gov/Pages/default.aspx
Executive Branch (Governor)	www.governor.arkansas.gov/
Legislative Branch	www.arkleg.state.ar.us/assembly/2009/2010F/Pages/Home.aspx
Constitution	www.arkleg.state.ar.us/assembly/Summary/ArkansasConstitution1874.pdf
Statutory Code	www.arkleg.state.ar.us/bureau/Publications/Arkansas%20Code/ARCodeMainDoc.pdf
Judicial Branch (the courts)	courts.state.ar.us/
Appellate Court opinions/Case Law*	courts.state.ar.us/opinions/opmain.htm
Administrative Code (regulations)	www.sosweb.state.ar.us/rules_and_regs/index.php/rules/search/new
State Bar Association	www.arkbar.com/

CALIFORNIA

Resource	URL
State's Homepage	www.ca.gov/
Executive Branch (Governor)	gov.ca.gov/
Legislative Branch	www.leginfo.ca.gov/ State Senate: www.sen.ca.gov/ State Assembly: www.assembly.ca.gov/defaulttext.asp
Constitution	www.leginfo.ca.gov/const.html
Statutory Code	www.leginfo.ca.gov/calaw.html
Judicial Branch (the courts)	www.courtinfo.ca.gov/
Appellate Court Opinions/Case Law*	www.courtinfo.ca.gov/opinions/ (supreme court and intermediate appellate opinions)
Administrative Code (regulations)	ccr.oal.ca.gov/linkedslice/default.asp?SP=CCR-1000&Action=Welcome (a search page for finding regulatory codes)
State Bar Association	www.calbar.ca.gov/state/calbar/calbar_home.jsp

COLORADO

Resource	URL
State's Homepage	www.colorado.gov/
Executive Branch (Governor)	www.colorado.gov/cs/Satellite/GovRitter/GOVR/1177024890353
Legislative Branch	www.leg.state.co.us/

(Cont'd.)

Finding the Answers to Legal Questions

COLORADO *(Continued)*

Resource	URL
Constitution	www.michie.com/colorado/lpext.dll?f=templates&fn=main-h.htm&cp=
Statutory Code	www.michie.com/colorado/lpext.dll?f=templates&fn=main-h.htm&cp=
Judicial Branch (the courts)	www.courts.state.co.us/
Appellate Court Opinions/Case Law*	www.courts.state.co.us/Courts/Court_Of_Appeals/Case_Announcements/Index.cfm Can also be found here: www.cobar.org/opinions/index.cfm?CourtID=1
Administrative Code (regulations)	www.sos.state.co.us/CCR/Welcome.do
State Bar Association	www.cobar.org/

CONNECTICUT

Resource	URL
State's Homepage	www.ct.gov/
Executive Branch (Governor)	www.ct.gov/governorrell/site/default.asp
Legislative Branch	www.cga.ct.gov/
Constitution	www.cga.ct.gov/asp/Content/constitutions.asp www.cga.ct.gov/asp/Content/constitutions/CTConstitution.pdf (pdf file)
Statutory Code	w3.nexis.com/sources/scripts/info.pl?4931 search.cga.state.ct.us/dtsearch_pub_statutes.html (this is the search statutes link)
Judicial Branch (the courts)	www.jud.ct.gov/
Appellate Court Opinions/Case Law*	www.jud.ct.gov/external/supapp/archiveAROap.htm (archive of appellate court opinions)
Administrative Code (regulations)	The full set of Connecticut state agency regulations (sometimes called the administrative code) is not available on the web. Some Connecticut state agencies have mounted selected regulations on their individual websites. A complete set of regulations in loose-leaf format (18 binders) or individual titles may be purchased from the Commission on Official Legal Publications.
State Bar Association	www.ctbar.org/

DISTRICT OF COLUMBIA

Resource	URL
State's Homepage	www.dc.gov/
Executive Branch (The District of Columbia is not a state. They elect a mayor rather than a governor.)	dc.gov/mayor/index.shtm?portal_link=hr Information about the mayor can also be found in print resources, such as on page 886 of the 2009-2010 Official Congressional Directory (111th Congress), which is published by the U.S. Government Printing Office.

(Cont'd.)

DISTRICT OF COLUMBIA *(Continued)*	
Resource	**URL**
Legislative Branch	www.dccouncil.washington.dc.us/ Information about the Council can also be found in print resources, such as on page 889 of the 2009-2010 Official Congressional Directory (111th Congress), which is published by the U.S. Government Printing Office.
Constitution (The District of Columbia currently has a charter, not a state constitution, within its Home Rule Act. Drafts of a constitution were created in 1982 and 1987 by those advocating for statehood status.)	www.dccouncil.washington.dc.us/homeruleact
Statutory Code	government.westlaw.com/linkedslice/default.asp?SP=DCC-1000
Judicial Branch (the courts)	www.dccourts.gov/dccourts/index.jsp Information about the District of Columbia courts can also be found in print resources, such as on page 886 of the 2009-2010 Official Congressional Directory (111th Congress), which is published by the U.S. Government Printing Office.
Appellate Court Opinions/Case Law*	www.dcappeals.gov/dccourts/appeals/opinions_mojs.jsp
Administrative Code (regulations)	www.dcregs.dc.gov/
State Bar Association	www.dcbar.org/
DELAWARE	
Resource	**URL**
State's Homepage	delaware.gov/
Executive Branch (Governor)	governor.delaware.gov/
Legislative Branch	legis.delaware.gov/Legislature.nsf/Lookup/SenateHome?open&nav=senate legis.delaware.gov/Legislature.nsf/Lookup/House_Home?open&nav=house
Constitution	delcode.delaware.gov/constitution/index.shtml
Statutory Code	delcode.delaware.gov/
Judicial Branch (the courts)	courts.delaware.gov/Courts/?index.htm#arms courts.delaware.gov/ courts.delaware.gov/Courts/Supreme%20Court/ courts.delaware.gov/Courts/Superior%20Court/
Appellate Court Opinions/Case Law*	courts.delaware.gov/Courts/Court%20of%20Chancery/ courts.delaware.gov/Courts/Court%20of%20Common%20Pleas/ courts.delaware.gov/Courts/Justice%20of%20the%20Peace%20Court/ courts.delaware.gov/AOC/?index.htm
Administrative Code (regulations)	regulations.delaware.gov/AdminCode/
State Bar Association	www.dsba.org/

(Cont'd.)

FLORIDA

Resource	URL
State's Homepage	www.myflorida.com/
Executive Branch (Governor)	www.flgov.com/
Legislative Branch	www.leg.state.fl.us Senate: www.flsenate.gov House of Representatives: www.myfloridahouse.gov/
Constitution	www.leg.state.fl.us/Statutes/index.cfm?Mode=Constitution&Submenu=3&Tab=statutes&CFID=150461196&CFTOKEN=55228804
Statutory Code	www.leg.state.fl.us/Statutes/index.cfm?Mode=View%20Statutes&Submenu=1&Tab=statutes&CFID=150461196&CFTOKEN=55228804
Judicial Branch (the courts)	www.flcourts.org/
Appellate Court Opinions/Case Law*	www.flcourts.org/# www.floridasupremecourt.org/index.html
Administrative Code (regulations)	https://www.flrules.org/default.asp
State Bar Association	www.floridabar.org/tfb/flabarwe.nsf

GEORGIA

Resource	URL
State's Homepage	www.georgia.gov
Executive Branch (Governor)	gov.georgia.gov/02/gov/home/0,2218,78006749,00.html
Legislative Branch	www.legis.state.ga.us/
Constitution	sos.georgia.gov/elections/2003_constitution.pdf
Statutory Code	www.lexis-nexis.com/hottopics/gacode/
Judicial Branch (the courts)	www.georgiacourts.org/
Appellate Court Opinions/Case Law*	www.gaappeals.us/ www.gasupreme.us/
Administrative Code (regulations)	rules.sos.state.ga.us/cgi-bin/page.cgi?d=1
State Bar Association	www.gabar.org/

HAWAII

Resource	URL
State's Homepage	www.ehawaii.gov/dakine/index.html (can just type: www.ehawaii.gov)
Executive Branch (Governor)	hawaii.gov/gov

(Cont'd.)

Appendix 3: State Law Resources Online

HAWAII (Continued)	
Resource	**URL**
Legislative Branch	www.capitol.hawaii.gov/
Constitution	hawaii.gov/lrb/con/
Statutory Code	www.capitol.hawaii.gov/site1/hrs/default.asp
Judicial Branch (the courts)	www.courts.state.hi.us/
Appellate Court Opinions/Case Law*	www.courts.state.hi.us/opinions_and_orders/index.html
Administrative Code (regulations)	hawaii.gov/ltgov/office/adminrules hawaii.gov/lrb/desk/hi3.html
State Bar Association	www.hsba.org/

IDAHO	
Resource	**URL**
State's Homepage	www.idaho.gov/
Executive Branch (Governor)	gov.idaho.gov/
Legislative Branch	www.legislature.idaho.gov/
Constitution	www.legislature.idaho.gov/idstat/IC/Title003.htm www.legislature.idaho.gov/idstat/idstat.htm
Statutory Code	www.legislature.idaho.gov/idstat/TOC/IDStatutesTOC.htm www.legislature.idaho.gov/idstat/idstat.htm
Judicial Branch (the courts)	www.isc.idaho.gov/
Appellate Court Opinions/Case Law*	www.isc.idaho.gov/search/ www.isc.idaho.gov/opinions/
Administrative Code (regulations)	adm.idaho.gov/adminrules/agyindex.htm
State Bar Association	isb.idaho.gov/

ILLINOIS	
Resource	**URL**
State's Homepage	www.illinois.gov/
Executive Branch (Governor)	www.illinois.gov/gov/
Legislative Branch	www.illinois.gov/government/gov_legislature.cfm
Constitution	www.ilga.gov/commission/lrb/conmain.htm
Statutory Code	www.ilga.gov/legislation/ilcs/ilcs.asp

(Cont'd.)

ILLINOIS *(Continued)*

Resource	URL
Judicial Branch (the courts)	www.illinois.gov/government/judiciary.cfm www.state.il.us/court/
Appellate Court Opinions/Case Law*	www.state.il.us/court/Opinions/recent_supreme.asp www.state.il.us/court/Opinions/recent_appellate.asp www.state.il.us/court/Opinions/default.asp
Administrative Code (regulations)	www.ilga.gov/commission/jcar/admincode/titles.html
State Bar Association	www.isba.org/

INDIANA

Resource	URL
State's Homepage	www.in.gov/
Executive Branch (Governor)	www.in.gov/gov/
Legislative Branch	www.in.gov/legislative/index.htm
Constitution	www.in.gov/legislative/ic/code/const/
Statutory Code	www.in.gov/legislative/ic/code/
Judicial Branch (the courts)	www.in.gov/judiciary/
Appellate Court Opinions/Case Law*	www.in.gov/judiciary/opinions/
Administrative Code (regulations)	www.in.gov/legislative/iac/
State Bar Association	www.inbar.org/

IOWA

Resource	URL
State's Homepage	www.iowa.gov/
Executive Branch (Governor)	www.governor.iowa.gov/index.php/governor/
Legislative Branch	www.legis.state.ia.us/
Constitution	www.legis.state.ia.us/Constitution.html search.legis.state.ia.us/NXT/gateway.dll/ic/2010const/1?f=templates&fn=default.htm
Statutory Code	Historical www.legis.state.ia.us/IACODE/1999SUPPLEMENT/ Current coolice.legis.state.ia.us/Cool-ICE/default.asp?category=billinfo&service=IowaCode Advanced search.legis.state.ia.us/NXT/gateway.dll/ic/2010const/1?f=templates&fn=default.htm

(Cont'd.)

IOWA *(Continued)*

Resource	URL
Judicial Branch (the courts)	www.iowacourts.gov/
Appellate Court Opinions/Case Law*	www.iowacourts.gov/Court_of_Appeals/Opinions/
Administrative Code (regulations)	www.legis.state.ia.us/IAC.html search.legis.state.ia.us/NXT/gateway.dll/ic/2010const/1?f=templates&fn=default.htm
State Bar Association	iabar.net/

KANSAS

Resource	URL
State's Homepage	www.kansas.gov/
Executive Branch (Governor)	governor.ks.gov/
Legislative Branch	www.kslegislature.org/legsrv-legisportal/index.do
Constitution	www.kslib.info/constitution/index.html
Statutory Code	www.kslegislature.org/legsrv-statutes/index.do
Judicial Branch (the courts)	www.kscourts.org/
Appellate Court Opinions/Case Law*	www.kscourts.org/Cases-and-Opinions/default.asp
Administrative Code (regulations)	www.kssos.org/pubs/pubs_kar.aspx
State Bar Association	www.ksbar.org/

KENTUCKY

Resource	URL
State's Homepage	kentucky.gov/Pages/home.aspx kentucky.gov/government/Pages/branches.aspx
Executive Branch (Governor)	governor.ky.gov/
Legislative Branch	www.lrc.ky.gov/house.htm www.lrc.ky.gov/senate.htm
Constitution	www.lrc.ky.gov/legresou/constitu/intro.htm
Statutory Code	www.lrc.ky.gov/statrev/frontpg.htm
Judicial Branch (the courts)	courts.ky.gov/
Appellate Court Opinions/Case Law*	apps.courts.ky.gov/supreme/sc_opinions.shtm
Administrative Code (regulations)	www.lrc.ky.gov/kar/frntpage.htm
State Bar Association	www.kybar.org/

(Cont'd.)

LOUISIANA

Resource	URL
State's Homepage	www.louisiana.gov/
Executive Branch (Governor)	www.louisiana.gov/Government/Executive_Branch/gov.louisiana.gov/
Legislative Branch	www.louisiana.gov/Government/Legislative_Branch/senate.legis.state.la.us/default.asp house.louisiana.gov/
Constitution	senate.legis.louisiana.gov/Documents/Constitution/Default.htm
Statutory Code	www.legis.state.la.us/lss/tsrssearch.htm
Judicial Branch (the courts)	www.lasc.org/
Appellate Court Opinions/Case Law*	LA Court of Appeals First Circuit (Baton Rouge) www.la-fcca.org/index.php/opinions LA Court of Appeals Second Circuit (Shreveport) www.lacoa2.org/ LA Court of Appeals Third Circuit (Lake Charles) www.la3circuit.org/opinions.htm LA Court of Appeals Fourth Circuit (New Orleans) www.la4th.org/Opinions.aspx LA Court of Appeals Fifth Circuit (Gretna) www.fifthcircuit.org/Opinions.aspx
Administrative Code (regulations)	doa.louisiana.gov/osr/lac/lactitle.htm
State Bar Association	www.lsba.org/

MAINE

Resource	URL
State's Homepage	www.maine.gov/
Executive Branch (Governor)	www.maine.gov/portal/government/governor.html
Legislative Branch	www.maine.gov/legis/
Constitution	www.maine.gov/legis/const/
Statutory Code	www.mainelegislature.org/legis/statutes/
Judicial Branch (the courts)	www.courts.state.me.us/
Appellate Court Opinions/Case Law*	www.courts.state.me.us/maine_courts/supreme/index.shtml www.courts.state.me.us/maine_courts/superior/index.shtml
Administrative Code (regulations)	www.maine.gov/sos/cec/rules/rules.html
State Bar Association	www.mainebar.org/

(Cont'd.)

Appendix 3: State Law Resources Online

MARYLAND

Resource	URL
State's Homepage	www.maryland.gov/
Executive Branch (Governor)	www.governor.maryland.gov/
Legislative Branch	mlis.state.md.us/
Constitution	www.msa.md.gov/msa/mdmanual/43const/html/const.html
Statutory Code	mlis.state.md.us/asp/web_statutes.asp
Judicial Branch (the courts)	www.mdcourts.gov/
Appellate Court Opinions/Case Law*	www.mdcourts.gov/coappeals/index.html www.mdcourts.gov/cosappeals/index.html
Administrative Code (regulations)	www.michie.com/maryland/lpext.dll?f=templates&fn=main-h.htm&2.0
State Bar Association	www.msba.org/

MASSACHUSETTS

Resource	URL
State's Homepage	www.mass.gov/?pageID=mg2homepage&L=1&L0=Home&sid=massgov2
Executive Branch (Governor)	www.mass.gov/?pageID=gov3homepage&L=1&L0=Home&sid=Agov3
Legislative Branch	www.mass.gov/legis/
Constitution	www.mass.gov/legis/const.htm
Statutory Code	www.mass.gov/legis/laws/mgl/index.htm
Judicial Branch (the courts)	www.mass.gov/courts/
Appellate Court Opinions/Case Law*	massreports.com/
Administrative Code (regulations)	www.lawlib.state.ma.us/source/mass/cmr/index.html
State Bar Association	www.massbar.org/

MICHIGAN

Resource	URL
State's Homepage	www.michigan.gov/
Executive Branch (Governor)	www.michigan.gov/gov/
Legislative Branch	www.legislature.mi.gov/(S(dkg5d1bexrqned45lfioo3i3))/mileg.aspx?page=home senate.michigan.gov/ house.michigan.gov/

(Cont'd.)

MICHIGAN *(Continued)*	
Resource	**URL**
Constitution	www.legislature.mi.gov/(S(42s0tpnej4mom5rylx5xmn45))/mileg.aspx?page=MCLconstitutionSearch
Statutory Code	www.legislature.mi.gov/(S(dkg5d1bexrqned45lfioo3i3))/mileg.aspx?page=ChapterIndex
Judicial Branch (the courts)	www.courts.michigan.gov/
Appellate Court Opinions/Case Law*	coa.courts.mi.gov/resources/opinions.htm
Administrative Code (regulations)	www.michigan.gov/dleg/0,1607,7-154-10576_35738---,00.html
State Bar Association	www.michbar.org/

MISSISSIPPI	
Resource	**URL**
State's Homepage	www.mississippi.gov/
Executive Branch (Governor)	www.governorbarbour.com/
Legislative Branch	billstatus.ls.state.ms.us/
Constitution	www.sos.state.ms.us/ed_pubs/constitution/constitution.asp www.sos.state.ms.us/ed_pubs/Constitution/ (keyword searching link)
Statutory Code	www.sos.state.ms.us/ed_pubs/pub_statutory_pubs.asp www.sos.state.ms.us/ed_pubs/mscode/ (link via Lexis to unannotated codes) www.mssc.state.ms.us/mscode/mscode.html
Judicial Branch (the courts)	Supreme Court: www.mssc.state.ms.us/appellate_courts/sc/sc.html
Appellate Court Opinions/Case Law*	Court of Appeals www.mssc.state.ms.us/appellate_courts/coa/coa.html Clerk of Appellate Courts www.mssc.state.ms.us/appellate_courts/clerk/clerk.html www.mssc.state.ms.us/trialcourts/trialcourts.html Circuit Court www.mssc.state.ms.us/trialcourts/circuitcourt/circuitcourt.html Chancery Courts www.mssc.state.ms.us/trialcourts/chancerycourt/chancerycourt.html County Courts www.mssc.state.ms.us/trialcourts/countycourt/countycourt.html Justice Courts www.mssc.state.ms.us/trialcourts/justicecourt/justicecourt.html Drug Courts www.mssc.state.ms.us/trialcourts/drugcourt/drugcourt.html

(Cont'd.)

MISSISSIPPI (Continued)	
Resource	**URL**
Appellate Court Opinions/Case Law* (Cont'd.)	Municipal Courts www.mssc.state.ms.us/trialcourts/municipalcourt/municipalcourt.html Youth Courts www.mssc.state.ms.us/trialcourts/youthcourt/youthcourt.html About the Courts www.mssc.state.ms.us/aboutcourts/aboutcourts.html www.mssc.state.ms.us/appellate_courts/appellatecourts.html www.mssc.state.ms.us/aoc/aoc.html
Administrative Code (regulations)	www.mssc.state.ms.us/mscode/mscode.html www.mssc.state.ms.us/rules/msrules.html www.mssc.state.ms.us/state_library/statelibrary.html www.mssc.state.ms.us/state_library/statelibrary_history.html Administrative code resource www.sos.ms.gov/regulation_and_enforcement_admin_procedures2.aspx Once a rule has been proposed, finalized, and has become effective through the processes outlined in the Mississippi Administrative Procedures Law and the rules promulgated by the secretary of state's office, the rules are published in the administrative code. This code will be an online publication. It will be available soon. The following are links to the index of titles for the administrative code. www.sos.ms.gov/regulation_and_enforcement_admin_procedures3.aspx www.sos.ms.gov/links/reg_enf/admin/Index_of_Titles.pdf
State Bar Association	www.msbar.org/
MINNESOTA	
Resource	**URL**
State's Homepage	www.state.mn.us/portal/mn/jsp/home.do?agency=NorthStar
Executive Branch (Governor)	www.governor.state.mn.us/
Legislative Branch	www.leg.state.mn.us/
Constitution	https://www.revisor.mn.gov/pubs/ www.mnhs.org/library/constitution/index.html www.house.leg.state.mn.us/cco/rules/mncon/preamble.htm
Statutory Code	https://www.revisor.mn.gov/pubs/
Judicial Branch (the courts)	
Appellate Court Opinions/Case Law*	Courts www.mncourts.gov/default.aspx Supreme Courts www.mncourts.gov/?page=550

(Cont'd.)

MINNESOTA (Continued)

Resource	URL
Appellate Court Opinions/Case Law* (Cont'd.)	Court of Appeals www.mncourts.gov/?page=551 District Courts www.mncourts.gov/?page=238 State Court's Administrator www.mncourts.gov/?page=244 Judicial Council www.mncourts.gov/?page=297
Administrative Code (regulations)	https://www.revisor.mn.gov/pubs/
State Bar Association	www.mnbar.org/

MISSOURI

Resource	URL
State's Homepage	www.mo.gov/
Executive Branch (Governor)	governor.mo.gov/
Legislative Branch	www.mo.gov/Government/Legislative/
Constitution	www.moga.mo.gov/homecon.asp www.sos.mo.gov/pubs/constitution.asp
Statutory Code	www.moga.mo.gov/statutesearch/
Judicial Branch (the courts)	www.courts.mo.gov/
Appellate Court Opinions/Case Law*	Court of Appeals www.courts.mo.gov/page.jsp?id=261 Opinions www.courts.mo.gov/page.jsp?id=12086&dist=Opinions Supreme Court www.courts.mo.gov/page.jsp?id=27 Supreme Court opinions www.courts.mo.gov/page.jsp?id=12086&dist=Opinions%20Supreme
Administrative Code (regulations)	www.sos.mo.gov/adrules/csr/csr.asp
State Bar Association	www.mobar.org/

MONTANA

Resource	URL
State's Homepage	mt.gov/
Executive Branch (Governor)	governor.mt.gov/

MONTANA *(Continued)*

Resource	URL
Legislative Branch	leg.mt.gov/css/Default.asp
Constitution	leg.mt.gov/css/Laws%20and%20Constitution/Current%20Constitution.asp
Statutory Code	data.opi.state.mt.us/bills/mca_toc/index.htm
Judicial Branch (the courts)	courts.mt.gov/default.mcpx
Appellate Court Opinions/Case Law*	fnweb1.isd.doa.state.mt.us/idmws/custom/sll/sll_fn_home.htm (Montana does not have intermediate appellate courts; appeals from the trial courts go to the supreme court.)
Administrative Code (regulations)	www.mtrules.org/
State Bar Association	www.montanabar.org/

NEBRASKA

Resource	URL
State's Homepage	www.nebraska.gov/
Executive Branch (Governor)	www.governor.nebraska.gov/ www.ltgov.ne.gov/ www.sos.ne.gov/ www.auditors.state.ne.us/ www.treasurer.org/ www.ago.ne.gov/
Legislative Branch	nebraskalegislature.gov/
Constitution	uniweb.legislature.ne.gov/laws/browse-constitution.php
Statutory Code	uniweb.legislature.ne.gov/laws/laws.php
Judicial Branch (the courts)	www.supremecourt.ne.gov/
Appellate Court Opinions/Case Law*	www.supremecourt.ne.gov/opinions/index.shtml?sub2
Administrative Code (regulations)	www.sos.ne.gov/rules-and-regs/regsearch/
State Bar Association	www.nebar.com/

NEVADA

Resource	URL
State's Homepage	www.nv.gov/
Executive Branch (Governor)	gov.state.nv.us/
Legislative Branch	leg.state.nv.us/

(Cont'd.)

NEVADA (Continued)

Resource	URL
Constitution	www.leg.state.nv.us/const/nvconst.html
Statutory Code	leg.state.nv.us/law1.cfm
Judicial Branch (the courts)	www.nevadajudiciary.us/
Appellate Court Opinions/Case Law*	www.nevadajudiciary.us/index.php/advancedopinions www.nevadajudiciary.us/index.php/viewdocumentsandforms/Supreme-Court-Files/Unpublished-Orders/
Administrative Code (regulations)	www.leg.state.nv.us/nac/CHAPTERS.HTML
State Bar Association	www.nvbar.org/

NEW HAMPSHIRE

Resource	URL
State's Homepage	www.nh.gov/
Executive Branch (Governor)	www.governor.nh.gov/
Legislative Branch	www.gencourt.state.nh.us/ www.gencourt.state.nh.us/house/default.htm www.gencourt.state.nh.us/Senate/default.html Note: NH's bicameral legislature is called "The General Court."
Constitution	www.nh.gov/constitution/constitution.html
Statutory Code	www.gencourt.state.nh.us/rsa/html/indexes/default.html
Judicial Branch (the courts)	www.courts.state.nh.us/
Appellate Court Opinions/Case Law*	www.courts.state.nh.us/supreme/opinions/index.htm (The New Hampshire Supreme Court is the state's only appellate court—it reviews cases directly from the state's trial courts, which are called superior courts.)
Administrative Code (regulations)	www.gencourt.state.nh.us/rules/default.htm
State Bar Association	www.nhbar.org/

NEW JERSEY

Resource	URL
State's Homepage	www.state.nj.us/
Executive Branch (Governor)	www.state.nj.us/governor/
Legislative Branch	www.njleg.state.nj.us/Default.asp

(Cont'd.)

NEW JERSEY (Continued)

Resource	URL
Constitution	www.njleg.state.nj.us/lawsconstitution/consearch.asp
Statutory Code	lis.njleg.state.nj.us/cgi-bin/om_isapi.dll?clientID=22801046&depth=2&expand headings=off&headingswithhits=on&infobase=statutes.nfo&softpage=TOC_ Frame_Pg42
Judicial Branch (the courts)	www.judiciary.state.nj.us/
Appellate Court Opinions/Case Law*	www.judiciary.state.nj.us/opinions/index.htm lawlibrary.rutgers.edu/search.shtml
Administrative Code (regulations)	www.state.nj.us/oal/rules.html
State Bar Association	www.njsba.com/

NEW MEXICO

Resource	URL
State's Homepage	www.newmexico.gov/
Executive Branch (Governor)	www.governor.state.nm.us/index2.php
Legislative Branch	www.nmlegis.gov/lcs/
Constitution	www.nmlegis.gov/lcs/
Statutory Code	www.conwaygreene.com/nmsu/lpext.dll?f=templates&fn=main-h.htm&2.0
Judicial Branch (the courts)	www.nmcourts.gov/
Appellate Court Opinions/Case Law*	coa.nmcourts.gov/ www.nmcompcomm.us/nmcases/
Administrative Code (regulations)	www.nmcpr.state.nm.us/nmac/ www.nmcpr.state.nm.us/nmregister/
State Bar Association	www.nmbar.org/

NEW YORK

Resource	URL
State's Homepage	www.state.ny.us/
Executive Branch (Governor)	www.state.ny.us/governor/index.html www.nysegov.com/citguide.cfm?superCat=102&cat=449&content=main
Legislative Branch	public.leginfo.state.ny.us/frmload.cgi?MENU-56857094 www.nysenate.gov/ assembly.state.ny.us/

(Cont'd.)

NEW YORK (Continued)

Resource	URL
Constitution	public.leginfo.state.ny.us/LAWSSEAF.cgi?QUERYTYPE=LAWS+&QUERYDATA= **CNSAS +&LIST=LAW+&BROWSER=BROWSER+&TOKEN=17132499+& TARGET=VIEW
Statutory Code	public.leginfo.state.ny.us/menugetf.cgi?COMMONQUERY=LAWS
Judicial Branch (the courts)	www.courts.state.ny.us/
Appellate Court Opinions/Case Law*	www.nycourts.gov/reporter/Decisions.htm www.courts.state.ny.us/courts/lowerappeals.shtml
Administrative Code (regulations)	www.dos.state.ny.us/info/nycrr.html public.leginfo.state.ny.us/menugetf.cgi?COMMONQUERY=LAWS
State Bar Association	www.nycbar.org/index.htm

NORTH CAROLINA

Resource	URL
State's Homepage	www.ncgov.com/
Executive Branch (Governor)	www.governor.state.nc.us/
Legislative Branch	www.ncga.state.nc.us/
Constitution	www.ncga.state.nc.us/legislation/constitution/ncconstitution.html
Statutory Code	www.ncga.state.nc.us/gascripts/statutes/statutes.asp
Judicial Branch (the courts)	www.nccourts.org/
Appellate Court Opinions/Case Law*	www.aoc.state.nc.us/www/public/html/opinions.htm www.aoc.state.nc.us/www/public/sc/calendar.html
Administrative Code (regulations)	ncrules.state.nc.us/ncac.asp
State Bar Association	www.ncbar.gov/

NORTH DAKOTA

Resource	URL
State's Homepage	www.nd.gov/
Executive Branch (Governor)	governor.nd.gov/
Legislative Branch	www.legis.nd.gov/
Constitution	www.legis.nd.gov/constitution/const.pdf
Statutory Code	www.legis.nd.gov/information/statutes/cent-code.html

(Cont'd.)

NORTH DAKOTA *(Continued)*

Resource	URL
Judicial Branch (the courts)	www.ndcourts.com/court/brochure.htm www.ndcourts.com/court/Districts/Districts.htm
Appellate Court Opinions/Case Law*	www.ndcourts.com/Search/Opinions.asp
Administrative Code (regulations)	www.legis.nd.gov/information/rules/admincode.html
State Bar Association	www.sband.org/

OHIO

Resource	URL
State's Homepage	ohio.gov/
Executive Branch (Governor)	governor.ohio.gov/
Legislative Branch	www.legislature.state.oh.us/
Constitution	www.legislature.state.oh.us/constitution.cfm
Statutory Code	codes.ohio.gov/orc
Judicial Branch (the courts)	www.supremecourt.ohio.gov/
Appellate Court Opinions/Case Law*	www.supremecourt.ohio.gov/ROD/
Administrative Code (regulations)	codes.ohio.gov/oac
State Bar Association	www.ohiobar.org/

OKLAHOMA

Resource	URL
State's Homepage	www.ok.gov/
Executive Branch (Governor)	www.gov.ok.gov/
Legislative Branch	www.lsb.state.ok.us/
Constitution	www.lsb.state.ok.us/ok_constitution.html
Statutory Code	www.lsb.state.ok.us/osStatutesTitle.html
Judicial Branch (the courts)	www/oscn.net/
Appellate Court Opinions/Case Law*	www.oscn.net/applications/oscn/index.asp?ftdb=STOKCS&level=1
Administrative Code (regulations)	https://www.sos.ok.gov/oar/online/viewCode.aspx
State Bar Association	www.okbar.org/

(Cont'd.)

OREGON	
Resource	**URL**
State's Homepage	www.oregon.gov/
Executive Branch (Governor)	governor.oregon.gov/
Legislative Branch	www.leg.state.or.us/
Constitution	www.leg.state.or.us/orcons/
Statutory Code	www.leg.state.or.us/ors/home.htm
Judicial Branch (the courts)	www.oregon.gov/OJD/courts/index.page
Appellate Court Opinions/Case Law*	www.publications.ojd.state.or.us/supreme.htm
Administrative Code (regulations)	arcweb.sos.state.or.us/banners/rules.htm
State Bar Association	www.osbar.org/

PENNSYLVANIA	
Resource	**URL**
State's Homepage	pa.gov/
Executive Branch (Governor)	www.governor.state.pa.us/
Legislative Branch	www.legis.state.pa.us/
Constitution	sites.state.pa.us/PA_Constitution.html
Statutory Code	government.westlaw.com/linkedslice/default.asp?SP=pac-1000
Judicial Branch (the courts)	www.courts.state.pa.us/
Appellate Court Opinions/Case Law*	www.courts.state.pa.us/T/SupremeCourt/SupremePostings.htm www.courts.state.pa.us/T/SuperiorCourt/SuperiorCourtOpinions.htm www.courts.state.pa.us/T/Commonwealth/Commonwealth Opinions.htm
Administrative Code (regulations)	www.pacode.com/ www.pabulletin.com/
State Bar Association	www.pabar.org/

RHODE ISLAND	
Resource	**URL**
State's Homepage	www.ri.gov/
Executive Branch (Governor)	www.governor.ri.gov/

(Cont'd.)

Appendix 3: State Law Resources Online

RHODE ISLAND *(Continued)*	
Resource	**URL**
Legislative Branch	www.rilin.state.ri.us/Genmenu/ www.rilin.state.ri.us/House/ www.rilin.state.ri.us/Senate/
Constitution	www.rilin.state.ri.us/RiConstitution/
Statutory Code	www.rilin.state.ri.us/Statutes/
Judicial Branch (the courts)	
Appellate Court Opinions/Case Law*	Judiciary of Rhode Island/Supreme Court www.courts.ri.gov/supreme/publishedopinions.htm Findlaw's site for Rhode Island Supreme Court opinions www.findlaw.com/11stategov/ri/rica.html Judiciary of Rhode Island/Superior Court www.courts.ri.gov/superior/publisheddecisions.htm
Administrative Code (regulations)	sos.ri.gov/rules/
State Bar Association	https://www.ribar.com/

SOUTH CAROLINA	
Resource	**URL**
State's Homepage	sc.gov/Pages/default.aspx
Executive Branch (Governor)	governor.sc.gov/ governor.sc.gov/executive/
Legislative Branch	www.scstatehouse.gov/index.html www.scstatehouse.gov/html-pages/house2.html www.scstatehouse.gov/html-pages/senate2.html www.scattorneygeneral.org/opinions/index.html
Constitution	www.scstatehouse.gov/scconstitution/scconst.htm
Statutory Code	www.scstatehouse.gov/code/statmast.htm
Judicial Branch (the courts)	
Appellate Court Opinions/Case Law*	Court of Appeals www.judicial.state.sc.us/appeals/ Published opinions 1997-current index www.judicial.state.sc.us/opinions/indexCOAPub.cfm Unpublished opinions 2004-current index www.judicial.state.sc.us/opinions/indexCOAUnPub.cfm Supreme Court www.judicial.state.sc.us/supreme/

(Cont'd.)

SOUTH CAROLINA *(Continued)*	
Resource	**URL**
Appellate Court Opinions/Case Law* *(Cont'd.)*	Published opinions 1997-current index www.judicial.state.sc.us/opinions/indexSCPub.cfm Unpublished opinions 2004-current index www.judicial.state.sc.us/opinions/indexSCUnPub.cfm
Administrative Code (regulations)	www.scstatehouse.gov/coderegs/statmast.htm
State Bar Association	www.scbar.org/

SOUTH DAKOTA	
Resource	**URL**
State's Homepage	sd.gov/
Executive Branch (Governor)	www.state.sd.us/governor/
Legislative Branch	
Constitution	legis.state.sd.us/statutes/Constitution.aspx
Statutory Code	legis.state.sd.us/statutes/TitleList.aspx
Judicial Branch (the courts)	
Appellate Court Opinions/Case Law*	ujs.sd.gov/ ujs.sd.gov/sc/Default.aspx ujs.sd.gov/cc/circuithome.aspx
Administrative Code (regulations)	legis.state.sd.us/rules/RulesList.aspx
State Bar Association	www.sdbar.org/

TENNESSEE	
Resource	**URL**
State's Homepage	www.tennesseeanytime.org/government/
Executive Branch (Governor)	www.tennesseeanytime.org/governor/Welcome.do;jsessionid=89ECA983D770149 49ED3001866F84ABD
Legislative Branch	
Constitution	www.tennessee.gov/sos/bluebook/07-08/47-Constitution,%20Tennessee.pdf www.michie.com/tennessee/lpext.dll?f=templates&fn=main-h.htm&cp=tncode
Statutory Code	www.michie.com/tennessee/lpext.dll?f=templates&fn=main-h.htm&cp=tncode
Judicial Branch (the courts)	
Appellate Court Opinions/Case Law*	www.tsc.state.tn.us/ www.tsc.state.tn.us/geninfo/Courts/AppellateCourts.htm

(Cont'd.)

TENNESSEE (Continued)

Resource	URL
Administrative Code (regulations)	www.state.tn.us/sos/rules/rules2.htm
State Bar Association	www.tba.org/index.php

TEXAS

Resource	URL
State's Homepage	test.texasonline.com/portal/tol
Executive Branch (Governor)	www.governor.state.tx.us/
Legislative Branch	www.capitol.state.tx.us/
Constitution	www.statutes.legis.state.tx.us/ (available from drop-down menu on same page as statutes)
Statutory Code	www.statutes.legis.state.tx.us/ (available from drop-down menu on same page as constitution)
Judicial Branch (the courts)	www.courts.state.tx.us/
Appellate Court Opinions/Case Law*	www.courts.state.tx.us/searchable.asp www.courts.state.tx.us/courts/coa.asp www.findlaw.com/11stategov/tx/courts.html
Administrative Code (regulations)	www.sos.state.tx.us/tac/ info.sos.state.tx.us/pls/pub/readtac$ext.ViewTAC
State Bar Association	www.texasbar.com/Template.cfm

UTAH

Resource	URL
State's Homepage	www.utah.gov/index.html
Executive Branch (Governor)	www.utah.gov/governor/index.html
Legislative Branch	www.le.state.ut.us/
Constitution	www.le.state.ut.us/UtahCode/chapter.jsp?code=Constitution
Statutory Code	www.le.state.ut.us/UtahCode/title.jsp www.le.state.ut.us/~code/code.htm
Judicial Branch (the courts)	www.utah.gov/government/judicial.html www.utcourts.gov/lawlibrary/research/#judicial (specific site for courts)
Appellate Court Opinions/Case Law*	www.utcourts.gov/opinions/ www.utcourts.gov/lawlibrary/docs/caselaw_website.pdf
Administrative Code (regulations)	www.rules.utah.gov/publicat/code.htm
State Bar Association	www.utahbar.org/ (Utah State Bar Association official site)

(Cont'd.)

Finding the Answers to Legal Questions

VERMONT	
Resource	**URL**
State's Homepage	www.vermont.gov/
Executive Branch (Governor)	governor.vermont.gov/
Legislative Branch	vermont.gov/portal/government/index.php?id=34
Constitution	www.leg.state.vt.us/statutes/const2.htm
Statutory Code	www.leg.state.vt.us/statutes2.htm
Judicial Branch (the courts)	www.vermontjudiciary.org/
Appellate Court Opinions/Case Law*	libraries.vermont.gov/law/supct
Administrative Code (regulations)	bgs.vermont.gov/adminpolicies
State Bar Association	https://www.vtbar.org/index.asp

VIRGINIA	
Resource	**URL**
State's Homepage	virginia.gov/
Executive Branch (Governor)	www.governor.virginia.gov/AboutTheGovernor/
Legislative Branch	virginia.gov/cmsportal3/government_4096/branches_of_state_government_4097/legislative_branch.html
Constitution	legis.state.va.us/Laws/search/Constitution.htm
Statutory Code	leg1.state.va.us/cgi-bin/legp504.exe?000+cod+TOC
Judicial Branch (the courts)	virginia.gov/cmsportal3/government_4096/branches_of_state_government_4097/judicial_branch.html
Appellate Court Opinions/Case Law*	www.courts.state.va.us/courts/cav/home.html
Administrative Code (regulations)	leg1.state.va.us/000/reg/TOC.HTM
State Bar Association	www.vsb.org/

WASHINGTON	
Resource	**URL**
State's Homepage	access.wa.gov/
Executive Branch (Governor)	www.governor.wa.gov/
Legislative Branch	www.leg.wa.gov/pages/home.aspx
Constitution	www.leg.wa.gov/LawsAndAgencyRules/Pages/constitution.aspx

(Cont'd.)

WASHINGTON *(Continued)*

Resource	URL
Statutory Code	apps.leg.wa.gov/rcw/
Judicial Branch (the courts)	www.courts.wa.gov/
Appellate Court Opinions/Case Law*	www.courts.wa.gov/opinions/index.cfm?fa=opinions.recent www.courts.wa.gov/opinions/index.cfm?fa=opinions.displayAll www.legalwa.org/
Administrative Code (regulations)	apps.leg.wa.gov/wac/
State Bar Association	www.wsba.org/

WEST VIRGINIA

Resource	URL
State's Homepage	www.wv.gov/Pages/default.aspx
Executive Branch (Governor)	www.wvgov.org/
Legislative Branch	www.wv.gov/Pages/your-government.aspx#legislative
Constitution	www.legis.state.wv.us/WVCODE/WV_CON.cfm
Statutory Code	www.legis.state.wv.us/WVCODE/Code.cfm
Judicial Branch (the courts)	www.state.wv.us/wvsca/ www.state.wv.us/wvsca/circuits/map.htm www.legis.state.wv.us/magistrate_rules.cfm www.state.wv.us/wvsca/overview.htm
Appellate Court Opinions/Case Law*	www.state.wv.us/wvsca/opinions.htm
Administrative Code (regulations)	www.legis.state.wv.us/Bill_Status/bill_status.cfm www.state.wv.us/wvsca/rules/rulesindex.htm
State Bar Association	www.wvbar.org/

WISCONSIN

Resource	URL
State's Homepage	www.wisconsin.gov/state/index.html
Executive Branch (Governor)	www.wisgov.state.wi.us/
Legislative Branch	www.legis.state.wi.us/
Constitution	www.legis.state.wi.us/rsb/2wiscon.html
Statutory Code	www.legis.state.wi.us/rsb/stats.html
Judicial Branch (the courts)	www.wicourts.gov/

(Cont'd.)

WISCONSIN *(Continued)*	
Resource	**URL**
Appellate Court Opinions/Case Law*	www.wicourts.gov/opinions/appeals.htm www.wicourts.gov/opinions/supreme.htm
Administrative Code (regulations)	https://health.wisconsin.gov/admrules/public/Home
State Bar Association	www.wisbar.org/

WYOMING	
Resource	**URL**
State's Homepage	www.wyoming.gov/
Executive Branch (Governor)	governor.wy.gov/
Legislative Branch	legisweb.state.wy.us/
Constitution	legisweb.state.wy.us/statutes/constitution.aspx
Statutory Code	legisweb.state.wy.us/titles/statutes.htm
Judicial Branch (the courts)	www.courts.state.wy.us/
Appellate Court Opinions/Case Law*	www.courts.state.wy.us/Opinions.aspx www.ck10.uscourts.gov/clerk/opinions.php
Administrative Code (regulations)	soswy.state.wy.us/rules/rule_search_main.asp
State Bar Association	www.wyomingbar.org/

The authors recognize that the hundreds of URLs provided in this appendix are likely to change quickly. This book's companion website, www.GetLaw.net, provides updates to these links. Anyone who finds obsolete or broken links is encouraged to contact the authors so the website can be as accurate as possible.

Index

Page numbers followed by "f," "t," and "s" indicate figures, tables (resources recaps), and sidebars, respectively.

About the Authors

Virginia Tucker is a county law librarian in Bellingham, Washington, and is on the faculty at the School of Library and Information Science at San José State University, where she teaches courses in information retrieval and online searching.

Her career in information services began as research branch librarian at the Stanford University Physics Library. She went on to become manager of client training at Dialog/Thomson (now ProQuest), where she gave training seminars, developed multimedia tutorials, and wrote user manuals. After many years of working directly with clients, Tucker moved behind the scenes to be an information architect and consultant for search engine interface design. She developed search prototypes, translation protocols, and online help systems.

Tucker received the prestigious Liberty Bell Award in 2010 from her local bar association for her "outstanding work in helping the public gain a better understanding of the law." As a volunteer, she has created websites for both the Whatcom County Bar Association and LAW Advocates, the local legal aid group. She also served for three years on the board of the Whatcom Dispute Resolution Center and has taught continuing legal education workshops on legal research in Bellingham and Seattle.

She has a master's degree in library and information science from the University of California at Berkeley, a bachelor's degree from Stanford University, and a paralegal certificate; she is currently a PhD student at Queensland University of Technology. She is a member of the American Association of Law Libraries (AALL), Law Librarians of Puget Sound (LLOPS), and Special Libraries Association (SLA).

Marc Lampson was admitted to the practice of law in 1985. In addition to his law degree, he holds a master of library and information science degree with a specialization in law librarianship from the University of Washington. He has worked at the Library at California State University, Sacramento, the Library at Richard Hugo House, the Antioch School of Law Library, and the University of Washington's Gallagher Law Library.

He taught legal research, legal writing, and other courses at Seattle University School of Law for 11 years and also has taught legal research at the University of Washington's School of Law, the two UW Paralegal Programs at Seattle and Tacoma, at paralegal programs at two community colleges, and at the Washington State Corrections Center for Women. He also has taught many continuing legal education courses regarding legal research and writing for the King County Bar Association and the Washington State Bar Association.

Since 2003 he has taught courses, including the legal resources course, for San Jose State University's School of Library and Information Science. As a doctoral student he taught courses on information behavior, information policy, and research methods at the University of Washington's Information School. He is the author of a book on local legal history, *From Profanity Hill: The King County Bar Association's Story*, published in 1993, and he was the principal writer of the first edition of the American Bar Association's monograph *Mental Disability Law: A Primer*. He is currently the executive director of the Unemployment Law Project, a nonprofit law firm that provides free legal assistance to people who are seeking unemployment benefits.